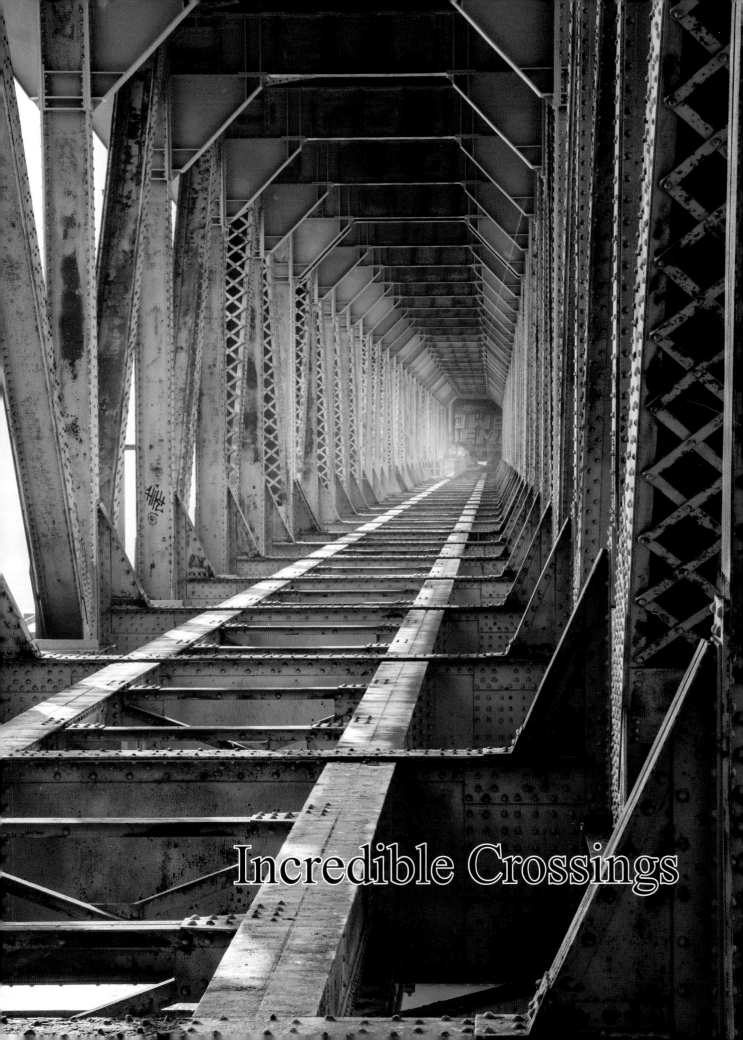

Incredible Crossings

Incredible
Crossings

The History and Art of the Bridges,
Tunnels and Inland Ferries
That Connect British Columbia

Derek Hayes

HARBOUR
PUBLISHING

Harbour Publishing Ltd.
P.O. Box 219, Madeira Park, BC, V0N 2H0
www.harbourpublishing.com

All photographs by Derek Hayes except where otherwise noted.
Editing by Iva Cheung.
Design and layout by Derek Hayes.
Cover design by Dwayne Dobson.
Printed and bound in South Korea.

 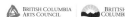

Harbour Publishing Ltd. acknowledges the support of the Canada Council for the Arts, the Government of Canada, and from the Province of British Columbia through the BC Arts Council.

Library and Archives Canada Cataloguing in Publication

Title: Incredible crossings : the history and art of the bridges, tunnels and inland ferries that connect British Columbia / Derek Hayes.
Names: Hayes, Derek, 1947- author.
Description: Includes bibliographical references and index.
Identifiers: Canadiana 20220245797 | ISBN 9781550179903 (hardcover)
Subjects: LCSH: Transportation—British Columbia—History. | LCSH: Transportation—British Columbia—Pictorial works. | LCSH: Bridges—British Columbia—Pictorial works. | LCSH: Tunnels—British Columbia—Pictorial works. | LCSH: Ferries—British Columbia—Pictorial works. | LCGFT: Photobooks.
Classification: LCC HE215.Z7 B72 2022 | DDC 388.09711—dc23

Note: References in *italics* refer to names or images, or, in a map caption, to words actually present on a map.

•••• *For Atifa* ••••

Acknowledgements

The author thanks the following for their input or assistance (in no particular order): Dan Farrell, City of Richmond Archives; D. Allan Blair, Museum and Heritage Services, New Westminster; Chelsea Bailey, City of Surrey Archives; Jessica Bushey, Daien Ide and Nina Patterson, North Vancouver Archives; Shea Henry, Maple Ridge Museum and Community Archives; Hilary Bloom and Rachel Bergquist, Squamish Public Library; Alex Code, PoCo Heritage Museum and Archives; Jenn Kuhn, McElhanney Ltd.; Reto Tschan, West Vancouver Archives; Tristan Evans, Chilliwack Museum and Archives; Lorinda Fraser and Kelly-Ann Turkington, BC Archives; Chak Yung, City of Vancouver Archives; Maria Martins, Central BC Railway and Forestry Museum, Prince George; John Fortoloczky, District of Hope; Al Lill; Henry Ewert; Alysa Routtenberg, Jewish Museum and Archives of BC; Cathy English, Revelstoke Museum and Archives; Eric Sakowski, highestbridges.com; Priscilla Lowe, Cowichan Valley Museum and Archives; Martin Wilson Christiansen, COWI; Doug Smith, kamloopstrails.net; Lorraine Buchanan, Mike Dunham-Wilkie, Robert Hunter, and the late Dave Wilkie; Owen Laukkanen; Matthew Robson; Mike Danneman; Garry and Roz Miller; Marty Bernard; Chris Harris; Tom Parkin; Doug Mayer; Gary Farnden, Chief Bridge Engineer, Province of BC; Terry K. MacKay, Senior Bridge Inspection Technician, Province of BC; Kristen Reimer, Information Officer, Ministry of Transportation and Infrastructure, Province of BC; Eric Julien, Area Manager, Bridges, Revelstoke; Waheed Sarwar, McCall Engineering; Jessica McWilliams, Emil Anderson Group; Kelly Sekhon, Nature Vancouver; and Ken Favrholdt, who also read the manuscript. Finally, thanks to my editor, Iva Cheung, who helped make the book much more readable.

To contact the author:
www.derekhayes.ca   derek@derekhayes.ca

Other books by Derek Hayes:

Historical Atlas of British Columbia and the Pacific Northwest
First Crossing: Alexander Mackenzie, His Expedition across North America, and the Opening of the Continent
Historical Atlas of the North Pacific Ocean
Historical Atlas of Canada: Canada's History Illustrated with Original Maps
Historical Atlas of the Arctic
America Discovered: A Historical Atlas of Exploration
Canada: An Illustrated History
Historical Atlas of Vancouver and the Lower Fraser Valley
Historical Atlas of Toronto
Historical Atlas of the United States
Historical Atlas of California
Historical Atlas of the American West
Historical Atlas of Washington and Oregon
Historical Atlas of the North American Railroad
British Columbia: A New Historical Atlas
Historical Atlas of Early Railways
        (UK edition: The First Railways; US edition: The First Railroads)
Iron Road West: An Illustrated History of British Columbia's Railways

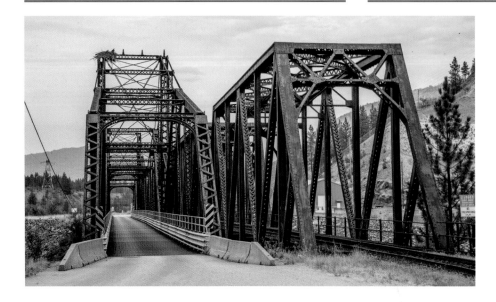

Half-title page. Hope Bridge.
Title page. Port Mann Bridge.

Left. British Columbia's oldest bridge of any size is the road bridge (left) at Waneta, over the Pend d'Oreille River at its confluence with the Columbia River near the US border. It was built in 1893 as a railway bridge, then converted to a road bridge in 1947 when a replacement railway bridge (at right) was built. A family of ospreys have built their nest right on top of the older bridge and can be seen guarding it. See page 266.

Right. The essentially unique covered Canadian Pacific Railway bridge across the Columbia River at Revelstoke, probably about 1903. See page 279.

CONTENTS

To find a specific bridge, see Bridge Finder, page 312

Why Bridges?

I have been taking photos of bridges for many years, attracted by their often elegant geometry, their lines and curves, and their structural composition. This book came about by circumstances, however. I was working on a book on high-speed trains and was booked to fly to Japan in March 2020 as part of the research for that. Well, we all know what happened that month: Covid-19 suddenly reached us, and we were suddenly in a locked-down environment. That summer, restrictions were eased enough to allow travel within the province, and this followed through to 2021. So, looking for a Covid project, I decided to put my collection of artistic-type photos together with my work as a historian, and voilà!—a book covering both the history of bridges and images of them as art.

One thing quickly became apparent—there are thousands of bridges in British Columbia, of all shapes and sizes. The BC Ministry of Transportation and Infrastructure has a database called the Bridge Management Information System (BMIS), and it contains information on an amazing 2,973 bridges and 73 tunnels. Some 2,264 of these are over rivers, creeks or lakes and 144 over railway lines.

And a startling statistic: if these bridges were all placed end to end, they would span over 150 km! Even as early as 1928 the total would have been 106 km. This figure reflects the vast number of streams, rivers, bays and other infrastructure over which bridges are needed. Of course, this also includes many small bridges, a great deal of which are not noticed by motorists, but there are nonetheless a significant number of impressive bridges not to be overlooked even by a much less observant driver.

Add to this the many railway bridges in the province, plus numerous municipal and private footbridges—not to mention 14 inland ferries—and it is clear the total must be at least 3,500. So this book is necessarily very selective, and I have tried to focus on bridges that have a story, feature an interesting structure to photograph, or are simply likely not to be there in a few years.

Road and rail bridges are what is known as "critical infrastructure." Without them there may be no other possible route. Where, for instance, would the Lower Mainland, essentially several peninsulas bounded by Burrard Inlet and the various distributaries of the mighty Fraser River, be without its bridges? Its economy would simply hemorrhage.

There have been bridge collapses—luckily very few. In neighbouring Washington State the bridge carrying Interstate 5 across the Skagit River collapsed in 2013, causing traffic mayhem for a while. And the Second Narrows Bridge collapsed in 1958

while under construction, instantly killing 18 workers; it is now the Ironworkers Memorial Bridge. And there is a bridge in the province designed by the same person who designed the freeway bridge in Genoa, Italy, that collapsed without warning in August 2018, killing 39 workers. The BC bridge was inspected and found to still be safe, but who would have anticipated such an event? In 1991 a much smaller bridge at Sayward suddenly collapsed when a full dump truck was driven over it; luckily the driver escaped by sitting on top of the partially sunken vehicle. A truss bridge near Merritt collapsed under the weight of a low-bed truck carrying a bulldozer in October 1980; a Bailey bridge replacement was in place within a week.

And then in November 2021 came the "atmospheric river," which dumped so much rain in a short time that major sections of important arterial roads—the Coquihalla Highway and Highway 8 between Merritt and Spences Bridge—were washed away, along with their bridges (see page 306).

And then, not nearly as serious but still a problem, there are ice bombs, big chunks of ice falling from the cables of both the Port Mann and Alex Fraser Bridges, injuring people and damaging cars and requiring the installation of special ice-clearing devices to run along the cables.

Settlers often built ferries as a matter of expediency, ranging from rowboats to those that could carry a horse and cart. But the government soon understood that it should be its responsibility to provide ferries, just as it provided roads. By 1936 there were some 45 inland ferries operated by, or subsidized by, the provincial government, and they carried 373,000 cars, buses, motorcycles and trucks. But the rise of the automobile in the 1920s spelled the end of many ferries because of traffic levels they were incapable of servicing properly. The 1928 annual report of the Department of Public Works stated "the increasing extent to which our highways are being used… has created a demand for better crossing facilities where ferries are now used." The number of ferries increased slightly into the 1930s and then declined. Today, there are only 14 inland ferries left in the province.

Since the period just after World War II there has been a steady progression of new bridges built of steel, rather than wood. There is no doubt steel will outlast wood, but unfortunately this reality has resulted in the destruction and replacement of countless bridges. The process goes on today, but modern bridges are often made of steel and prestressed concrete and are by comparison soulless flat creatures. So the recording of some of the older structures is part of the rationale for this book.

Railway bridges have tended to be more strongly built, as they were more likely to be fabricated from steel to begin with. This was because the substantially greater weight of steam locomotives required it, and because early wooden trestles and bridges had a nasty habit of being set on fire by their users.

Left. This unusual view of the Alex Fraser Bridge is solarized, a digital version of an old technique that involved re-exposure of a film negative to light—the sun—thus partially reversing positive and negative tones. The original image was shot vertically through the open sunroof of a car travelling over the bridge. See page 63 for a different version.

This characteristic led the Canadian Pacific Railway, which arrived in BC in 1885, to replace most of its critical wooden structures in the Rockies and Selkirks within 10 years.

This is not a technical book. Readers can discover the many variations in construction types easily from the internet. The types of bridge, all represented in the province at one time or another, range from a simple log bridge used by pack animals all the way to modern suspension and cable-stayed bridges. In between is that essential component of the vast majority of bridges—the truss. The latter is simply a structural combination of wood or steel beams triangulated in both compression and tension, creating a bridge part that is stronger than the sum of its components.

Trusses come in a seemingly endless assortment, and many are named after their inventors: the Pratt truss is perhaps the most common, which has diagonals in tension and verticals in compression; the Howe truss, which is the reverse; and the Warren truss, which uses equilateral triangles. But there are rare examples too, like the Whipple truss found on only a single BC bridge and only three in Canada.

Of the modern designs, the concrete stringer-beam bridge is now the most common for short spans. Cantilever trusses, such as on the Ironworkers Memorial Second Narrows Crossing, were used 50 years ago, though less now. The tried-and-true suspension bridge is still sometimes used, though more often for pedestrian versions, but for long bridges the cable-stayed bridge has come to predominate all over the world. The Pitt River Bridge and the Port Mann Bridge are of this type, where an array of cables support the bridge deck directly, instead of via a main tower-to-tower cable as with a suspension bridge. Derided by some, cable-stayed bridges in many cases are very elegant-looking structures. They are used more today because the complex math they involve can be tackled with the aid of computers, yet the first one of this type was built in Italy in 1595. And there is the extradosed bridge, a combination of a prestressed box-girder bridge and a cable-stayed one. The Golden Ears Bridge is a good example of this type.

British Columbia has an amazing variety of bridges, many of which are works of art as well as engineering. This book takes a look at some of them.

Above. A simple felled-log pack bridge, northeastern BC, early 1920s.

Above. A US Army pontoon bridge forming part of the Alaska Highway in 1942. This type of bridge could be constructed very quickly and would serve until a replacement could be built later. Pontoons were used on a completely different scale for the two permanent bridges over Okanagan Lake (see page 251).

Above. Here's an unusual bridge photo, to say the least. It is a vertigo-inducing view from the top of the new south tower of the replacement Port Mann Bridge, completed in 2012, before the old bridge, at right, had been removed (see page 88). The fog isolates the main subjects, making for a compelling image.

Above. Bridge builders are justifiably proud of their achievements, and politicians want to broadcast what they have done for their constituents, so sometimes a monument is built as well. This one is the Donald Bridge, a modern concrete-and-steel-beam flat type bridge completed in 2012, which carries the Trans-Canada Highway over the Columbia River. The monument records federal-provincial co-operation and funding.

Above. The Chehalis River Bridge, near Harrison Mills in the Upper Fraser Valley, is being replaced by a concrete-and-steel flat bridge—much more efficient but with far less character. The 1950-built wooden-truss bridge it is to replace is at right, and some of the concrete-filled steel tube piers are in place. The steel tubes were made, like so many things these days, in China (*inset*). See page 176.

Right. In November 2021 a 3-day-long "atmospheric river" dumped rain on BC, leading to extensive flooding, mudslides, and collapse of roads, railways and bridges all over the southern part of the province. Highway 8 between Merritt and Spences Bridge and the southern part of the Coquihalla Highway were particularly badly hit, with many bridges and even whole sections of roads destroyed. Four Highway 8 bridges were wiped out, as were five on the Coquihalla. Here, in a Ministry of Transportation photo taken on 16 November 2021, one of the bridges on the Coquihalla Highway, across Juliet Creek, a modern-type steel-beam structure, has collapsed after its abutment was eroded. This pattern was repeated in many places: the bridges themselves were often more or less intact but collapsed when river banks were undercut by fast-flowing water. Despite this, after 24/7 repairs, the Coquihalla was reopened to essential traffic just 36 days later (see page 306).

Vancouver Harbour

In Vancouver's harbour, ferries preceded bridges, as will be seen in many other cases. At first—from the 1860s, when European settlement began on the shore of the inlet—they were simply private rowboats like the one belonging to "Navvy Jack" Thomas, a deserter from Britain's Royal Navy. From 1866 a steam tug called *Sea Foam* operated between the settlements of Burrard Inlet.

There were enough settlers on the North Shore by 1891 that they petitioned to incorporate as the District of North Vancouver. It covered the entire North Shore except Moodyville, where there was a sawmill. In 1893 the municipality reached an agreement with the Union Steamship Company to provide a regular ferry service across the inlet, initially only six crossings per day. As the population grew, the North Vancouver Ferry and Power Company took over. The City of North Vancouver was incorporated in 1907 following large real estate developments centred on the ferry landing. The ferry allowed real estate sales there to boom. The new city took over the ferries in 1908.

West Vancouver pioneer John Lawson purchased land at Ambleside in 1905 and subdivided it for sale. He commissioned two boats to carry potential purchasers and new residents, and a new company owned by Lawson, with three partners, the West Vancouver Ferry Company, was created in 1909. The population had increased enough by 1912 that the Municipality of West Vancouver was created, halving the size of the 1891 North Vancouver, and it took over the ferry company.

With the construction of the Second Narrows Bridge in 1925 and the Lions Gate Bridge in 1938, the ferries' days were numbered. West Vancouver's ferry service continued until 1947, and North Vancouver's until 1958.

Above. The *Senator* provided early North Vancouver ferry service, but it called at Lonsdale Quay en route from Moodyville, where the sawmill was located. It also serviced ships at anchor in the harbour and thus only provided ferry service on an unreliable schedule.

Above. North Vancouver No. 1, previously *Norvan*, crosses the harbour with sailing ships at anchor in the background. This ferry was launched in 1901 and was the first vessel to be purpose-built as a North Vancouver ferry.

Above. West Vancouver Ferry Company's diminutive first ferry, which ran from 1909 to 1915. It was previously a fishing boat named *Eileen*.

Above, right. West Vancouver Ferry No. 5. This ferry collided with the Canadian Pacific Railway steamer *Princess Alice*, inbound from Seattle, in thick fog on 4 February 1935. The ferry sank, killing one elderly passenger trapped below deck.

Right, centre. North Vancouver Ferry *St. George*, built in 1905. It was named after North Vancouver real estate owner and salesman Alfred St. George Hamersley. He created the North Vancouver Ferry and Power Company in 1903, which bought out the municipal system in 1904. The double loading ends of this ferry were then a unique feature. Hamersley sold the ferry company to the newly created City of North Vancouver in 1908.

Right. North Vancouver Ferry No. 3, equipped to carry vehicles, with a ramp either end. It was built in 1936.

Left. Lonsdale Quay ferry dock in 1917. At right is Wallace Shipyards. Streetcars waiting for passengers from the ferries can be seen just beyond the dock gates, at the foot of Lonsdale Avenue.

One of the last ferries, *North Vancouver No. 5*, built in 1941, was converted into the Seven Seas Restaurant in 1959. It dominated the foot of Lonsdale Avenue until the restaurant closed in 2001; it was scrapped the next year after a dispute with the city about what would happen if it sank. Yet when put in drydock to be dismantled, the hull was found to be in excellent shape and the vessel had posed no risk of sinking.

Of course, that was not the end of ferries between Vancouver and the North Shore; a modern equivalent, the Sea-Bus, began service in 1976. There were two vessels (MV *Burrard Otter* and MV *Burrard Beaver*). A third (MV *Burrard Pacific Breeze*) was added in 2009 in anticipation of heavier traffic during the 2010 Olympics, and a fourth (MV *Burrard Otter II*) in 2014. The original *Burrard Otter* was retired and MV *Burrard Chinook* entered service after some delay in 2021.

SeaBuses are all aluminum-hulled catamarans with a capacity of 385 passengers; they can make the journey from shore to shore in 10 minutes, though a 15-minute schedule (30 minutes on weekends and holidays) is normal. They are operated by Coast Mountain Bus Company, the same company that runs Metro Vancouver's buses.

Below. MV *Burrard Otter II*, built in Singapore in 2014, approaches the Vancouver terminal with the cranes and containers of Centerm looming in the background.

Above, top. The MV *Burrard Beaver* in mid-crossing, with a backdrop of the high-rises of Downtown Vancouver and the cruise ship terminal at Canada Place.
Above. A SeaBus in its terminal on the Vancouver side.

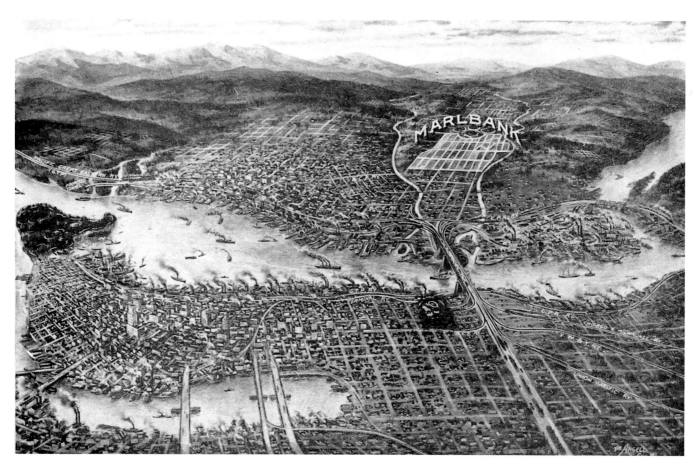

Above. At least seven bridges are shown in this bird's-eye view of Vancouver published in 1912 to promote a proposed residential subdivision, *Marlbank*, between Lynn Creek and the Seymour River in North Vancouver. The Second Narrows bridge shown here, however, was nothing but a developer's pipe dream, being only a proposal. It is shown carrying both a road and a myriad of railways that converge on that point. It might have become reality were it not for World War I, which began two years after this view was published, for Vancouver was expected to boom in the wake of the completion of the Panama Canal in 1913. A railway bridge is shown crossing Indian Arm (at right); this again was but a proposal that never went anywhere. At First Narrows a *Proposed Tunnel* is marked. False Creek shows four bridges that did exist: the Kitsilano Trestle, the Granville Street Bridge (the second one, completed in 1909), the Cambie Bridge, and the Westminster Avenue (Main Street) Bridge. The latter has another crossing just to the west (left) of it, seemingly another slip of the promotional artist's pen. The east end of False Creek is shown half reclaimed; although it was reclaimed over the next few years, it never looked like this, and certainly not in 1912. Note the Vancouver waterfront lined with smoky industry; smoke meant prosperity in those days!

Second Narrows

A bridge at Burrard Inlet's Second Narrows had been long desired by railway promoters. The then much less used waterfront beckoned to the railways competing with Canadian Pacific, for the latter had much of the south shore already tied up. In addition, before World War I there were several schemes promoted to construct railways to the Yukon goldfields via Indian Arm, the Capilano valley, or Howe Sound, all of which proposed crossing Burrard Inlet at the Second Narrows.

After the war, with the North Shore growing in population, the idea of a bridge was revived, and with financing from John Stewart, a long-time railway builder, it became feasible. Stewart had got himself into trouble with his last enterprise, the building of the Pacific Great Eastern by his company Foley, Welch and Stewart, and so he created another company, Northern Construction, to build this bridge.

The bridge, which had one span as a bascule bridge, opened for tolled automobile traffic on 7 November 1925, and to rail traffic a few months later. The bridge quickly proved to be a navigation hazard and

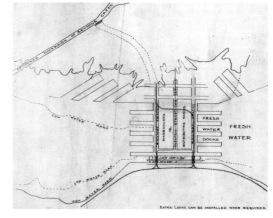

Above. A 1910 proposal to dam the Second Narrows is shown in this map. The idea was that it would be cheaper to dam than to build a bridge—unlikely at best. This scheme would have created a freshwater lake out of the eastern end of Burrard Inlet, and the idea also included a canal leading from Port Moody to the Pitt River. In 1920 the Vancouver Harbour Commission revived the idea, without the canal, but this also proved unworkable, which paved the way for the Second Narrows Bridge, completed in 1925.

resulted in a litany of accidents. On 10 March 1927 it was hit by a 10,000-ton freighter, the SS *Eurana*, causing considerable damage. The following year it was hit by another freighter, the SS *Norwich City*, and in April 1930 by yet another, the SS *Losmar*, which struck the south span.

Then, on 13 September 1930, the *Pacific Gatherer*, a former sailing ship converted to a log barge, became wedged under the fixed centre span and was lifted by the tide, destroying the span. This damage was more serious than before, and the bridge was closed until 1934. The closure had serious financial effects, proving to be a big problem for North Shore residents and businesses and even tipping the District of North Vancouver into bankruptcy. In 1933 the bridge was purchased by the provincial government, which installed a lift span

Left, top. The centre fixed span is placed into position on the concrete piers using floating supports constructed for the purpose.

Left, centre. The bridge approaches completion. The bascule section is raised, with the concrete counterweight just above the railway tracks.

Left. The completed bridge in late 1925. The camera angle shows quite well how the bascule worked, with the large concrete counterweight hanging over the tracks. In the distance, the small amount of dock development is evident.

Above, top. The bridge after being hit by SS *Losmar*.

Above, centre. The log barge *Pacific Gatherer* is wedged under the central fixed span and has lifted it up with a rising tide.

Above, bottom. The middle fixed span hits the water as *Pacific Gatherer* is pulled away by a tug. The spectacle now has an audience.

Above. This detailed photo of the first Second Narrows railway bridge under construction was taken on 28 April 1925. The south and centre fixed spans are in place, as is part of the south trestle, enough for single-track access, but the north trestle has yet to be constructed. Part of the lever mechanism for the bascule span lies in the foreground, and the structure to operate the bascule weight is partially complete.

Below. An aerial photo of the completed bridge shows the rather convoluted road approach across the CPR track (nearest to the camera).

Below. This 1928 map shows the detailed bridge road and rail layout. The roadways were outside of the truss spans on the southern half of the bridge, then on the east side on the northern (trestle) half.

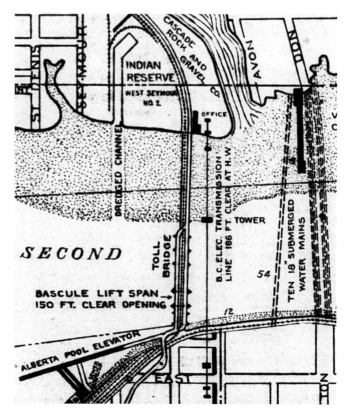

Above. The Second Narrows railway bridge after installation of the lift span in 1934.

to replace the bascule, hopefully to make it easier for ships to pass through. It seems to have worked, for there were far fewer accidents after that.

The bridge was purchased for $1 by Canadian National Railways (CN) and in 1963 converted to railway-only use. In 1968 CN replaced the old bridge with a higher and larger new bridge, also with a lift span. Instead of being angled across the inlet to turn sharply onto the south shore of the harbour, the new bridge directed the railway tracks into a new 3.4-km-long tunnel bored right under the higher parts of Burnaby, emerging beside Willingdon Avenue. This was completed in 1969 and was named the Thornton Tunnel, after Henry Thornton, the second president of the railway. The tunnel is interesting for its vertical ventilation shaft, which emerges in a residential neighbourhood but has been disguised to look like just another house.

The new bridge did not end the collisions with shipping, however. In October 1979 the freighter *Japan Erica* collided with the railway bridge in heavy fog, knocking a section of the bridge just north of the lift span into the water. The bridge was closed until March 1980.

Above. This back view of the "house" on the northeast corner of Ingleton Avenue and Frances Street in Burnaby shows the ventilation shaft outlet from the Thornton Tunnel below.
Right. The southern end of the Thornton Tunnel line joins the main line under the Willingdon Avenue bridge. The tunnel portal is hidden from view by the trees (on the curved line, centre).

Above, left, top. The Second Narrows rail bridge as it was between 1930 and 1934, minus fixed centre span.

Left, centre. The 1968 CN rail bridge in October 1979, following a collision by the freighter *Japan Erica*, which closed the bridge until March 1980.

Above. This photo, taken from the road bridge, shows how the post-1969 track crosses the CPR track beneath and goes directly into the Thornton Tunnel, just under the pedestrian trail bridge (now closed) at right.

Right. Taken on 22 April 1958, this photo shows the temporary falsework bent (the two steel piers in the foreground) that collapsed on 17 June that year, after three more truss sections had been added.

SECOND NARROWS BRIDGE
VANCOUVER B.C.
CONTRACT Nº S. 3703 E
DOMINION BRIDGE CO. LTD.
No 13-A   DATE APR. 22, 1958

After World War II, it became clear that the single-lane bridge, with frequent interruptions to road traffic by trains, not to mention bridge openings, would have to be replaced by something with greater capacity and reliability.

The new provincial government of W.A.C. Bennett, which came to power in 1952, was more oriented to road building for economic expansion than previous governments had been. And roads, of course, need bridges. The 1954 road program of Highways Minister Phil Gaglardi included a start on work for a new Second Narrows bridge and the Upper Levels Highway in North and West Vancouver. This time the bridge was to be a high-level bridge—no more encounters with wandering ships!

Engineering firm Swan Wooster designed the bridge, and construction was to be done by Dominion Bridge. It was to be a steel-truss cantilever bridge. Work began in 1956. Unfortunately, during construction two engineers made a mistake in calculating the load that would be applied to a temporary support, a falsework bent, that was to hold up the cantilevered truss only until the next permanent support pier was reached.

On 17 June 1958, the truss proved too much of a load for the bent, and came crashing down. Not only did the supported span collapse, but as it fell it dislodged the previous span from the concrete pier where both had been anchored. The collapse killed some 18 ironworkers on the structure at the time, plus a diver later searching for bodies.

The bridge construction was of course much delayed while various legal inquiries were held to find out the cause of the tragedy. Then the bridge was reconstructed.

The bridge finally opened on 25 August 1960, having taken over four years to build. The opening ribbon was cut not by some dignitary but by one of the survivors, Bill Wright. Just over six months later, on 4 March 1961, the connecting Upper Levels Highway opened.

The new bridge was unimaginatively called just the Second Narrows Bridge when it opened, the same as the bridge it was replacing, but in 1994 it was renamed the Ironworkers Memorial Second Narrows Crossing to honour those who died during its construction.

Above. Divers search for victims following the bridge collapse. Bodies were recovered for eight days after the disaster, and on 26 June diver Leonard Mott died while trying to cut a girder underwater.

Left. The two spans that collapsed, shown from the air. Span 5, nearest the camera, collapsed when the falsework bent temporarily holding it up buckled and gave way. As span 5 went down, it dislodged span 4 adjacent to it, causing it to also collapse. The toll booths of the old bridge can be seen in the background.

Second Narrows Bridge construction after the collapse:

Above. 11 May 1959.

Above, right. 23 June 1959.

Left. 24 May 1960.

Below. Two sections from contact, 3 June 1960.

Right. One truss section from contact, 7 June 1960.

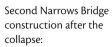

Above and *below*. Three bridges at Second Narrows. These two photos show a situation that existed only for a few months, between the completion of the Second Narrows Rail Bridge—the first train crossed on 6 May 1969—and the removal of the 1925 bridge, beginning in spring 1970. The angle of the new railway bridge leading to the Thornton Tunnel contrasts with the angle of the older bridge.

Above, top. This 1961 aerial photo shows the toll booths at the southern end. Tolls would be removed two years later as part of a widespread toll-removal policy of the W.A.C. Bennett government.

Above. Old and new bridges, November 1960.

Below and *right (3)*. The modern Ironworkers Memorial Second Narrows Crossing, including (*far right*) a photo showing two plaques: one placed by the Ironworkers Union listing the names of the dead—23 in total—and another one placed when the bridge was officially renamed in 1994.

Above. Taken at the end of March 2021, this photo of the two bridges at Second Narrows is only possible because the trees have not yet leafed up. They make a colourful contrast with each other and their blue environment.

Left. The always impressive view of the North Shore mountains as one drives north over the hump of the Ironworkers Memorial Bridge is even more so when the winter snows remain on a sunny day.

Right. Like many bridges, the Ironworkers Memorial has gained its share of graffiti, some of which, like that shown here on one of the east-side piers, might be considered artistic if photographed appropriately. Note that recording images from life such as this does not amount to approval of tagging.

Lions Gate

The First Narrows has always been an obvious place for a bridge, but until there was enough population on the North Shore, it was not likely to be economically viable. In 1927 a proposal for a road through Stanley Park to give access to a bridge even got as far as being put to a plebiscite in Vancouver, but it was resoundingly defeated.

It took the energies of one man to bring the bridge proposal to fruition. A.J.T. "Fred" Taylor, an engineer and real estate promoter (who simultaneously was involved in the construction of Earls Court Exhibition Centre in London, England), enlisted the help of a friend, Lord Southborough, to persuade the Irish beer-brewing Guinness family to invest in land in West Vancouver. They created a syndicate called British Pacific Properties (BPP) that purchased 1,620 ha from the District of West Vancouver in 1931, saving the district from bankruptcy in the process. But the land would be hard to develop without a bridge nearer than the Second Narrows. That bridge was out of commission at that time anyway.

In December 1933 a second bridge plebiscite was held in Vancouver and, largely because of a public appetite for anything that might create employment—this being the middle of the Great Depression—the result was a 70 percent victory for the bridge promoters.

In the meantime, in July 1933, Taylor had purchased the iconic Marine Building on Burrard Street and turned it into the headquarters of British Pacific Properties. Construction had begun in 1929, but its builders had been bankrupted by the onset of the Depression. Taylor acquired it for just 40 percent of what it cost to build.

Having received the approval of the City of Vancouver voters, BPP still had to obtain permission from the federal government, since the bridge would cross navigable waters. But the federal government was heavily influenced by the Canadian Pacific Railway, which had extensive land holdings in Vancouver and did not want to see anything that might compete with them. It took a change of government (R.B. Bennett's Conservatives to W.L. Mackenzie King's Liberals in 1935) and much personal persuasion by Taylor and his partners (Southborough was a friend of Mackenzie King) to overcome the powerful influence of the CPR. Taylor also enlisted the help of Gerald G. McGeer, who was conveniently both mayor

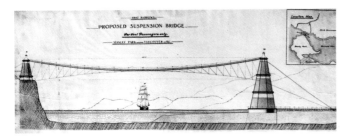

Above. A proposal for a pedestrian-only suspension bridge at First Narrows, 1909. There would have been a lot of stairs to climb within the north-end conical tower.

Above, top. Dated 3 August 1937, this photo shows the cleared right-of-way through Stanley Park.

Above, centre. By November 1937 the north approach had been cleared, footings for the approach viaduct poured, and a hoisting tower built at the north end of the suspended span.

Left. The south-end tower during construction, March 1938.

Above, left and right. The catwalks have been strung from tower to tower. Both views look north; the mountains are obscured, *left*. The north approach viaduct is also shown under construction, *right*. Both photos were taken in May 1938.

Below. An official portrait of the Lions Gate Bridge on completion and after installation of Charles Marega's lions at the southern end. Now it was truly "Lions Gate."

Above. The King of Great Britain and Canada, George VI, and his wife, Queen Elizabeth, are escorted over the new Lions Gate Bridge on 29 May 1939. They had travelled across Canada to boost support for Britain and the Empire just prior to World War II.

Above. The toll booths at the north end of the bridge in the 1950s.

Above. A commemorative postcard shows the completed bridge, with distinctly fewer vehicles than would be seen today! The lion sculptures that guard the southern bridge approach were commissioned from Charles Marega, a local sculptor who also worked on the decorative element of the Burrard Street Bridge and the statue of George Vancouver which stands outside Vancouver City Hall.

of Vancouver and a Liberal MP, a supporter of all manner of Depression make-work projects, including a new City Hall, to be completed in time for Vancouver's jubilee in 1936.

Taylor went so far as to suggest that if the bridge were not approved and the wishes of Vancouver voters did not prevail, then a public enquiry would be needed. This neither Mackenzie King nor Bennett, now leader of the Opposition, wanted to contemplate. On 29 April 1936, an order-in-council finally gave federal consent.

McGeer understandably wanted to name the bridge-to-be the "Jubilee Bridge," but this the promoters resisted, and it remained unnamed, despite construction having begun, un-til 2 October 1937, when the name "Lions Gate Bridge" was announced, named after the overlooking mountain and better for marketing purposes. The bridge was to be a suspension bridge. In April and May 1937 a right-of-way was cleared through the middle of Stanley Park, and the North Shore approaches were cleared as well. Also in April, work began on driving piles for rock cribs that would be used to lay foundations for the two bridge towers. From then work continued apace. On the Stanley Park side the cliff already had the road at the required height, but on the North Shore side a 700-m-long viaduct was required to bring the roadbed to that height; the first steel for that was erected on 25 November. The steel tower sections were fabricated at the Dominion Bridge plant in Burnaby and shipped by rail and scow to the site. By 10 March 1938 the south tower was complete, and the north tower by 29 April.

At 4:50 am on 2 May the First Narrows was closed to shipping for the first time ever to allow the first cables, to support a catwalk, to be strung from tower to tower. They were followed in the next weeks by multiple cables, each themselves composed of many prestressed wires, the whole then being clamped together to form a single massive—and very strong—single cable to which the wires holding the roadbed could be attached. The roadbed was made of U-shaped sections, each with Warren-type truss sides to ensure rigidity. They were raised from a scow below. The first was raised on 9 June 1938, and by 21 June some 174 sections were hung. By the end of the month the roadbed floor was being laid. The concrete roadbed itself was poured beginning on 16 August, with the work being carried out from both ends simultaneously to ensure equal loading on the cables.

The bridge was completed months ahead of schedule, the result of meticulous scheduling by the engineers and a streak of good weather. It opened to pedestrians on 12 November 1938, followed by cars two days later. The bridge was officially opened on 26 May 1939 in a little ceremony with Fred

Above. Another commemorative postcard tries to emphasize Vancouver's "modernity" by including an unlikely three planes—and not even float planes at that—as well as a luxury speedboat and sailboats.

Taylor present; three days later (on 29 May 1939) it was "honoured" by British King George VI and Queen Elizabeth, who drove over it, refusing to meet with Indigenous people from the Capilano Reserve at the north end of the bridge—on land surrendered to build it—or even slow down to allow a plaque to be revealed. Such it was in pre-war Imperial days when Vancouver and Canada were very much more "British" than today.

Toll booths had been built at the north end, for the intention was that the cost of the bridge construction be recouped. Tolls were 25 cents for a car or horse and carriage, and 5 cents for a pedestrian. In January 1955 the Guinness family, having recouped their investment in the bridge, sold it to the provincial government for the same amount as it had cost them to build it—a little less than $6 million. Tolls remained until 1963 and are said to have netted the government the cost of the bridge again; it was a standing joke that the bridge had been paid for twice.

In 1986, as an Expo gift, the Guinness family purchased mercury vapour decorative lights for the bridge; these were updated in 2009 to LED lights.

In 1975 the original concrete deck of the north viaduct was replaced with a stronger orthotropic (structurally reinforced) deck, and in 2000–2001 the suspended part of the bridge was rebuilt, with the original U-shaped sections being taken out one by one and lowered to a barge, with replacement sections hoisted in the same way. The new sections also had an orthotropic deck and cantilevered pedestrian walkways outside the suspension cables; the side trusses were replaced by under-the-deck structural steel. The difference is apparent from a comparison of older photos of the bridge with recent ones (page 26, *top left*, and page 28, *top*).

Below. A section of the new road deck is winched into position during the replacement of the deck in 2000–2001. The removal of the old sections was essentially the reverse of the way they had been installed, while the installation of the new sections was similar to the original installation, lifting them from a barge below, albeit no doubt made simpler with modern equipment and techniques. Nonetheless, extreme precision was necessary.

Above. The southern end of the bridge has a fantasyland of white trees around it in this image taken with an infrared camera. Infrared makes green foliage look white.

Left. The south tower soars above the granite-lined bridge foundations, inhabited by cormorants, while the bridge deck arches towards the North Shore mountains.

Below. The bridge now has a background of West Vancouver houses, the development foreseen when it was planned.

Right. Starkly outlined against a featureless sky, the underside of the bridge and the south tower make an interesting composition. The lateral stiffening truss under the orthotropic deck is clearly shown. This replaced the side vertical trusses when the bridge deck was renovated in 2000–2001.

The Third Crossing

After the province purchased the Lions Gate Bridge in 1955, there ensued a multi-year debate as to its adequacy to accommodate future traffic flows given the growth that was then happening on the North Shore. A government report released in 1955 considered a twin bridge within five years. Another, three years later, set a target date of 1966 for a new four-lane suspension bridge. The "Third Crossing," as any new bridge or tunnel across the harbour became known, was much in the news.

It was in this period (1956–60) that the new Second Narrows Bridge was built, and in 1965 money was allocated for a new Georgia Viaduct (completed in 1972; see page 50), which was intended to become part of a freeway system that would include the Third Crossing, though no one told that to the voters. (The eight-lane Granville Street Bridge, completed in 1954, was also intended to be part of this system.)

In 1967 Vancouver City Council received the first part of a comprehensive report called the *Vancouver Transportation Study*. It had been written by an American freeway planning consulting firm, which had been given as its parameters an assumed third crossing of Burrard Inlet, and connections to existing freeways to the south and east of the city. This study recommended a complex freeway system for Downtown Vancouver that included elevated freeways up to eight lanes wide along the waterfront connecting to a tunnel to the North Shore off Brockton Point in Stanley Park.

It was the freeways rather than the bridge or tunnel that killed off the idea. Swelling public opposition forced city council first to modify the freeway plans and finally to scrap them, and with them the Third Crossing. Seven hundred people turned out to a public meeting in January 1972, and there followed a memorable piece of verbiage from the mayor, Tom Campbell. The new crossing, he was reported as saying, "is on the verge of being sabotaged by Maoists, Communists, pinkos, left-wingers and hamburgers." The latter he defined for the *Vancouver Sun* as "persons without university degrees."

A petition with 21,000 signatures was presented to the provincial government in February, and a thousand people attended a marathon public meeting in March. Premier W.A.C. Bennett was voted out of office in August 1972. In November Campbell chose not to run for re-election and was replaced as mayor by Art Phillips, leader of a new municipal party, The Electors' Action Movement (TEAM), which had been born amid the freeway and third crossing furor. The freeways and the Third Crossing were dead.

The only options now were to secure and upgrade the Lions Gate and introduce transit options; the SeaBus began service in 1976 (see page 12).

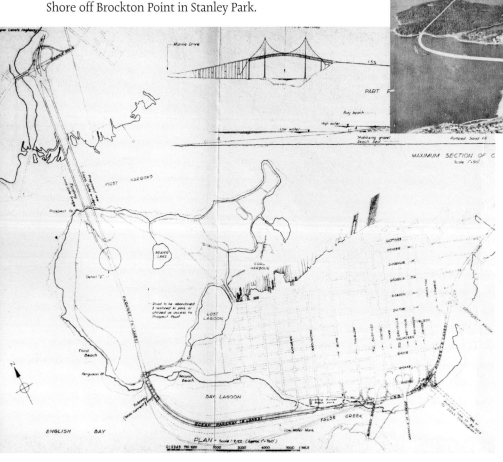

Left and *above*. Produced by engineering company Swan Wooster in October 1960 (with costs revised in 1964), this interesting proposal included a twinned Lions Gate Bridge and a completely new eight-lane southern approach road curving around the southern edge of the Downtown peninsula, swinging out into English Bay as an *Ocean Parkway*, and then following a new path through Stanley Park. The parkway was to have been created by pumped sand fill, as had been done in 1960 to create a causeway for ferries in Tsawwassen. This ocean parkway plan, with an estimated total cost of $33.6 million including the new bridge, was much cheaper than plans for a waterfront freeway, which would have cost $112 million, or those for a waterfront freeway and tunnel off Brockton Point, which would have cost $130 million. An interesting detail is the *Future Oak St Bridge to Deas Throughway* (at bottom right), which would have become another crossing of False Creek.

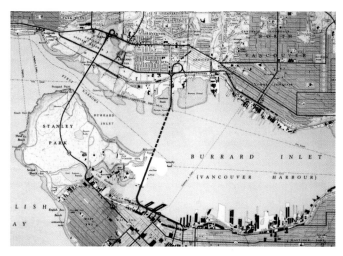

Above, left and right. The Brockton Point tunnel proposal by engineering company Christiani and Nielsen in 1963, four years after they had successfully completed the Deas Island Tunnel (see page 58). Various versions of this proposal included different uses for the island created for the southern tunnel portal, including high-rise apartments, shown here, and even an airport. It may seem over the top now, but in 1962 there was also a proposal for a "city" airport on Spanish Banks in English Bay.

Far left and *left.* A 1969 report contained this aerial photo mock-up and view of a Brockton Tunnel crossing without other development on the south portal island, although it would still have changed the nature of Downtown Vancouver forever.

Below. The Third Crossing on a map of proposed Downtown freeways contained in the 1968 *Vancouver Transportation Study* that caused major public revolt.

Below. By 1970, the date of this altered photo, the proposal for a Brockton Point tunnel had changed into a bridge. A beautifully designed bridge, it is true, but one destined to never come to fruition. It was designed by local bridge engineers Peter Buckland and Peter Taylor, who went on to form the company that would work on the upgrading of the Lions Gate Bridge.

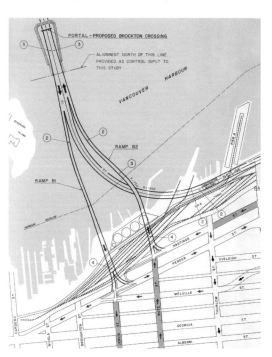

False Creek

False Creek has always been an integral part of Vancouver, but for much of its first hundred years within the city it was an industrial, polluted mess, only being reimagined to its current premier city residential location and major defining feature of Vancouver since the 1970s. In both incarnations, False Creek formed a barrier right in the centre of the city that had to be overcome by the use of bridges, both road and railway.

The Granville Street Bridge

The Granville Street Bridge was the second bridge to cross False Creek. The earliest Granville Street Bridge was completed by the Canadian Pacific Railway in 1889, using a convenient large sandbar. The railway intended to develop its land grant, and the bridge would help with that. The bridge was a simple trestle affair, with a movable span nonetheless, designed to link the city—at the time mainly confined to what is now the Downtown peninsula, with the road, also built by the CPR—to the new bridge at Marpole (see page 100) and hence to the farmlands and food sources of the Fraser Delta in Richmond. (The road was popularly called North Arm Road, though this became

Above, top. The first Granville Street Bridge, built in 1889 by the CPR.
Above. This 1891 photo of False Creek from Fairview shows the first Granville Street Bridge with the Kitsilano Trestle, the railway connection, built in 1886 (see page 40) behind.
Below, centre. An 1893 Admiralty hydrographic map shows the bridge and trestle with the enormous sandbar that would later become Granville Island.
Below, right. A 1911 map shows the first and second Granville Street Bridges as well as the trestle. The 1909 bridge was built at a slight angle to the first.

Left. The opening of the second bridge on 6 September 1909.
Below, bottom. The second Granville Street Bridge in 1916. A barrier wall has been built around the sandbar, and the infilling that would create Granville Island has begun.

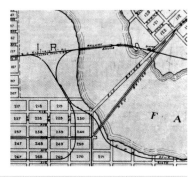

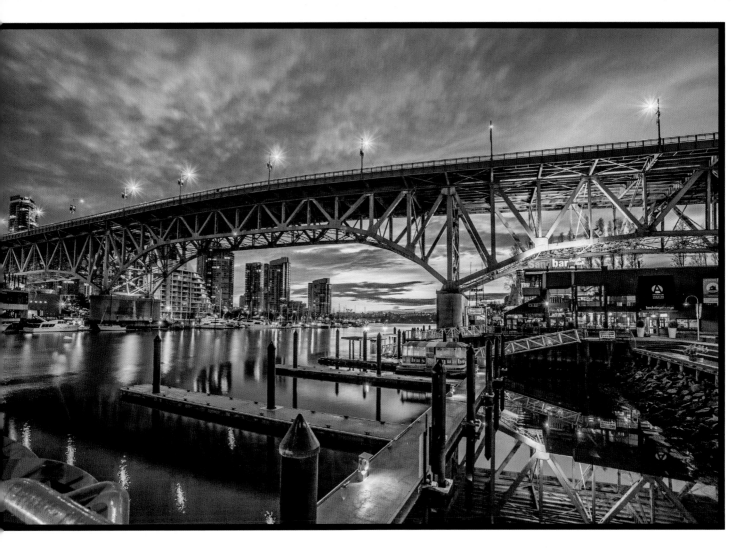

the official name for what was later Fraser Street, leading south to the Fraser Street Bridge, built in 1894; see page 113.)

The bridge was named after the road on the Downtown peninsula, Granville Street, itself named by CPR surveyor Lauchlan Hamilton after Granville Townsite (popularly Gastown), which in turn was named after a British earl—this being considered solidly British territory at the time. South of the bridge to the city boundary at 16th Avenue was called Centre Street, and South Granville Street after 1907. Point Grey municipality, established in 1908, renamed the portion south of 16th Avenue as South Granville Street, the whole becoming

Above. This view of the Granville Street Bridge was taken a few minutes after sunrise on a late-November morning from beside the ferry dock on Granville Island.

Below, left. The second bridge under construction in 1908. The railway tracks leading to the Kitsilano Trestle are in the foreground.

just Granville Street after Point Grey became part of the City of Vancouver in 1929.

The first bridge had rail lines laid across it in 1891 to allow Vancouver's first electric streetcar service to be launched—the Fairview Belt Line, which is credited with (slowly at first) encouraging the development of the CPR's lands at Fairview, to the south of False Creek.

By 1907 the bridge had become unable to handle the traffic and was replaced by the second bridge, a medium-level steel bridge with a through-truss centre swing span, officially opened in September 1909. It was built slightly to the east of the first bridge (on the alignment of today's Old Bridge Street on Granville Island).

In 1915–16, the sandbank at its south end was reclaimed by building a retaining wall and infilling the middle with sand. This, of course, was Granville Island, and all it did for False Creek was create more land for the smoky industries of the day that had come to inhabit its shores. The island's initial official name matched its use—Industrial Island.

Above. This is a view looking north from the control house on top of the second Granville Street Bridge, a photo taken on 6 June 1916. Granville Island is being created below. A retaining wall was built and sand dredged from False Creek deposited inside. The Kitsilano Trestle is visible at right.

A streetcar line was built across the bridge, running, as with the Connaught Bridge farther east, through the trusses of the middle span. This bridge is generally credited with expediting the development of Kitsilano and the Canadian Pacific–developed upscale Shaughnessy, just as the first bridge had helped the development of the railway's Fairview Slopes before it.

The upgrade to the present bridge began in 1949 with the appointment of a new City Engineer, John C. Oliver. At this time there was a movement afoot to fill in False Creek more or less entirely and thus eliminate the need for any bridges at all. Oliver, by comparing costs with the value of the land reclaimed, showed that this would not likely be an economical proposition. This was confirmed by a report published in 1956, which is perhaps just as well, since the bridge had already been completed by then.

Oliver then planned a new freeway-style bridge to replace the 1909 one; it would have multiple on- and off-ramps and be the first eight-lane bridge in Canada. In a sense he was

Below. The open movable span of the second bridge in 1952, looking west. At right, a derrick crane structure is being brought into False Creek on a barge pulled by a tug, no doubt the reason for the bridge opening.

ahead of his time, for the Eisenhower Administration's building of interstate highways in the US was still years away (they were authorized in 1956).

The new bridge followed almost exactly the alignment of the first bridge. Construction began in September

Below. Interurban streetcar *No. 1204* has just cleared the centre movable span of the second Granville Street Bridge about 1947, heading south for Steveston. This service would normally be routed across the Kitsilano Trestle, which was likely open for marine traffic or otherwise unavailable.

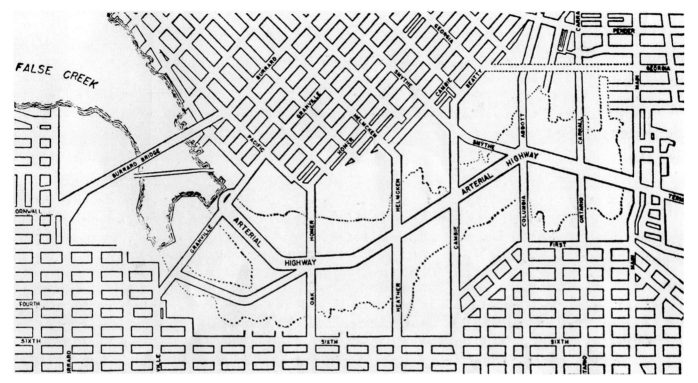

Above. The idea that False Creek could just be filled in and eliminate the need for any bridges save the Burrard Bridge was epitomized in this map produced by a Vancouver alderman, Jack Price, for his re-election campaign in December 1950. The concept was also supported by then Vancouver mayor Fred Hume. It shows an arterial highway right down the middle of False Creek. Price proposed dredging some 12 million cubic yards of sediment from the bottom of English Bay, at a cost of $4 million, compared with the $20 million cost of replacing the Granville and Cambie Bridges. "False Creek," he maintained, "is nothing more than a filthy ditch." City Engineer John Oliver showed that the cost of filling False Creek would be uneconomical in terms of the potential return. Luckily for thousands of present-day Vancouver residents, the infill plan went nowhere.

1951, and the new bridge opened three years later, on 4 February 1954. By the time it did, streetcars had almost disappeared from the Vancouver scene, and the new bridge was notable in being built trackless; it was clearly designed for cars. The new trolley buses would operate across it, but not streetcars. Now, with freeways in Vancouver long out of the picture, the city is reclaiming lanes on the bridge for pedestrian and bicycle use and has removed the circular off-ramps at the north end of the bridge.

Below. The steelwork of the north end of the third bridge under construction in 1953. This part of the steelwork can also be seen in the aerial photo, *right*.

Below. The third Granville Street Bridge is beginning to take shape just west of the second bridge in this aerial photo taken in 1953. The on- and off-ramps connecting the bridge with Howe Street and Seymour Street are particularly well advanced.

Above. The third and current Granville Street Bridge under construction: a view looking south on 9 April 1953. The old (second) bridge is at left, and traffic is diverted around one of the first piers for the Seymour Street off-ramp. A pair of Vancouver Brill trolley buses are in the foreground.

Left. An aerial view of the nearly complete bridge, November 1953.

Right, top. A view of the bridge under construction from the Howe Street on-ramp, 21 May 1953.

Right, centre. This photo taken on 5 February 1954 shows the new bridge is open, and the old closed off.

Right, bottom. The new bridge under construction, viewed from the old bridge, 12 March 1953.

Right. Later in 1954 the old bridge is being demolished. The difference in height of the two bridges is quite marked in this photo.

Above. The underside of the Granville Street Bridge in black and white showing the multiple truss supports.

Left. A demonstration calling for action against climate change closed the bridge in the afternoon of 2 May 2021. Police were heavily in attendance.

Left, bottom. Like many bridges, the Granville Street Bridge attracts graffiti, but this is deliberately painted art appropriate to the Granville Island location.

Below. During the bridge closure on 2 May 2021 this image was seen. It shows the bridge and the West End reflected in the side of a police van parked in the middle of the bridge.

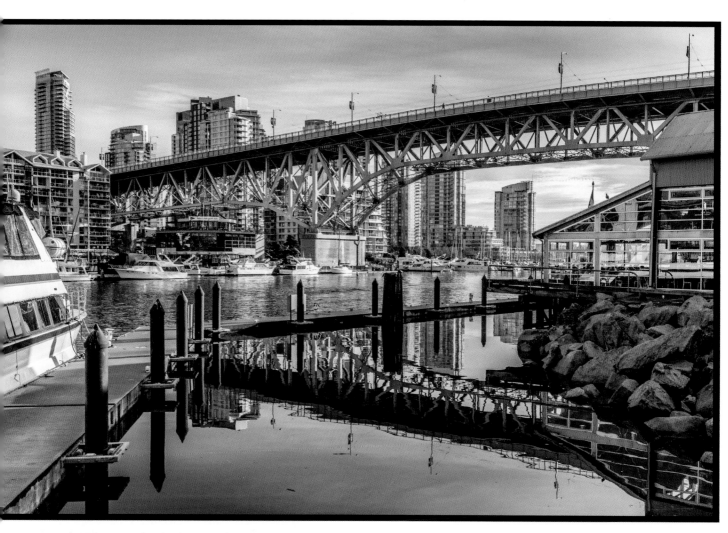

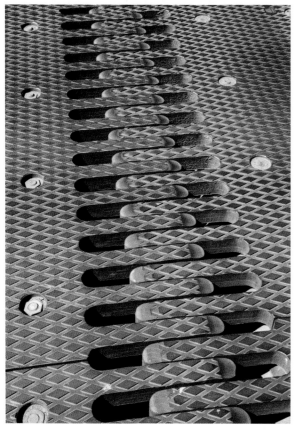

Above. The Granville Street Bridge from Granville Island, reflected in the still waters of False Creek behind the dock. The bridge is a cantilever truss-arch structure.

Left. A study of the expansion joints in the bridge deck.

Right. The sleek buildings of University Canada West that have been built to utilize space between the bridge and its ramps at the north end have a necessarily triangular shape and a "pointy end."

Above. An ocean liner built in 1929, HMS *Menestheus* is carefully eased through the Kitsilano Trestle in September 1945. The ship had been requisitioned from the Blue Funnel Line during World War II and had been used as a minelayer and later an amenities ship. She returned to civilian use after the war.

Kitsilano Trestle

In 1886, the same year Vancouver was incorporated, the CPR built a fixed trestle bridge over False Creek to connect with wharves and yards the railway proposed to build at Kits Point. The trestle became a navigational nuisance and not really required after the CPR built its yards on the north shore of False Creek and at Coal Harbour.

In 1901–02 the original trestle was demolished and a new one built that included a swing span. This was for a CPR subsidiary, the Vancouver & Lulu Island Railway, built along the Arbutus corridor and crossing into Richmond at a bridge over the North Arm of the Fraser (see page 102) to service the burgeoning salmon canning industry at Steveston.

In 1905 the line was leased to the British Columbia Electric Railway, which electrified the whole line and began operating an interurban service. BCER also began a streetcar service over the trestle to Kitsilano, an action credited with the development of that area as a residential district in the years just before World War I. Kitsilano streetcars ran until 1947 and interurban service to Steveston ended in 1958.

In 1982 the trestle was demolished as part of the transformation of False Creek prior to Expo 86.

Left, centre. A PCC streetcar travels across the Kitsilano Trestle about 1950. This design was introduced in 1939 as an attempt to improve comfort and efficiency, but the unions did not like them because they were one-man operated. The Burrard Bridge is in the background.

Left. A number of streetcars in BCER's Kitsilano yard in November 1949, with the Kitsilano Trestle (left) and the second Granville Street Bridge (right) in the background.

Burrard Bridge

A bridge at the entrance to False Creek had been proposed by town planning consultant Harland Bartholomew, who had included it as part of a proposed grand civic centre development on the north side of the bridge. Despite the amalgamation of Vancouver with Point Grey and South Vancouver in 1929, the onset of the Great Depression put an end to those plans. However, the bridge was built, starting in 1930 and being competed in 1932 (the civic centre—city hall—was eventually built at 12th Avenue and Cambie Street). In keeping with the original concept, the bridge was designed in a massive art deco form.

The two approach spans are below-deck Warren trusses, while the centre span is a Pratt through-truss, designed to allow greater height clearance for ships. The centre span is flanked by vertical extensions of the bridge's masonry piers designed to partially hide the steelwork of the span when viewed from either side. These are embellished with the arms of the city and ship prows and busts of British naval explorer George Vancouver and his friend Harry Burrard Neale, after whom Vancouver named Burrard Inlet. The whole forms an impressive starkly art deco structure.

Below. A pedestrian's view of the centre-span steelwork.

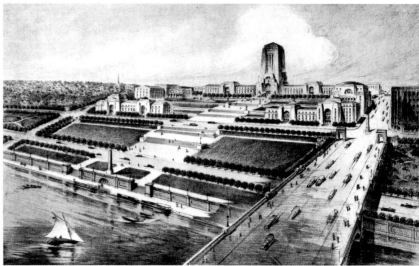

Above, top. A commemorative postcard produced soon after the bridge opened, on 1 July 1932.

Above. Harland Bartholomew's original 1928 concept for a magnificent civic centre included a bridge, though not the art deco structure that was built.

Below. The northern arch at the end of the centre span. These structures were intended to hide the above-deck steelwork of the span when viewed from street level.

Above. The centre span of the Burrard Bridge photographed with a fisheye lens and converted to black and white.

Below and *right*. Bridge details: the city coat of arms and the Harry Burrard Neale bust.

Far right. The bridge entrance column braziers were restored and relit in 2018. They originally honoured Canadian Forces personnel of World War I, who used braziers to keep warm in the trenches; now they honour all veterans. This is the invitation to the relighting ceremony.

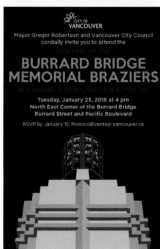

Above. The Burrard Bridge from the Hornby Street ferry dock. An Aquabus ferry is approaching the dock. This photograph shows selective colour, a technique where all but a detail, in this case the ferry, has been converted to black and white.

Right. Sometimes the most effective angle for photographing a bridge can be from above. This beautiful early-morning image of fog shrouding the bridge was taken from a high-rise apartment on the West End side.

Below. Detail of a lamp amongst the steelwork of the centre span.

Below, right. Railing and lamp on the southern approach span, photographed from under the bridge and converted to black and white.

Cambie Street Bridge

The first Cambie Street Bridge was built in 1891, two years after the Granville Street Bridge, and, similarly, was intended to open up the land on the south side of False Creek for development. It was constructed of wooden piles and had a truss swing span in the middle. Despite its simplicity, it lasted for 20 years.

The second bridge was a four-lane, medium-level steel bridge, with streetcar tracks and a through-truss swing span. It was completed in 1911 and opened to traffic on 24 May, although its official opening had to wait until the next year. On 20 September 1912 the Governor General, the Duke of Connaught, performed the honours. The bridge was renamed after him, although most people still referred to it as just the Cambie Bridge. In April 1915 the creosoted wood deck caught fire, leading to the collapse of one of the fixed spans.

In the 1980s, as Expo 86 approached, the city decided to replace the bridge with a non-opening one, financially helped by a contribution from Expo, but nothing from the provincial government (although later the government guaranteed Expo's debt and established Lotto 6/49 to deal with it). Amazingly for a large project such as this, the bridge was built 25 percent under budget and seven months ahead of schedule. The city had fast-tracked its construction because of the Expo 86 deadline.

Unusually for bridge construction, and only possible here because of the availability of alternate crossings, the 1911 bridge was closed in November 1984, before the new one had been completed, to allow for the alignment of the new bridge with existing approaches. It was opened on 8 December 1985.

Right, top. The Cambie Street Bridge on an 1898 bird's-eye map of Vancouver. The CPR's roundhouse and yards are at right.
Right, centre. The wooden bridge from the tower of King Edward School at 12th Avenue and Oak Street in 1905.
Right. This 1904 view looking towards Downtown from the bridge also has a ghostly horse and rider, unable to stay still for the relatively long exposure required.
Below. The bridge, now renamed the Connaught Bridge, on 20 September 1912, the day it officially opened.

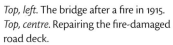

Top, left. The bridge after a fire in 1915.
Top, centre. Repairing the fire-damaged road deck.
Top, right. A bus crashed through the railing of the bridge on 1 September 1929. Here it lies upside down in the mud.

Colour photos on this page.
Photographs taken by the City Engineering Department of the construction of the new bridge, completed in 1985:
August 1983 (*top, left*);
October 1983 (*top, right*);
4 April 1985 (*centre, left*);
11 September 1985 (*centre, right*), Expo 86 structures are now seen on the north shore of False Creek;
18 November 1984 (*right*), which also shows what the 1911 bridge was like to cross, with its traffic lanes divided by the through-truss of the swing span.

Above, top. The Cambie Street Bridge at dusk, February 2010.

Above. A view of the bridge looking towards the high-rises of Downtown, August 2020.

Westminster Avenue/ Main Street Bridge

The Westminster Avenue Bridge, after 1910 the Main Street Bridge when the road name was changed, was the first bridge across False Creek, having been built about 1872 at the narrowest part of the inlet to carry a road to New Westminster. It was a simple wooden plank-and-pile trestle. This worked because the water here was very shallow, with the area east of the bridge drying to mud flats at low tide. In 1890, what was effectively another bridge was attached to the west side to carry Vancouver's first streetcar tracks over False Creek to Mount Pleasant.

More use of the eastern part of False Creek led to some dredging and, about 1905, the construction of a new steel bascule bridge to allow access for larger vessels. This new bridge lifted the entire road to near vertical. This bridge did not last very long, however, for plans were afoot to fill in the eastern creek to provide railway terminals and facilities, first for a partial fill by the Great Northern, approved by Vancouver voters in 1910, and then for filling the rest by the Canadian Northern Pacific in 1913. The bridge was progressively encroached on by fill and was demolished in 1921.

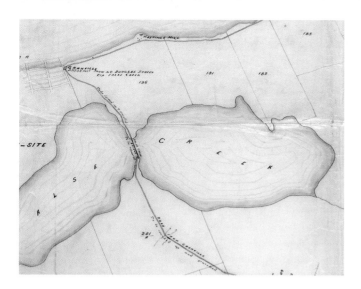

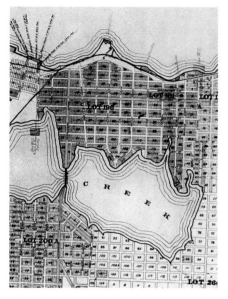

Above. This 1883 map from a provincial government road repair contract shows the first *False Creek Bridge* at what is now Main Street. The bridge has the notation *To be repaired*, and *The Road from Granville* is shown as *To be rounded up and gravelled*.

Left. The bridge in 1886. By this time the City of Vancouver had been created and much surveyed.

Above, top (1890), and *above* (1893). The Westminster Avenue (later Main Street) Bridge, a view south to Mount Pleasant. In 1890, when this streetcar service began, the rail bridge had been built attached to the road bridge, giving the divided bridge seen here. It must have been near high tide when this photograph was taken, as the area east (left) of the bridge appears as water rather than the mud flat it became at low tide. By 1917 it was filled in, and the need for much of the bridge disappeared (see photo *overleaf*). The imposing building to the right of the bridge in the 1890 photo is a stable that was built to house the horses intended to pull the first streetcars. They were never used, as the streetcar system was electric from the beginning.

Right. A view of the bridge in 1887 from Westminster Avenue (Main Street) and 7th Avenue.

Below. The bascule bridge under construction about 1905. The large round structures that would hold the massive counterweight are visible at either side.

Above. A colourized postcard of the Westminster Avenue bascule bridge, with streetcars crossing.   *Above.* The open bascule bridge.

Below and *below, bottom.* The bascule bridge's days are numbered as fill from the eastern part of False Creek encroaches on the bridge. *Below,* the Great Northern Railway station is visible in the background in this 1918 photo. These were some of the last streetcars to cross, and temporary streetcar tracks can be seen on the fill behind the bridge, to which the streetcars would be diverted. *Below, bottom,* the temporary streetcar tracks are still on the fill and the bridge is about to be demolished. The photo was taken on 30 June 1921 from the new Canadian National (successor to Canadian Northern Pacific) station, still there today. The GNR trestle and swing bridge are in the background. The February 1913 agreement between Canadian Northern and

the City of Vancouver called for the building of a seawall 270 feet (80 m) west of the Main Street Bridge, and the filling in of the land behind it. The agreement was put to a plebiscite, and on 15 March 1913 Vancouver voters approved it 5,032 to 1,385. (The agreement also called for the building of a first-class hotel, something that was not achieved until the current Hotel Vancouver was completed in 1939, 26 years later.)

Great Northern Bridge

Another False Creek bridge that is no longer in existence was the Great Northern Railway trestle bridge, built by the railway's subsidiary, the Vancouver, Westminster & Yukon Railway (VW&Y), in 1905.

At the turn of the 20th century the Great Northern Railway had a problem: it needed access to Vancouver, but the land was all tied up by its bitter rival, the Canadian Pacific, which had been given much land as grants in 1885. By 1910 it had solved this problem by filling in part of eastern False Creek, but before that it obtained access via a line from New Westminster through swampy land north of Burnaby Lake and the line of the Grandview Cut (the cut was made later, in 1913, to improve the difficult grade). This was track built by the VW&Y.

An initial temporary station was at today's Main Street and First Avenue, but this was too far away from Downtown, and the railway built the trestle bridge with a swing span to access the north shore of False Creek, where a station and limited yards could be built. Today the station site is the Sun Yat-Sen Chinese Garden.

The Canadian Northern had the same access issue as the GNR until it also solved the problem by filling in more of False Creek. Its initial tri-weekly transcon-

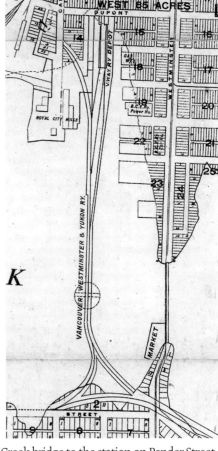

tinental service, begun in late 1915 after the transcontinental line was completed, ran into Vancouver using Great Northern lines, crossing on the False Creek bridge to the station on Pender Street. So the Great Northern False Creek bridge was for a brief period one of great significance, carrying trains both from the United States and Eastern Canada into Vancouver.

Above. This 1907 map shows the *Vancouver Westminster & Yukon* Bridge just to the west of the Westminster Avenue (Main Street) Bridge crossing the eastern end of False Creek. The station is on Dupont Street, renamed Pender Street in 1907.

Left. Taken from the north side of False Creek in 1917, the GN bridge is shown at left. A wharf is being built in the foreground. The atmosphere in False Creek at that time was smoky, just as depicted here. On the north side the bridge led to a station and yards, some track of which had to also be on trestles (see next page).

Below. A side view of the GN bridge from Main Street in 1916. The steel swing section contrasts with the wooden pile trestles on either side.

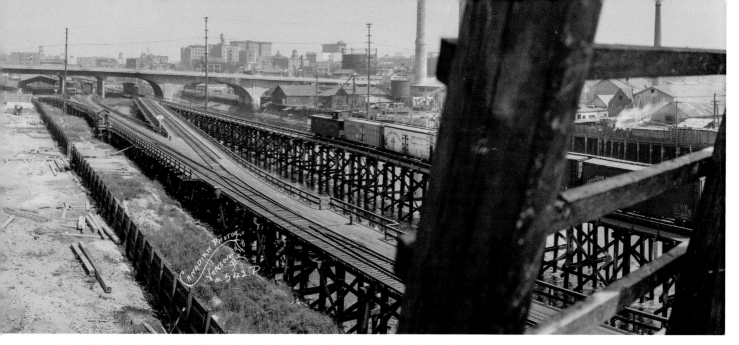

Above. The GN yards and station (at left, under the viaduct) leading north from the bridge shown on the previous page. The tracks led under the reinforced-concrete span of the first Georgia Viaduct, in the distance. This part of False Creek is radically different today!

Georgia Viaduct

The first Georgia Viaduct was the city's answer to Downtown access across the marshy flats surrounding False Creek. Opening in 1915, it was at first named the Hart McHarg Bridge after Lieutenant Colonel William Hart-McHarg, killed that year in World War I action, but it was commonly called the Georgia Harris Viaduct, because it connected those two streets. However, Harris Street was renamed East Georgia Street after the viaduct's completion, so simply Georgia Viaduct made more sense.

The design was initially considered to be an engineering marvel because it included a 25-m-long reinforced-concrete span over an arm of False Creek and some of the GN tracks, thought at the time to be the longest in North America. (The other part of the bridge was a steel-truss design.) It was

also hailed as "incombustible," which, in an age where many bridges were made of wood, seems to have been a big deal. Unfortunately, it turned out that too much sand had been included in the mix, and the bridge almost immediately suffered from structural safety concerns. Every other street light was removed to reduce weight, and streetcar tracks laid across the viaduct were never used.

The viaduct was demolished in 1972 and replaced by a more robust concrete structure that had been intended as a part of the Downtown freeway system, advanced by the *Vancouver Transportation Study* of 1968. Despite freeways being thoroughly rejected in 1972 by Vancouver voters, the new Georgia Viaduct had somehow survived, perhaps because work on it had already begun by 1967, including the levelling of 15 blocks in the Chinatown area, including Hogan's Alley, a Black neighbourhood. The twin, one-way viaducts opened

Below. The Georgia Viaduct under construction in 1914. The CPR rail yards are in the foreground.

Right. In this 1939 photo the concrete part of the Georgia Viaduct spans the northeast arm of False Creek, long since filled in. Looking almost idyllic, the water was in fact highly polluted.

on 9 January 1972 amid protesters who tried to prevent Mayor Tom Campbell's limousine from driving across the structure.

The southernmost viaduct leads east from Georgia Street, while the other is for westbound traffic and leads onto Dunsmuir Street; for this reason it is often referred to as the Dunsmuir Viaduct.

It seems, however, that the anti-freeway activists will finally win the day, 50 or so years later, for in 2015 Vancouver City Council voted to tear down the twin viaducts and replace them with ground-level roads, having discovered from traffic surveys that only about 10 percent of the traffic entering or leaving Downtown actually uses the viaducts, probably because the east ends merge onto normal city streets.

Above. A panoramic view of the new first Georgia Viaduct taken on 1 July 1915 from the GNR tracks below. The steel-truss part of the bridge is at left.

Below. The Georgia Viaduct in 1926. The never-used streetcar tracks run down the centre of the road.

Below. The old Georgia Viaduct and the proposed new viaduct as part of the Downtown freeway system, as shown in the 1968 *Vancouver Transportation Study*. The second viaduct was built on the routing shown here, connecting to Georgia and Dunsmuir Streets, though without the several on- and off-ramps on this map.

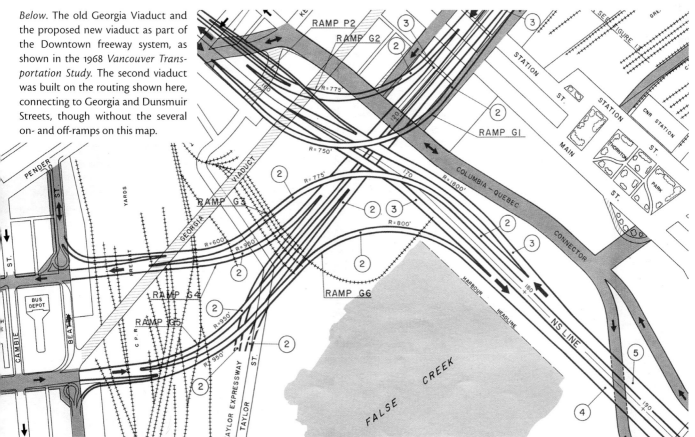

52 INCREDIBLE CROSSINGS

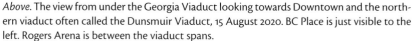

Above. The view from under the Georgia Viaduct looking towards Downtown and the northern viaduct often called the Dunsmuir Viaduct, 15 August 2020. BC Place is just visible to the left. Rogers Arena is between the viaduct spans.

Above, right. A railway line footbridge with an interesting origin. In 1909, just north of what used to be the eastern end of False Creek, the Great Northern Railway built a line from its False Creek yards to Vancouver Harbour, thus gaining the access long denied it by the Canadian Pacific monopoly. In 1970, Raymur Place housing project was built to the west of the line. The children of the mainly single mothers from the project began risking their lives every day crossing the line to get to their school, Admiral Seymour Elementary, on the east side of the railway. A long protest demanding a footbridge over the rail line by "militant mothers of Raymur" ended with three blockades between January and March 1971 before the city and the two rail companies now using the line, Burlington Northern and Canadian National, agreed to construct the bridge, which they did later that year; it was named the Keefer Street Pedestrian Overpass. In 2019, the City of Vancouver officially changed the name of the bridge to the Militant Mothers of Raymur Overpass in honour of the women.

Opposite, top, left. The second Georgia Viaduct under construction on 1 November 1970.

Opposite, top, right. The railings at the western end of the Dunsmuir Street viaduct pay homage to the design of the first viaduct.

Left. An aerial photo of False Creek taken in 1954 shows six bridges. From the top they are the Burrard Bridge, the third Granville Street Bridge with the second still visible below it, the Connaught (Cambie) Bridge, and the first Georgia Viaduct. The industrial mess that was once False Creek is evident. Log booms in the water feed the several mills that lined the shores.

Above. The magnificent Canoe footbridge in Southeast False Creek, part of the development that began life as the Olympic Athletes' Village in 2010. The Canoe Bridge was completed in 2009 and was designed to emulate the ribs of a canoe or kayak, and it bulges in the middle like a canoe. It has a mesh-iron grid deck to maximize light for the marine habitat below. The illuminated sphere of Science World is seen in the background.

Bridge stories typically start with ferries and end with bridges. False Creek is the other way around. In 1981 Brian and Laura Beesley began to run four passenger-only electric ferries from Granville Island. The following year the company was sold to George McInnis and George Pratt and became False Creek Ferries. In 1985 Pratt sold his share to McInnis, but the following year his son, Jeff Pratt, started up a rival ferry service, the Aquabus, which could carry bikes. The rivalry continues today, resulting in excellent service for passengers. False Creek Ferries operates 17 ferries, while Aquabus operates 14 vessels. Both add to the amazing modern False Creek environment—and make great subjects for photographers!

There is one other crossing of False Creek that might be overlooked: the SkyTrain Canada Line tunnel between the Yaletown–Roundhouse Station on the north side and Olympic Village Station on the south.

These are twin tunnels, bored by a 440-tonne, 86-m-long Lovat Tunnel Boring Machine, which could bore at the rate of about 10 m a day. They were part of the much longer tunnel in which the SkyTrain runs for the majority of its route in Vancouver, though to the south the tunnel was constructed by the cut-and-cover method.

The breakthrough of the second tunnel under False Creek was on 2 March 2008. It was opened as part of the entire Canada Line on 17 August 2009, easily in time for the 2010 Winter Olympics held in Vancouver and Whistler the following year.

Opposite, top. An Aquabus ferry in front of BC Place, 11 November 2015.

Opposite, bottom. Aquabus, again with BC Place as a backdrop, 12 December 2020. This type of ferry can carry bicycles, hence the prominent bike displayed on the bow.

Above. False Creek Ferries' *Spirit of False Creek 10*, built in Richmond in 2002, approaches the Granville Island dock early in the morning of 24 November 2013 as the sun illuminates the Burrard Bridge behind it.

Below. A False Creek Ferry heads westward on 12 December 2020.

Lower Fraser River

Long before any bridge or tunnel crossings were contemplated across the lower reaches of the Fraser, ferries plied back and forth, initially intermittently and often unreliably, as in winter ice floes can be dangerous for small vessels. At New Westminster the first formal ferry ran in 1884, and in 1891 it connected with the newly completed New Westminster Southern Railway, which ran from the US border to a point across the river from the city (see page 75). At Ladner, in the early 1890s Union Steamships began a service from Steveston to Ladner once a day.

Most of the early ferries connected Ladner to Steveston, but by 1912 Woodward's Landing, at the southern end of No. 5 Road, was also included. There were plans for a large ferry dock at Woodward's built by the Canadian Northern Pacific Railway, but this railway only ran for a short time before a trestle over boggy ground on Lulu Island caught fire, ending that service; the dock idea was abandoned along with the railway.

In November 1913, after trials since January that year, a government-run ferry service began using a paddleboat with a barge attached. The passengers were carried in the boat, vehicles and livestock on the barge. The 20-minute crossing became four hours on one sailing a month later when the boat struck a sandbar and damaged the paddlewheel. A bus connected to Vancouver at Woodward's, though poor Richmond road conditions in winter (remedied in the mid-1930s) often led to long journeys.

In the 1920s and '30s, several new ferries were used on the run, and in 1932 a screw-propelled vessel took over from the previous stern-paddlewheelers. The original ferry landing was in Ladner, but in 1931 a new landing at what is today Captain's Cove Marina was built, along with a paved Ferry Road—still named that today. As a result the crossing time was reduced to 10 minutes.

In 1949, the *Delta Princess*, a permanent ferry capable of carrying 36 cars, entered service, and the ferry dock was extended across Deas Slough to the western tip of Deas Island. The *Delta Princess* ran until 1959, when the new tunnel opened. The vessel became part of BC Ferries' fleet in 1961 and was renamed the MV *Saltspring Queen*.

Above, top. Side-loading stern-paddlewheeler *Ladner-Woodward's Ferry No. 3* in February 1931.

Above. An aerial photo taken about 1946 shows the second ferry dock at the end of Ferry Road, with a ferry leaving from Woodward's Landing. The photo has been marked up to show the then proposed *New Landing* at the western end of Deas Island, which would reduce the crossing time to 10 minutes.

Below. A 1949 government topographic map shows the landing extension built that year. The route of the ferry is shown, before the new landing became operational. The sandbars and islands of this part of the Fraser Delta shift over time. What looks like solid land in the photo is shown on the map as *Ladner Marsh* and is subject to flooding.

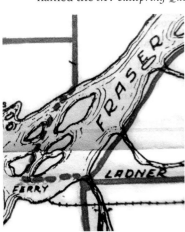

Left. The pre-1932 ferry route to Ladner is shown on this road map from about 1925.

Below. A car leaves the Ladner ferry dock on 15 July 1931.

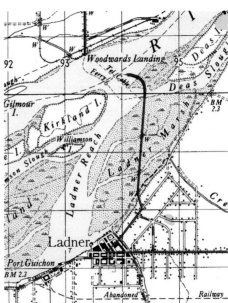

Above. The extended ferry dock is packed with waiting cars in this aerial photo from about 1950. In 1958–59, the last full year of operation, the ferry made 15,475 round trips, carrying 492,623 cars, 39,525 trucks, 3,887 trailers and semis, and 2,904 buses. Small wonder there was a demand for a fixed crossing here.

Above. The lineup is long on Richmond's No. 5 Road in this aerial photo from the fifties.

Below. The *Delta Princess* at Woodward's Landing in 1957. The ferry made its last crossing on 23 May 1959, the day the Deas Island Tunnel opened.

Above. The remains of the second ferry dock can still be seen on the Ladner side. This photo was taken in 2011, as was the photo, *right, centre*, which shows the remains of the piles that guided the ferry to the ramp (also visible in the older black-and-white photos here).

Below. On the Richmond side a few of the guide piles (farthest from camera) survive today.

Massey Tunnel

A tunnel was particularly suited to the location at Woodward's, close to the Fraser River's outlet to the sea, because of the immense deposits of sediment here, which made finding secure footings for a large bridge problematic.

A bridge had been proposed here before, notably in 1927, when a charter to build the bridge had been granted. In 1933 construction had begun, and in November 1934 a provincial government agreement with the Ladner Bridge Company allowed the company to collect tolls. However, pressure was building from New Westminster supporters, and the main proponent of the Ladner location, Premier S.F. Tolmie, had lost the 1933 election. His successor, T.D. ("Duff") Pattullo, was more inclined to build a bridge at New Westminster. He refused to allow the Ladner bridge to proceed, backing what became the Pattullo Bridge in 1937 (see page 80).

In the 1950s, provincial highways department engineers conducted a three-year study to determine where a new *bridge* should be built; sites considered included Port Mann and Annacis Island. They recommended a bridge at the location of today's Alex Fraser Bridge without even considering a tunnel at any location.

The tunnel—rather than a bridge—was the brainchild of George Massey, after whom the tunnel would be renamed in 1967. He was a Ladner resident and MLA for Delta from 1956 to 1960. He searched the world for information about tunnels under rivers, then launched a tireless campaign for a tunnel based on one that had been built in Rotterdam in 1942, the Maastunnel. At first, his campaign was supported only by the mayor and council of Delta, and his idea was derided by almost everyone else.

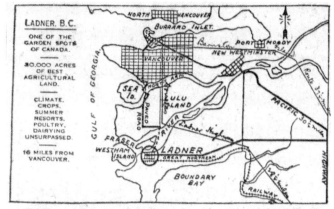

The above sketch map shows the comparative distances of the Barnston Island route, a distance of 37.5 miles, and Ladner Highway route via Lulu Island and the proposed Ladner bridge over Deas Island, to Ladner Highway, a distance of 28.5 miles.

Above, top. The *Delta Princess* has just left the 1949 ferry dock on the Ladner side about 1950. Pile driving appears to be in progress.

Above. This map appeared in the *Vancouver Sun* on 21 February 1931 in support of a bridge at Ladner.

Except Phil Gaglardi, then Minister of Highways. He had a study done by Foundation of Canada, and they recommended Massey's idea of a tunnel because of the potential issues with finding a good footing for bridge piers. Gaglardi then approved this proposal, which was contrary to the advice of his own engineers. Several of them, including chief engineer Neil McCallum, quit in protest.

The Deas Island Tunnel was to be a critical link in a new provincial highway—a freeway—from Vancouver at the Oak Street Bridge to the US border at Blaine, where it would link to Interstate 5 and the whole American interstate system being built at the time.

The innovative construction process began in 1957 and involved fabricating tunnel tubes on land and then floating them out into the river and sinking them into a specially prepared bed of gravel, where they were connected, backfilled, and drained. The sections were joined up with a specially developed sealing device resembling a huge bicycle inner tube. Six concrete tunnel sections were built on the north shore of the river. Each was just over 100 m long, 24 m wide and 7 m high. Television monitors were provided from the beginning, together with an extensive ventilation system.

The completed tunnel was opened to traffic on 23 May 1959. The first two days were toll-free, and that was so popular it immediately caused a traffic jam—perhaps an augur of things to come. The connecting freeway to Blaine would not be complete for another two years, so Ladner experienced the brunt of the sightseer traffic. An official opening ceremony was held a few weeks later, on 15 July, with the Queen attending the ceremony.

By the early 21st century, development south of the river had increased to the point that the newspapers described the tunnel as the worst bottleneck in Canada. A replacement bridge was announced by the (Liberal) provincial government in September 2013, and a groundbreaking ceremony took place on 5 April 2017. However, the project was cancelled by a new (NDP) government after its election later that year. Currently a new eight-lane replacement tunnel is planned, but not scheduled for completion until 2030.

Above. George Massey points out the location of the Deas Island Tunnel—later the Massey Tunnel—on a large, hand-painted map that he created to illustrate his case at public meetings.

Below. The north entrance to the Deas Island Tunnel is beginning to take shape in this photo from above the tunnel portal taken in 1957.

Above. The tubular sections that make up the tunnels being assembled on land. They would be floated out into the river, sunk, then sealed together.

Below. A section of the bridge over Deas Slough, connecting the mainland with Deas Island and the tunnel, is floated into position in 1958. The route of the nascent freeway (Highway 99) is in the background.

Above, left. A tunnel ramp nears completion.

Above, right. One of the special cranes that lowered the tunnel sections to the riverbed.

Right. This map appeared in the *Vancouver Sun* on 21 May 1959, two days before the tunnel opened. The *Rejected Route* would later be built as the Alex Fraser Bridge. The *Present Route* is the Pattullo Bridge.

Below. The transition at the north end of the tunnel.

Below, bottom. A plaque commemorating the opening of the tunnel by the Queen on 15 July 1959.

The Deas Island Tunnel was the first in North America to use immersed-tube technology and is the only road tunnel below sea level in Canada. Its roadway is thus the lowest in Canada also.

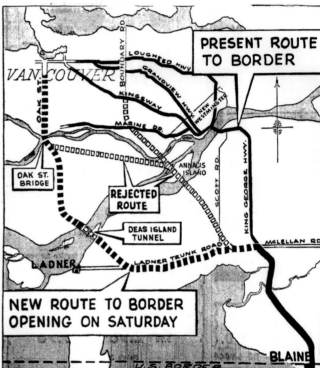

Above. In 2013 the (Liberal) provincial government announced plans to replace the aging Massey Tunnel with a 10-lane cable-stayed bridge, shown here, but after the 2017 election a new NDP government scrapped that plan in favour of a new 8-lane tunnel, writing off $100 million in site preparation already spent. The Liberals have stated their intention to revive the bridge plan if they win the next election, slated for 2024. Either way, it will be many years before anything is built.

Above and *right*. Views from above the Massey Tunnel, facing south, show the massive ventilation shaft and the ironwork above the tunnel portal intended to provide a gradual transition from daylight to tunnel and vice versa.

Alex Fraser Bridge

The Alex Fraser Bridge, named after the provincial Transportation and Highways Minister under whose watch the project began, is the centrepiece of a system of new major roads built within a few years of each other. The planning began in the 1970s; in 1973 the required right-of-way on the north side was acquired from Grosvenor, the owner of the land on Annacis Island (see page 69), who no doubt realized the bridge was likely to add considerable value to their land.

The bridge was completed in 1986 and connected a new Highway 91 from interchanges with Highway 99 in Richmond in the north to another in Delta to the south, thus creating a new route to the US boundary. The southern part was completed in 1986 at the same time as the bridge, as was a connection north to the Queensborough Bridge (now Highway 91A), but the link on Lulu Island, now usually referred to as the East-West Connector, was not completed until 1989.

The Alex Fraser Bridge is a cable-stayed bridge, which at the time of completion was the longest of this type in the world, a record it held for 19 years. With towers 154 m high it was also the highest structure in Metro Vancouver, equivalent to a 50-storey building. This record has long since been lost to many relatively recent buildings in Downtown Vancouver, where the height limit now stands at 200 m.

The towers sit on steel piles, which on the north side had to be driven down 90 m to find a solid footing, perhaps not so surprising since the whole of Annacis Island is but a sandbar in the river. The pilings had to be then topped with caps that required 450 truckloads of concrete, which for reasons of structural integrity needed to be all poured in a single pour. This necessitated the utilization of virtually every available cement truck in the entire region. The base of the towers can in theory withstand an impact by a large freighter moving at 12 knots, likely faster than a large ship would be moving at this location.

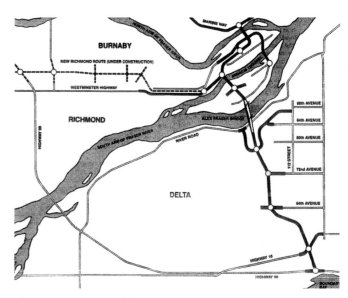

Above. The Alex Fraser Bridge was opened on 22 September 1986 by Premier Bill Vander Zalm. Two days before, the provincial government published this map showing the bridge in the context of all the highway improvements being made. The main north–south route from the Queensborough Bridge to Highway 99 at Boundary Bay is complete, but the *New Richmond Route* (the East-West Connector) is still under construction and would not be complete for another three years. Even then there were traffic lights at the Highway 91/91A intersection and at the 72nd Avenue intersection; the latter would only be removed in 2018. A connection with the new South Fraser Perimeter Road (Highway 17), which runs parallel to River Road under the south end of the bridge, was made in 2013.

A provincial government brochure calculated that the road system to and from the bridge required some 7 million cubic metres of sand, dredged from the Fraser River, and that amount would fill a train of coal cars stretching from Vancouver to Calgary!

Right. The Alex Fraser Bridge is a photographer's delight. Here, with a cloudless sky, the south tower with its accompanying cables is photographed vertically through the sunroof of a moving car using a fisheye lens, then converted to high-contrast black and white. See also page 6.

Attached to the towers are some 192 specially manufactured steel cables from 50 to 237 m in length that were imported from the UK. Each cable is made up of 283 strands of galvanized steel about the thickness of a pencil. The cables support a bridge deck that is 930 m long, and it has been estimated that if laid end to end they would be 26 km long. The multiple fans of cables make the Alex Fraser Bridge one of the Lower Mainland's most photogenic bridges.

The bridge construction was not without some controversy. In 1984 the St. Mungo Cannery site at the south end of the bridge was bulldozed for construction despite it being a significant historical site and an ancient Indigenous midden. And in the summer of 1985, to the outrage of many, a sewer line was accidentally cut while an access ramp was being prepared, dumping millions of litres of raw sewage into the river.

Above, top. The construction method for a cable-stayed bridge is well demonstrated in this photo of the Alex Fraser under construction. First the supporting towers are built, then the bridge deck is built out away from the tower in each direction at the same time, to maintain balance. Each new piece of deck is supported by new cables that reach higher and higher up the tower.

Above. When the bridge was complete, a provincial government brochure proudly compared its size to other tall structures. The bridge towers are 154.3 m above the pile cap, the height of a 50-storey building. By comparison, (the first) BC Place was 60 m, the Statue of Liberty 72 m, the Lions Gate Bridge 109 m, and Harbour Centre, the tallest building in Downtown Vancouver at the time, 148 m.

Left. In 1986, the bridge nears completion as crews lay the roadbed.

Right. Two views of the Alex Fraser, a vertical view and a side view. The latter particularly emphasizes the intricate patterns formed by the cables.

Above. The Alex Fraser Bridge from New Westminster. A car-carrying ship is unloading on Annacis Island in the foreground.

Left. A near-silhouette of the bridge seen from below.

Above. In 2019 the six-lane bridge was changed to seven lanes by narrowing the existing lanes a little, enabling the creation of a counterflow lane in the centre. The counterflow lane changes directions using this "zipper" truck, unique to Western Canada, which can move the specially created short-length median blocks over one lane's width as required.

An aerial view of the Alex Fraser Bridge in May 2018, looking south-southwest. Annacis Island is nearest to the camera, and Burns Bog can be seen in the middle distance.

Above. The approach spans are large bridges in their own right. This is the East Bridge across Annacis Channel, the main feeder onto the Alex Fraser from the East-West Connector (Highway 91). It is viewed from an observation deck on South Dyke Road in Queensborough. To the bridge's left an inlet can be seen. This was once the channel between Annacis Island and Patrick Island, a small island in the Annacis Channel now incorporated into the larger island.

Right. The West Bridge over the Annacis Channel from the north carries Highway 91A from the Queensborough Bridge and the Annacis Island off-ramp from Highway 91 onto the Alex Fraser. Almost directly underneath are these quite new houses, pleasantly situated on the river bank but subject to constant traffic noise from the bridge.

Below, left. The curves of the East Bridge over Annacis Channel, viewed from the west side.

Below, right. Another, less conventional view of the East Bridge, taken vertically from underneath with a fisheye lens and converted to black and white.

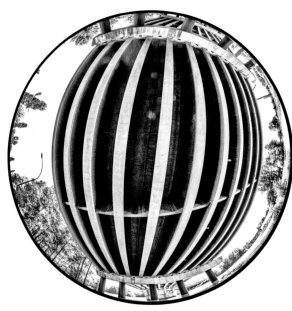

Annacis Island Bridge

In 1953, Grosvenor, a British real estate development company (owned by the Duke of Westminster, then the third-richest man in the world!) purchased the whole of Annacis Island, some 485 ha, with the intention of developing it as Canada's first industrial park. At the time there were no bridges to the island, and so Grosvenor built a combination causeway and trestle across the northeastern end of Annacis Channel. This was facilitated by the simultaneous reclamation of the small Robson Island, plus a sandbank that is now the entire northern tip of Annacis Island, today home to a huge vehicle importing dock, storage and shipping area.

The bridge, named the Annacis Causeway but sometimes referred to as the Pembina Causeway (since Pembina was the road that led onto the crossing), was opened on 22 July 1955, allowing the development of Annacis Island to begin. It carried both road and rail.

In 1984, with Annacis Island growing apace, the trestle and causeway were replaced by a more substantial structure, the Annacis Island Swing Bridge.

Right, top and centre. Two views of the Annacis Causeway under construction in 1955.

Below, left. This map extract from 1949 shows the situation before development of Annacis Island began, with the small *Robson* Island, which was connected to Annacis by filling and provided the stepping stone for the 1955 trestle. The water area at the northern tip of *Annacis Island* (where the "b" of *Queensborough* is on the map) was also filled and is now filled with imported cars waiting to be shipped to the rest of Canada. Note also on this map a footbridge to *Poplar I.* in the North Arm. This island was home to shipyards during World War I and at the time of this map was owned by Rayonier, a forestry company. It became a nature reserve in 1995.

Below, right. This map shows the same area in 1962, with a bridge to *Annacis I.* Also shown are the CNR Lulu Island Bridge, over the North Arm at left; the then new third Queensborough Bridge; the second Queensborough (BCER) Bridge, still shown as a road; the Pattullo Bridge; and the New Westminster (rail) Bridge.

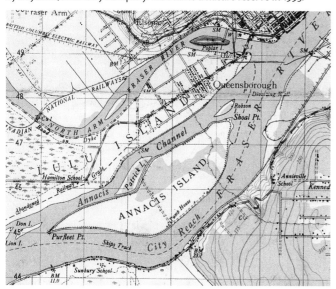

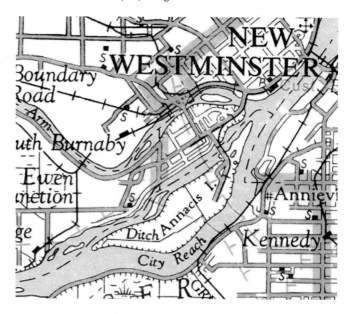

Above. Detail of the Annacis swing span construction: many bolts that hold part of the bridge together, painted with now-weathered light blue paint against corrosion, make an interesting photograph.

Left. Another detail: the joint between the swing span and the fixed span on the railway track. Heavy locomotives and freight cars need as small a gap as possible—here it is about 10 cm—and are locked in position by what could best be described as "flaps" of steel that are raised when the bridge is opened. Again, rail traffic is less tolerant of misaligned rails than rubber-tired road traffic would be.

Opposite, top. Two Southern Railway of BC (Rail Link) locomotives return across the bridge after making a delivery to Annacis Island. The bridge control tower is in the background.

Opposite, bottom. This aerial photo was taken in 1955, just after the first bridge had been completed. The "half-causeway-half-bridge" nature of this crossing can be seen. Robson Island has disappeared, but the northern tip of Annacis is still in the process of being reclaimed. Just a few buildings have been built. In the background is the North Arm of the Fraser with the second Queensborough (BCER) Bridge. The dense patch of trees is Poplar Island.

Westham Island Bridge

A complete change of pace, the bridge connecting Westham Island to the mainland in Delta over Canoe Pass in the Lower Fraser River is well over a hundred years old and recognized as a heritage structure. It was completed in 1909 and officially opened on 29 March 1910, superseding a small and irregular ferry. The bridge's principal purpose was to allow island farmers to transport their produce to market.

The bridge is significant as a rare surviving example of a Howe-truss swing bridge, unique in the Lower Mainland. It was built with a combination of heavy timber diagonal beams (for compression) with vertical iron roads to control tension; it has been modified somewhat over the years and is now partly a steel-truss structure. The swing span was manually operated until 1974, when it was electrified.

The bridge provides the only access to the Reifel Migratory Bird Sanctuary, and its enduring structural form has led to its being featured in many movies; of course, it is also an interesting location for photographers.

Above, top. The wood-and-metal rod structure is seen in this span of the bridge, as is the wooden road deck.

Above. The whole 325-m length of the bridge is seen in this view across marshlands from River Road West.

Above. A tractor crosses the bridge. It was originally built so that island farmers could easily get their produce to market.

Above. A classic full fisheye of the bridge appears to bend the truss members nearest the camera. *Left*. The steel swing span. *Right*. The east wooden span was replaced with another wooden span on 13 June 1924. Here it is being floated into place. The photo is from the annual report of the BC Department of Public Works for 1924–25.

New Westminster's Three Bridges

Given New Westminster's status, until the founding of Vancouver in 1886, as the only city on the mainland of British Columbia, it is perhaps surprising that, before 1883, there was no ferry; people wishing to cross the river mostly got someone to row them across in a small open boat. Transport of anything like a farm cart had to involve one of the steam riverboats plying the Fraser River at that time, but there were few schedules and little reliability.

The first ferry began in 1883 but was notoriously unreliable. It used an old threshing machine engine for propulsion and was operated

Above. New Westminster's three bridges in February 2017. Nearest to the camera is SkyBridge, opened in 1990, then the Pattullo Bridge, opened in 1937, and, lower than the others, New Westminster Bridge, opened in 1904.

Left. The ferries *K de K* (*top*) and *Surrey*.

Below. A span of the New Westminster Bridge is carefully manoeuvred into position on 11 November 1903.

by Peter Byrne, later a reeve of Burnaby. The vessel's antics gave it the local name of "The Sudden Jerk." Byrne only ran his ferry if there was no more profitable venture available that day!

The following year the city voted to authorize borrowing of money to enable a contract for a regular ferry service to be signed. Captain Angus Grant began operating the *K de K*, still a rather rickety affair, on a two-hour schedule. Despite its appearance, the *K de K* provided a reasonably reliable service.

In 1891 New Westminster acquired a much more imposing ferry. A double-hulled catamaran, *Surrey* began service in February 1891, the same month the Great Northern Railway–sponsored New Westminster Southern Railway completed its line from a connection with the Fairhaven & Southern Railroad at Blaine to Liverpool—and then Brownsville and South Westminster—all on the Fraser River opposite New Westminster.

The Canadian Pacific Railway, which had arrived in New Westminster in 1886 as a branch line from the main line to its own creation—Vancouver—promptly withdrew its connecting service to Vancouver to try to hobble GN. Pas-

sengers had to struggle to reach a less conveniently located interurban terminal to continue to Vancouver. (The interurban also opened to New Westminster in 1891.)

All this changed in 1904, with the opening of the New Westminster Bridge, a steel railway bridge with a wooden roadway for vehicles above. Premier James Dunsmuir committed to building a bridge in 1901 to forestall the possibility that GN might build its own bridge farther upstream, bypassing New Westminster altogether. (Vancouver, Westminster & Yukon Railway, another GN subsidiary, had begun service between New Westminster and Vancouver on 31 December 1903 via a line north of Burnaby Lake.) Bridge construction began in July 1902, and the bridge was completed and opened two years later, on 23 July 1904.

Right. A commemorative postcard published when the New Westminster Bridge opened.

Below. The first train to cross the New Westminster Bridge, on opening day, 23 July 1904. The line connected to the GN subsidiary New Westminster Southern, but the train is from Victoria, having arrived at Port Guichon (Ladner) on the Victoria Terminal & Ferry Co. ferry from Vancouver Island, another Great Northern–controlled company. The locomotive is Victoria & Sidney Railway *No. 2*, and at least one of the coaches is from the Vancouver, Westminster & Yukon Railway, all GN controlled. The north-side span, on which the train is posed, is a "Y" to allow trains to come off the bridge in either direction.

Above. The New Westminster Bridge was an important landmark that warranted postcard views, like this one from soon after the bridge opened. Note the upper roadway.

Left. GN was joined by two other railways using the bridge: BCER, with its interurban line to Chilliwack, in 1910, and transcontinental Canadian Northern Pacific (later Canadian National) in 1915. Here a CN train, *The Confederation*, with a sightseeing car at the rear, is about to leave New Westminster Station and cross the bridge. This locomotive would pull the train only to Port Mann, where a faster locomotive would take over. The stronger but slower locomotive shown here (an N Class built in 1913) was used west of Port Mann because of the 1.1 percent grade in the Grandview Cut, the steepest part of the entire line west of Winnipeg.

Above. A two-car BCER interurban train has just left the west "Y" of the New Westminster Bridge in this 1948 photo.

Below. At the other end of the bridge the line splits into three, all on trestles: the GN line to the US border (left), the BCER line to Chilliwack (centre), and the CN transcontinental line (right). This 1949 photo shows an interurban on the junction, with the Pattullo Bridge, completed in 1937, at left.

Left. Over the years the bridge has had a number of mishaps. Here the main fixed span has been destroyed by an empty log barge that broke away from its moorings on Boxing Day afternoon, 1975. The collapsing span took with it high-voltage power lines above. So mangled was the span that a new one had to be made; this was placed into position on 21 April 1976.

Below. You might think that steel bridges cannot catch fire, but of course there is plenty of wood involved with their construction. On 29 May 1982, shortly after a CN train had passed, the creosoted ties were on fire. The fire quickly spread, engulfing the control tower; a traffic jam ensued on the adjacent Pattullo Bridge as spectators gawked. After the fire was extinguished, the swing span was hand cranked open to allow ships to pass while repairs took place. When the track was replaced, it was with new concrete ties. Trains were able to resume using the bridge on 23 June.

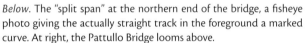

Below. The "split span" at the northern end of the bridge, a fisheye photo giving the actually straight track in the foreground a marked curve. At right, the Pattullo Bridge looms above.

The New Westminster Bridge as it is today, still federally owned, with the track used by all railways. *Above*, a view of the entire bridge from Front Street, with a Canadian Pacific freight crossing, 8 August 2020. *Below*, a CN freight crosses on 18 September 2019, viewed from the south bank.

BC Premier Thomas Dufferin "Duff" Pattullo decided to build a new bridge at New Westminster after he was elected to office in November 1933, refusing to continue with building a bridge lower down the Fraser (at the site where the Massey Tunnel would later be built; see page 58) authorized by his predecessor, Simon Tolmie. It was a bold decision in the midst of the Depression.

The estimated cost was $4 million, which was equal to the entire budget for road building and maintenance in 1929, the last "normal" year before the Depression began. Even that was an underestimate, as the final cost was $6 million. But it was probably necessary, as it replaced the road part of the 1904 bridge, by then subject to load restrictions and frequent openings of its swing span, causing much congestion.

Plans were drawn up for a steel-truss through-arch bridge, but Pattullo ran into a problem with the federal government, which decided that a bridge so close to the 1904 one would present a navigational hazard. They insisted on the replacement of the swing span of the 1904 bridge with a lift span. Pattullo outmanoeuvred the federal government by serving notice on CN, BCER and GN that he was going to close the 1904 bridge down (they had signed a contract years earlier allowing for this). The federal government was responsible for CN and knew it required a bridge, so a compromise was reached whereby the 1904 bridge would be turned over to the federal government free of charge. Pattullo could proceed with his new bridge, which was completed and officially opened on 15 November 1937, exactly four years after Pattullo's election.

The new Pattullo Bridge charged tolls that were very much disliked by many people, who had previously been able to cross the river free, earning the bridge the name "Pay-tolla." After farm trucks were allowed to cross for free, more than a few motorists cut the backs of their cars down and, perhaps with a bale of hay in the back, were able to qualify for a "K" licence, which meant they were legally a truck. Tolls lasted until 1952, when the new W.A.C. Bennett government removed them.

Left, top. The Pattullo Bridge under construction in 1937.

Left, centre. The south approach under construction, as seen from the 1904 bridge approach.

Left, bottom. The main arch is half complete in this early-1937 photo.

Below. A Pattullo Bridge "commutation" toll ticket.

Right. The Pattullo Bridge viewed from under the 1904 bridge at Front Street.

Below, bottom. A veritable symphony of multicoloured steel: the two bridges.

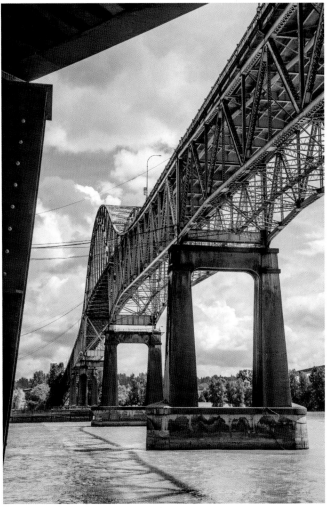

Above. The mass of steel in the Pattullo Bridge is evident in this telephoto image of the main span. The narrowness of the lanes with no proper divider can also be seen.

Below. This attempt at an artistic view of the bridge was created by moving a zoom lens during exposure.

Above, top. A postcard photo of the bridge soon after it opened in 1937 shows the lack of much development on the Surrey side of the river.

Above. In 2008, TransLink, responsible for regional transit and some roads and bridges, including the Pattullo, decided to replace the bridge rather than re-habilitate it, although some work was necessary just to ensure the bridge remained functional until a new one arrived. In 2020 a contract was signed. Work began in February 2021, and a new Pattullo Bridge is expected to be open in 2024, though its name will likely be a new one.

Right. A view from immediately under the bridge shows the massive concrete piers and the steel trusses under the road deck.

Above. SkyBridge under construction in 1989. The portion of the bridge attached to the southernmost tower was completed first, then the north-side one. This aerial view looks towards New Westminster and the southern half is nearing completion. All three bridges can be seen.

The third bridge across the Fraser at New Westminster was SkyTrain's SkyBridge, a cable-stayed structure. Metro Vancouver's Advanced Light Rapid Transit (ALRT) system began with the completion of the Expo Line from Downtown Vancouver to New Westminster, which opened in time for Expo 86 on 11 December 1985. In 1987 construction began on an extension to Surrey. SkyBridge opened on 16 March 1990, allowing SkyTrain to run to Scott Road Station; in 1994 the terminus was extended to King George Station.

At the time of its construction, the 616-m-long SkyBridge was the longest cable-stayed transit-only bridge in the world; it is still the second-longest, having been surpassed in 2019 by the Egongyan Rail Transit Bridge in Chongqing, China.

Right. The southern approach spans of SkyBridge form a graceful and very slender structure, an engineering achievement in its own right.

Opposite. Anglers take in the view right under SkyBridge on the Surrey bank of the Fraser. On the far side is the iconic "Big W," a 2015 public art installation by Brazilian artist José Resende; this was removed in September 2020 following a disastrous fire on the New Westminster waterfront.

Above. SkyBridge, like most bridges, has its share of artistic graffiti.

Above. A view of the SkyBridge from below on the eastern side of the New Westminster end. This angle manages to exclude the visual confusion of the other two adjacent bridges.

Opposite. Sometimes visual confusion is what the photographer wants. Here four(!) bridges can be seen—with SkyBridge being reflected in the foreground rain puddle. Conversion to black and white ensures that emphasis remains on the shape, form and pattern of the bridges. Even the foreground railing helps.

Above and *right*. The footbridge on the New Westminster waterfront gives access to the riverside part across the tracks. SkyBridge can be seen in the background. The photo was taken because of the footbridge's interesting design, but a view of the whole retains a portable toilet, which detracts from the image. The wonders of Photoshop could have removed it, of course, but then the image would not be true to life. The real aim of the photographer here, however, was the distinctive steelwork of the bridge, which has been captured in the cropped image at right. The pattern is made even more interesting by the mesh covering.

Central Lower Fraser

Port Mann Bridge

There have been two Port Mann Bridges, the first opening in 1964 and the second in 2012. The first bridge, a through-arch structure, was part of the freeway system envisaged at that time, and was built as a connection from the first urban freeway in Burnaby and Coquitlam across the Fraser River to the rest of Canada via the Trans-Canada Highway, Highway 1 (401 until 1973).

More significantly, the Port Mann Bridge opened up the Fraser Valley to the residents north of the river in a way not seen since the opening of the New Westminster Bridge in 1904. But now travel was by car rather than rail, or, after 1910, interurban, and the numbers were much higher. Surrey stores immediately began advertising their new accessibility. Guildford Town Centre, the third-largest shopping centre in the province, opened in 1966, its viability assured by the new bridge.

Though planned about the same time as the Deas Island Tunnel (see page 58), construction did not begin until 1959, and completion of the entire freeway and bridge system was slated for 1962. But unexpected engineering challenges with the bridge footings in the difficult river sediments, plus labour unrest issues, delayed the official opening until June 1964, although parts of the freeway had opened the previous year.

On opening day, 12 June 1964, Premier W.A.C. Bennett and his Highways Minister "Flyin' Phil" Gaglardi opened the bridge and then roared up the freeway to Chilliwack at 70 mph (113 km/h). Gaglardi was infamous for his collection of speeding tickets; that very day he raised the speed limit on the freeway from the planned 65 mph (105 km/h) to 70, then boasted that you could now drive from Vancouver to Chilliwack in 45 minutes—without breaking the speed limit (you can't).

The first Port Mann Bridge was the last riveted bridge in British Columbia. It was designed by hand, but it was also the first bridge in which computers were extensively used to aid the construction process. It was also the first orthotropic steel deck in North America—that is, one made with a roadbed foundation of structural steel, which allowed it to contribute to the

[continued on page 94]

Opposite. This aerial photo, looking from Coquitlam over the river to Surrey, was taken on 29 September 1961. The supports for the bridge approaches on both sides of the river are nearly complete, as is the earth berm on the north side. Note the CN Port Mann rail yard on the far bank and the lack of any development on the Coquitlam side.

Below. Temporary arch supports as seen from the bridge deck, 12 September 1963.

Above. Construction of the first Port Mann Bridge, May 1963. Note the temporary steel towers (also *left, bottom*) to support the arches of the main span until they connect. Note also the Pitt River road and rail bridges in the background.

Below. The bridge nears completion on 11 June 1964; the bridge deck has been laid.

Above. A postcard of the 1964 Port Mann Bridge published that year shows an almost rural landscape on the Coquitlam (nearest camera) side.

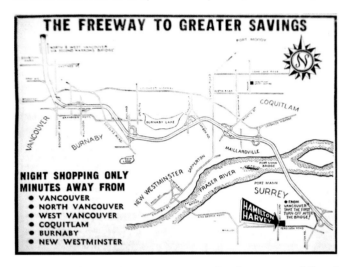

Above. One of many advertisements promoting the new accessibility of Surrey to the rest of Vancouver north of the river. This one appeared in the *Vancouver Sun* the day before the bridge opened.

Above, right, top. The government ad announcing the bridge's opening.

Below. The new bridge takes shape in this view from the top of the south tower in 2010. Note the temporary access pier.

Right, centre. In 2001, the bridge underwent a seismic upgrade, and an eastbound high-occupancy vehicle (HOV) lane was added by removing the pedestrian walkways and rebuilding them outside the road deck. This photo shows the new rebuilt walkway.

Announcing –
The opening of the Port Mann Bridge and lower mainland FREEWAY section of the Trans-Canada Highway.

Right, top. A photo taken on 24 June 2012, the new bridge (at right) would soon be open, and views of the old one like this would be gone forever.

Right, bottom. Crossing the old bridge on 24 June 2012.

Far right, bottom. For environmental reasons the old bridge was removed by reverse construction. This fisheye view taken on 12 November 2014 vertically through the sunroof of a moving car on the new bridge shows (at right) the temporary tower built to hold up the structure of the old bridge during its dismantling. This is the same procedure, in reverse, used when the bridge was constructed (see photos, *previous page*).

Below. The 1964 bridge.

Right. The Port Mann Bridges at the halfway point of the construction of the new bridge, 12 September 2011. Only a relatively small number of the cables that would support the new bridge's deck are in place at this point, despite already looking like a veritable cable forest. The bridge deck is being built out in both directions from both towers. The principle of cable-stayed bridge construction is that the cables are anchored in the main support towers rather than going right over them to an anchor point on shore as with a suspension bridge.

load bearing of the whole bridge structure and also allowed the bridge to expand or contract as much as a metre. Gaglardi pushed for this design after seeing it employed on bridges in Germany.

In 2006 the provincial government unveiled the Gateway Program, which included a considerably upgraded freeway from McGill Street in Vancouver to 216th Street in Langley and a new bridge across the Fraser at Port Mann. The originally envisaged idea was to twin the existing bridge, but the government instead decided to build a new 10-lane replacement bridge. The new bridge and improved freeway were to relieve what was then considered the worst bottleneck in British Columbia. The bridge project was initially to be a public-private partnership (PPP), but the terms could not be agreed upon, and so the province funded the entire project.

The eastbound lanes of the new cable-stayed structure opened to traffic on 18 September 2012. The bridge initially held an unusual record as the world's widest long-span bridge (it is 65 m wide), though this record was lost to the San Francisco–Oakland Bay Bridge a year later. The bridge is 2.02 km long and, with its 470 m distance between the main towers, it was one of the longest cable-stayed bridges in the world, though it has now been superseded by dozens of bridges, particularly in China.

Between December 2012 and October 2015, the old bridge was completely removed using a reverse construction process for environmental reasons.

In order for the province to recoup its cost of building the new bridge, tolls were collected electronically; sensors were placed on a structure on the Surrey side. During the 2017 provincial election the NDP promised to remove them if they were elected. After they won, all tolls were removed on 1 September 2017. (They were also removed from the Golden Ears Bridge at the same time.)

Below. Old and new bridges, 24 June 2012.

Opposite. Four ways of photographing the cables of the cable-stayed Port Mann Bridge: *clockwise from top left*: with a fisheye lens, with a telephoto lens, as a reflection in an industrial building below the bridge, and as a side view, here transformed to look like a pen-and-ink sketch.

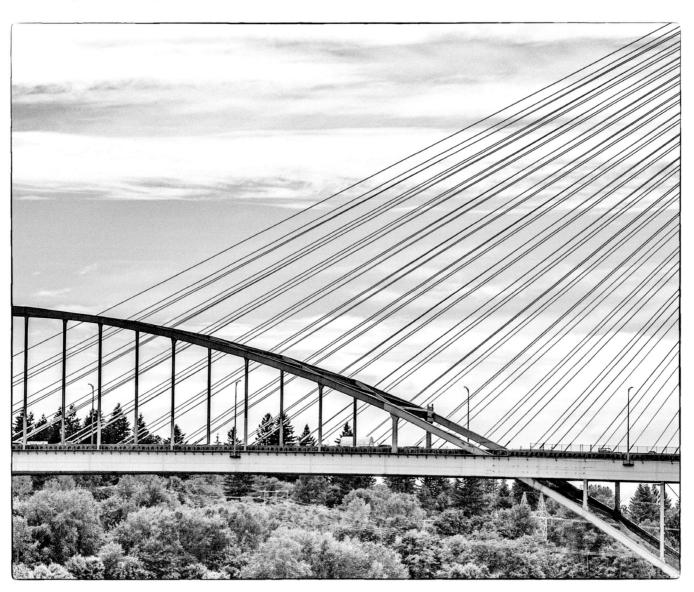

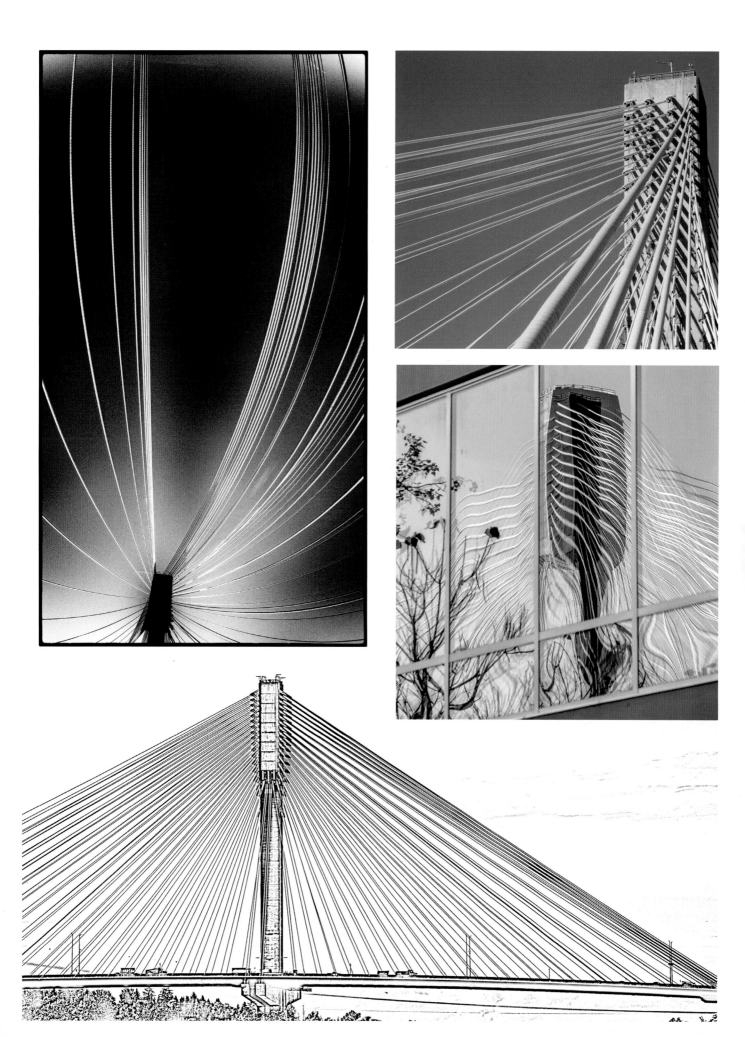

Above. A study of the Port Mann Bridge against a clear blue sky. The photo was taken from the south approach on 5 December 2018.

Golden Ears Bridge

The Golden Ears Bridge is an extradosed bridge—that is, a combination of a prestressed box-girder bridge and a cable-stayed bridge. It connects north Langley with Pitt Meadows and Maple Ridge. When completed, it was the longest extradosed bridge in North America, with four towers spanning over 2 km.

The bridge was built to replace the Albion Ferry, which operated upstream between McMillan Island at Fort Langley and the Albion neighbourhood of Maple Ridge. The ferry began service on 2 June 1957 and was closed down on 31 July 2009, after the bridge opened.

The first ferry was MV *T'Lagunna*, which had been transferred here from the Agassiz–Hope route after that bridge opened in 1956. Originally named MV *Agassiz*, it was built in 1931 and had a capacity of only 16 vehicles (see photo page 187). In 1978 another ferry, MV *Kulleet*, able to carry 26 vehicles, was put into service with *T'Lagunna*, and in 1985 MV *Klatawa* replaced *T'Lagunna*. Both *Kulleet* and *Klatawa* were K Class ferries previously operated on short routes in the Gulf Islands by the BC Ministry of Highways, taken over by BC Ferries in 1985.

Klatawa was converted to run on natural gas and when licensed on 16 December 1985 became the first natural gas–powered ferry in the world.

With traffic rapidly becoming too much for the ferries to handle, a new bridge was planned some 9 km downstream. Built as a public-private partnership (PPP), construction began in mid-2006 and included building 14 km of connecting roads both north and south of the river.

The bridge, unusually, opened for traffic without fanfare at two in the morning on 16 June 2009. Two days before, however, pedestrians had been allowed on the new bridge, and the result, as CBC News reported, was the bridge's "first traffic jam and it didn't involve a single car," as thousands crammed onto the bridge deck to take a first look.

Above. MV *Klatawa*, the first natural gas–powered ferry in the world.

Below. MV *Kulleet* leaves the McMillan Island dock en route for Albion on 14 June 2009, the very day the Golden Ears Bridge opened for pedestrians. Not everyone wanted to see ferry service here end, as can be seen by the sign at left. Juxtaposition of the sign and ferry makes for a great historical photo.

As with the Port Mann Bridge built three years later, the (electronic) tolls were removed in 2017 following an NDP victory at the provincial polls that year.

The Golden Ears Bridge, with its multiple cable-stayed spans, does not have the high towers of the Port Mann or Alex Fraser but still manages to provide some interesting photographic opportunities.

Above. Golden Ears Bridge from the Langley side. The perspective of this telephoto view emphasizes the many cables.

Right. The bridge from Emmeline Mohun Park in Maple Ridge. This more side-on view makes the cables less visible.

Barnston Island Ferry

Barnston Island, a large island in the Fraser between the Port Mann and Golden Ears Bridges, has never had a large population but, because of river flooding, has good farming land. By 1915 the island had its own school, and a foot ferry became a vehicle ferry in 1916—a barge pushed by a small boat. In 1921 the government purchased a fishing boat to use as a ferry; every morning before starting regular service it sailed right around the island picking up milk from several farms (including Avalon Dairy, which began in 1906), returning the empty cans before stopping running for the night.

The ferry remains a barge pushed by a small boat today, though the barge is somewhat more sophisticated. There has been some demand for a bridge to replace the ferry because of isolation after the ferry shuts down at night, but others fear it might lead to industrialization. In 2006 an application to remove most of Barnston Island's land from the Agricultural Land Reserve had been rejected.

Above, left. Two schoolteachers wait for the ferry in 1915.

Above, right. From 1921 vehicles could be carried by this barge pushed by a fishing boat, basically the same as today. Note the milk can at left.

Right and *below*. Three views of the Barnston Island Ferry in operation today. The boat is attached to the barge with ropes. *Below, right*, loading on the island side requires motorists to reverse onto the ferry barge.

North Arm of the Fraser

Marpole Bridge

The fertility of Richmond was apparent early on in Vancouver's modern history, and in 1889 a connection with Vancouver—what is now Downtown Vancouver—was made with the completion of the Granville Street Bridge across False Creek, which allowed easy access to a trail to Marpole—along what became Granville Street. Marpole did not receive that name until 1916. Before that, settlements on both the north and south sides of the Fraser were known as Eburne.

From northernmost Eburne a bridge was built in two parts: one across the North Arm of the river to Sea Island, and one across the Middle Arm from Sea Island to Lulu Island, the main part of Richmond. The bridge never appeared to receive an official name, being variously called the Eburne Bridge, the Sea Island Bridge, the Marpole Bridge, or, separately, the North Arm Bridge and Middle Arm Bridge—none being very inspiring names!

Before the bridge was built, there was a great deal of squabbling between the provincial government, Vancouver and Richmond as to who would pay for it. And permission had to be obtained from the federal government, which had legal jurisdiction over the navigable river.

Despite all the wrangling, the need for a bridge here was clear, and in reality everyone wanted it—they just didn't want to pay for it. The $17,500 bridge contract was given to the San Francisco Bridge Company, and the bridge was completed in late November 1889. However, on 3 January 1890, about six weeks after the bridge had been completed, a large sheet of ice floated up the river on a rising tide and wiped out the swing span on the Middle Arm part of the bridge. It was

Above. Pictured being rebuilt in 1891, the Eburne Bridge, as it was then, sports the notice about speed referred to in the text (page 102).

repaired, but was out of service for most of 1890, and, soon after it was back in service, the same swing span fell into the river, for no obvious reason.

In 1902, the two spans were replaced because the existing structures were rotting. Then, again, in 1924–25 both spans of the bridge were completely replaced with steel and wood, and an asphalted road surface was added in 1926.

The Marpole Bridge lasted many years (until its replacement by the Oak Street Bridge in 1957), but this pattern repeated itself all too frequently and was a constant irritant to Richmond and to the provincial government, which took over responsibility for the bridge in 1901 (though Richmond had to pay an annual fee until 1921, when the government accepted that the bridge had become of use to many people farther afield than Richmond). Both parts of the bridge changed shape over the years, being replanked, repainted and even partly rebuilt.

Below. The Eburne Bridge soon after its construction. A family takes a boating trip in the river beneath.

Left. A very early aerial photo, taken 27 May 1919, shows the Middle Arm part of the Marpole Bridge nearest the camera. The bridge originally used the island (Duck Island) as a stepping stone to Lulu Island (at right); the slough between was filled in during the 1960s, after the bridge had gone. (The slough is now the location of Richmond Night Market.) The BCER bridge (see next page) is in the background. Compare with a modern aerial photo (looking in the reverse direction) on page 122.

Below, centre. The North Arm part of the Eburne Bridge in 1911. At this time land in Eburne (Marpole) seen in this photo, looking north, was being heavily promoted for sale, and (at left) a lumber mill had been built.

Above. On a misty morning sometime around 1930, a lone car crosses the twice-rebuilt North Arm part of the bridge. The Middle Arm portion can just be seen in the distance.

Left. An aerial view of the Marpole Bridges taken in 1954, three years before the Oak Street Bridge opened, looking north. The North Arm bridge is at centre top left, from Marpole to Sea Island. The Middle Arm bridge in the foreground, from Sea Island to Duck Island, and then to Lulu Island (not seen in this image). Duck Island is now part of Lulu Island.

In 1891, after the second time the swing span needed repair, a notice had been posted: "Parties Driving Faster than a Walk Will Be Prosecuted According to the Law." Sixty years later, with much heavier traffic, a committee campaigning to get a new bridge posted another sign. It read: "Notice! Parties Walking over This Bridge Will Get There Faster than Driving!"

Despised by motorists and mariners alike, the Marpole Bridge was finally replaced by the Oak Street Bridge and Moray Bridge in 1957. The North Arm part was removed right away, but the Middle Arm portion remained until 1965–66.

CPR–BCER Marpole Bridge

Also known as the Marpole Bridge was the railway bridge built by the Canadian Pacific Railway in 1902 for its subsidiary the Vancouver & Lulu Island Railway, which ran from the CPR yards in Downtown Vancouver, across False Creek on the Kitsilano Trestle (see page 40), crossing the North Arm of the Fraser in a single span at Marpole, then known as Eburne. The line was intended to service the salmon canneries that had been established at Steveston. In July 1902 the railway began operating a twice-a-day service to Steveston.

In 1905 the CPR leased the line to the British Columbia Electric Railway Company (BCER), which electrified the line and began an interurban service, both for passengers and freight, to Steveston. The first electric tram crossed the river on 4 July 1905. Soon known as the Sockeye Limited, the service opened up the area between Sea Island and Steveston to increased settlement. The Steveston interurban ran until 28 February 1958, when the service finally succumbed to the automobile and the bus.

After that, much of the track in Richmond was abandoned, though some industrial areas still retained service. In 1986 BCER relinquished its lease. By 2010, all the track was disused. North of the bridge, after much negotiation with the City of Vancouver, the right-of-way was sold and has been converted into the Arbutus Greenway pedestrian and cycle path.

A probably intentionally set fire in 2014 destroyed a 100-m section of the south approach trestle, the smoke temporarily closing the Oak Street Bridge and impacting flights at Vancouver International Airport. In 2016 a barge collided with the bridge, prompting CP to remove the swing span, and the swing platform was removed the following year.

Above. An interurban train at the south end of the CPR–BCER Bridge about 1957, a view now possible after the Oak Street Bridge opened that year.

Above. The CPR–BCER Bridge in 1956. The Oak Street Bridge is under construction in the background.

Above. Another aerial photo, taken in the mid-1950s, shows the CPR–BCER Bridge in the foreground, and the Marpole Bridges behind it, including a clear view of Duck Island. In the background is the Dinsmore Bridge to Dinsmore Island (later part of Sea Island), the wartime community of Burkeville, and the runways of Vancouver Airport, when the main terminal was at the location of the south airport now.

Left. The remains of the CPR–BCER Bridge on 17 September 2017, after the swing span had been removed but before its platform was also removed.

Below. An interurban train crosses the CPR–BCER Bridge about 1957. The Oak Street Bridge, completed that year, is in the background.

Above. Sometime in 1957, a BCER interurban train heads for Richmond over the south trestle of the CPR–BCER Bridge in the evening light, with a newly completed Oak Street Bridge in the background.

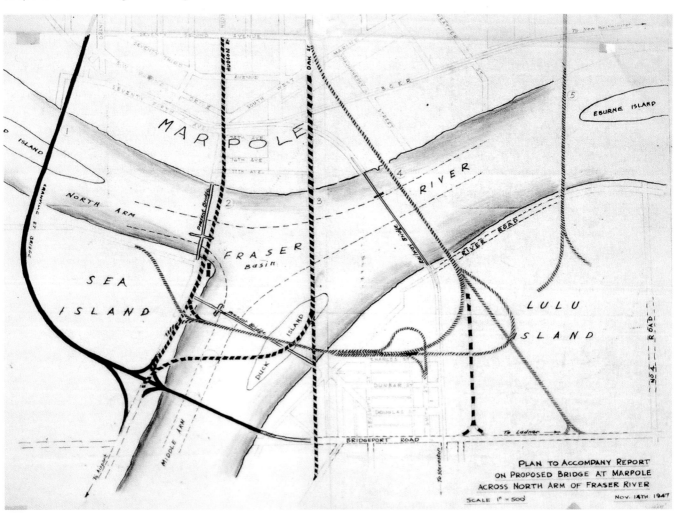

Oak Street Bridge

After World War II, Richmond began to grow, and traffic on the Marpole Bridge was increasing every year, with much grumbling about the frequent traffic jams, particularly a problem when either of the spans was opened for marine traffic. Indeed, traffic was increasing almost everywhere. The new W.A.C. Bennett Social Credit provincial government, elected in 1952, introduced a highways program in 1954 that included a new bridge over the Fraser at Marpole. Of simple haunched-girder design, at first it was called simply the New Marpole Bridge but was eventually named, no more imaginatively, the Oak Street Bridge.

The provincial government paid the entire $10 million cost of building the Oak Street Bridge, despite many protestations to Ottawa that it provided access to the federally owned (after 1962; it was owned by the City of Vancouver before that) Vancouver Airport. The federal government did contribute $400,000 to a new bridge system but specified it be used for the $1 million Moray Channel Bridge (see page 122).

The Oak Street Bridge was opened on 1 July 1957 (for pedestrians only; 3 July for traffic), the same day as the Moray Channel Bridge, with the announcement that a toll of 25 cents would be charged for bridge crossing for twelve and a half years. This caused so much uproar that the premier had to backtrack, though in fact the tolls stayed until 31 March 1964. The tolls were such a big deal that the day after the Oak Street Bridge opened there were major traffic jams on the ancient Fraser Street Bridge (see page 113) 2.5 km upriver as commuters tried to avoid the new toll.

Two years later the Deas Island Tunnel and a connecting freeway from the Oak Street Bridge were opened, making the bridge even more critically located, although the continuing freeway to the US border waited another two years after that.

In 1956 Richmond's population was 25,978, and had been growing at a rate of around 600 persons per year, but in 1961, four years after the Oak Street Bridge opened, it had risen to 42,323, an increase of almost 4,500 per year. Such is the power of accessibility.

The nearly 70-year-old Oak Street Bridge has proven to be one of the most long-lived of the critical bridges of the Lower Mainland. It has undergone many improvements and seismic upgrades. Most visible to drivers were concrete dividers down the middle of the road and new guardrails on the sides, both installed in 1995.

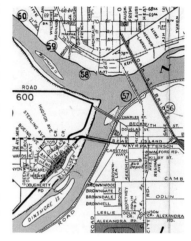

Left. This map was produced in 1947 as the realization set in that a new bridge would be required to cross the Fraser at Marpole. It shows the options considered. The route shown in green is the one ultimately used—the Oak Street Bridge. Other options shown (west to east) are an extension of Granville Street to Sea Island; an extension of Hudson Street, also to Sea Island; and a direct southward extension of Oak Street. The first two required a further bridge from Sea Island to Lulu Island. The route chosen was the one most easily able to connect with the Deas Island Tunnel and provide a route to the airport as a side benefit; this materialized as the Moray Channel Bridge, which was built at the same time and opened simultaneously with the Oak Street Bridge (see page 122). Two other river crossings are shown: the CPR–BCER *Railway Bridge*, and the Fraser Street Bridge (at right, unnamed).

Below. An aerial view of the Oak Street Bridge under construction.

Right. The bridges at Marpole by 1960. The North Arm part of the Marpole Bridge has been removed, but the Middle Arm part remains. The *Oak St. Bridge* and the Moray Channel Bridge are shown.

The Oak Street Bridge under construction.

Above, left. Supports for the south approach, 1955.

Above. A record photo for the bridge contractor, Dominion Bridge, shows the main spans under construction 22 August 1956. The haunched-girder design (steel beams, thicker where they meet the bridge piers) can be seen.

Left. By March 1957, three months away from opening, the road deck has yet to be laid. The photo, taken looking towards Vancouver, gives the impression of a bridge in the air.

Arthur Laing Bridge

Some 18 years after the Marpole Bridge, the original link between Vancouver and Richmond, had disappeared, the Arthur Laing Bridge was completed in more or less the same location. Built as the Hudson Street Bridge, it was renamed before it opened for Arthur Laing, a local MP and cabinet minister, who had promoted the idea of a new bridge in this location but had died a few months before it opened.

The bridge was controversial. In 1971, while it was still in the planning stages, the federal government, which mainly intended to improve access to the airport, made two changes to the original plans: first, that it would have no tolls—fine with most people—but second, that ramps at the south end of the bridge that would have provided access to Richmond, without having to drive into the airport first, had to be removed. This caused consternation in Richmond but was approved of by Vancouver City Council.

The Arthur Laing Bridge, 1,676 m long with a main span of 270 m, opened to traffic on 27 August 1975 but was officially opened on 15 May 1976 by its namesake's widow. As a federally owned bridge its official name includes the French: Pont Arthur Laing.

Even after the bridge opened, the mayor of Vancouver, Jack Volrich, made it clear Vancouver did not want Richmond commuters clogging up Granville Street. As a result of Vancouver's unwillingness to accept Richmond traffic, by 1979 the bridge was operating at only 10 percent of its capacity, while the Oak Street Bridge was jammed. Disputes between levels of government dragged the arguments on, and it was not until 1986 (following a change of federal government in 1984) that the required ramps were built at the south end of the bridge and Richmond commuters could finally use it. Richmond population surges were noted both following the bridge's opening in 1975 and after 1986, when the new access ramps were added.

In May 1981 a single-engine plane approaching Vancouver Airport ran out of gas and flew (or glided, really) under the Granville Street exit overpass at the north end of the bridge, made a sharp left turn and crash-landed on the bridge deck. Amazingly, no one, including the pilot, was injured.

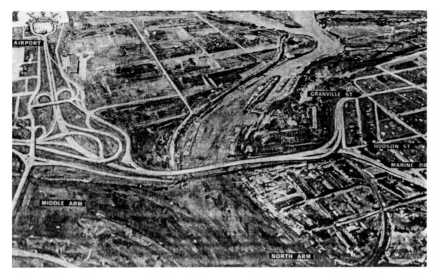

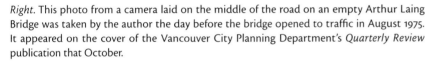

Above. This rough map, or aerial view, of the proposed bridge appeared in the *Richmond Review* on 4 November 1970 under the headline "$21.2 Million Cure for Traffic Headache" when the bridge was first announced by the federal Public Works Minister—Arthur Laing, no less. It included a spaghetti-like mass of roadways at the Sea Island end to allow connections to Lulu Island. But they were not to be, at least until 1986.

Right. This photo from a camera laid on the middle of the road on an empty Arthur Laing Bridge was taken by the author the day before the bridge opened to traffic in August 1975. It appeared on the cover of the Vancouver City Planning Department's *Quarterly Review* publication that October.

Below. The Arthur Laing Bridge, viewed from the south bank of the Fraser. The bridge is a cantilever design.

North Arm SkyTrain Bridge

Between 1990 and 1993, transportation planners evaluated possible routes for the next phase of rapid transit in Vancouver, a line to Richmond and Vancouver International Airport, which would have to include a bridge over, or a tunnel under, the North Arm of the Fraser. The need for a decision became more urgent with the prospect of the 2010 Winter Olympics to be held in Vancouver.

In 2001 the federal government established an infrastructure fund that would pay for its contribution to the new line, an amount that would be increased three years later. There was much negotiation over funding between levels of government—the provincial government ultimately made almost the same contribution as its federal counterpart, and the Vancouver Airport Authority, TransLink, and the City of Vancouver all added contributions—work began on the line in October 2005. In 2007 TransLink approved the addition of a pedestrian and bicycle path to the bridge. Construction was completed in August 2009, ahead of schedule, and the first service train crossed the bridge on opening day, 17 August 2009.

The North Arm SkyTrain Bridge is an extradosed bridge (a combination of cable-stayed and prestressed girder construction). It uses the westernmost tip of Mitchell Island (Twigg Island until 1927, when the two were connected) as a footing for its northernmost tower. Its main span is 180 m long and the whole bridge 562 m. Its elegant curved lines and accessibility via the pedestrian path make it a favourite with photographers.

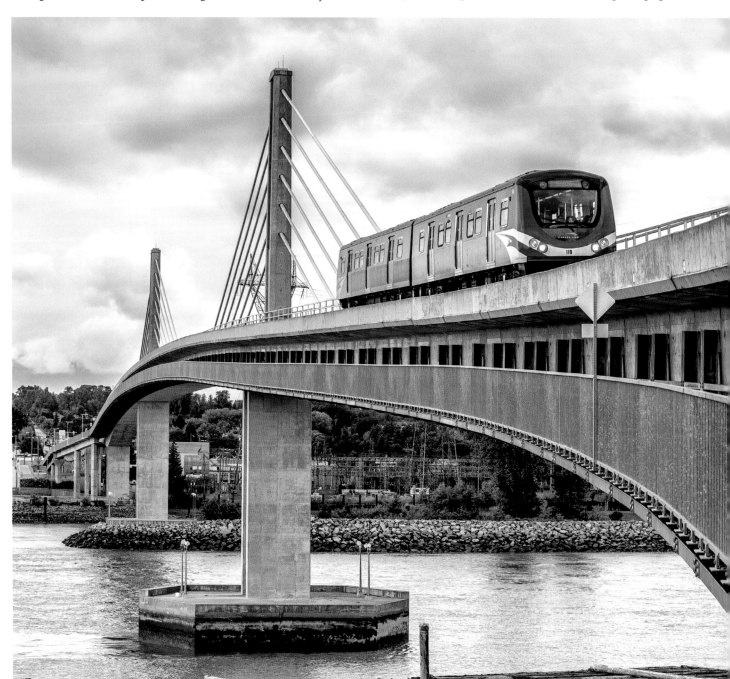

Above. The south approach to the bridge passes the maintenance yard (lowest ramp, with track showing), which, in addition to the Oak Street Bridge behind, adds to an apparent jumble of bridges.

Left. Two SkyTrains pass at the southern end of the bridge.

Opposite. A Canada Line train heads for Richmond in this photo taken from the pedestrian walkway in June 2012. Note the pier on the west point of Mitchell Island.

Above. SkyTrains, being automated, allow passengers to look out from the front of the train. Here is a close-up of the bridge cables, in the middle of the tracks, from a train.

Below. The silhouetted curves of the main bridge (top) and the pedestrian walkway railing lead the eye to a lone figure walking across the bridge.

Above. This aerial photo, taken on 16 July 2018, shows nine bridges, plus the Massey Tunnel in the background. The view is almost due south. From left (east): the remains of the Twigg Island Railway Bridge from Mitchell Island to Vancouver; across the North Arm of the Fraser, the North Arm SkyTrain Bridge (with the middle pier on the tip of Mitchell Island); the Oak Street Bridge, leading to the Highway 99 freeway south to the tunnel; and the Arthur Laing Bridge to Sea Island (at middle right). On the Middle Arm, between Sea Island and Lulu Island, are the Middle Arm SkyTrain Bridge; the Airport Connector Bridge; the Moray Channel Bridge; the Dinsmore Bridge; and the No. 2 Road Bridge (see page 124).

Twigg Island Rail and Road Bridge

The Twigg Island Bridge is probably the least known of all the Lower Mainland's major bridges, but it has a very intriguing history. For it is actually part of the road bridge installed across the Pitt River in 1915, which before that was the 1907 CPR Pitt River Bridge (see page 126), which had replaced the first wooden one from 1883, the latter made of that material to get the transcontinental line open as quickly as possible.

Until the mid-1950s the part of Mitchell Island that had been Twigg Island until the two were joined in 1926 was not occupied other than by pioneering settlers. The name Twigg Island, after local farmer and 1905–06 Richmond councillor J.J.C. Twigg, was rescinded in 1951.

In December 1956 Western Canada Steel purchased what had been called Twigg Island to build a new steel smelter and rolling mill, since the island offered potential easy docking facilities for iron-ore carriers. The company already owned manufacturing facilities opposite the island on the Vancouver shore; in fact it owned the entire 400-block of SE Marine Drive.

As part of this enterprise, a steel swing-span bridge was built to carry a rail line joining the mill with the BC Hydro rail line along Kent Avenue in Vancouver (the line originally built from Eburne to New Westminster by the CPR for the BCER in 1909).

In 1957 the company purchased three sections, including the swing span, of the 1915-built Pitt River (now road) Bridge, which was replaced that year, and on a Sunday morning in March 1958, when tide and wind conditions were right, floated it downstream in three sections to its new location. By April the bridge was installed, but adjustments continued until June, when it was opened. This was a quick solution for the company, since access to the island was needed before significant construction could start on the steel mill.

Since the rail bridge was built by the company for the company, it was a private bridge and was named as such on Vancouver City Engineer's maps. To allow its trucks to avoid the weight restriction on the Fraser Street Bridge, the rail bridge deck was boarded to enable vehicles to also cross the bridge.

Left. On 12 December 2020 the remains of the Twigg Island Railway Bridge, the two fixed spans, are forlornly reflected in the waters of the Mitchell Island north channel of the Fraser River in Richmond. The middle swing span was removed soon after the bridge was closed, to facilitate navigation. The truss structures provided a solid base for the electricity pylons.

Above. The swing span is open in this 1977 photo.

By 1963 Western Canada Steel's operation on Twigg Island boasted the world's largest induction furnace, for making steel ingots, and had an annual production of some 100,000 tons of steel ingots and employed 500. It was truly one of Vancouver's now-forgotten industrial giants!

After the new Knight Street Bridge opened, on 31 January 1974 the provincial government ended vehicle access to the Twigg Island Railway Bridge at the same time as the old Fraser Street Bridge, since easy access was now available from the new bridge.

In 1988 the steel mill closed, putting an end to steel-making aspirations in British Columbia; the swing span was removed to facilitate navigation on the river. The southern arm of the bridge and some adjacent land on the island became Mitchell Island Pier park, and the arm was used as a popular pier for fishing, a use which has recently stopped because of safety concerns with the aging bridge. But the somewhat picturesque structure remains.

Above. The south span of the Twigg Island Railway Bridge was used as a fishing pier as part of a Richmond park until the structure became unsafe. The north span can be seen on the other side of the river.

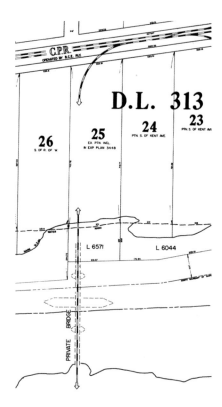

Above. A Vancouver City Engineer's map dated 1967 shows the branch line from the Marpole–to–New Westminster rail line (*C.P.R. Operated by B.C.E. Rly*) and the bridge to the steelworks as a *Private Bridge.*

Above, left. An aerial photo taken in 1977 shows the bridge, and the steelworks at the far end of Twigg Island. The line first curves eastward, so a train would reverse its load back to the works. *Above*, an enlarged part of the photo shows the bridge detail: three spans with the middle a swing span.

Left. The distorted reflections of the bridge truss make an interesting abstract image converted to black and white.

Fraser Street Bridge

The Fraser Avenue Bridge—from the mid-1940s called the Fraser Street Bridge—was the second bridge to be built from Vancouver to Richmond, opening in 1894 from what was then (and until 1929) the Municipality of South Vancouver. It consisted of two bridges meeting on Twigg Island, which after 1926 was joined to the larger Mitchell Island, later assuming that name.

The northernmost span had a manually operated swing section to allow for navigation on the river. It was notoriously difficult to close in some wind conditions, and the bridge tender was known to occasionally enlist the help of members of the public waiting to cross. Except for some concrete piers and steel on the swing span the entire bridge was made of wood. (It remained so for most of its life; the southern fixed span was replaced with steel in 1967, just seven years before it would be closed.)

The bridge was opened just in time for it to be battered by the great Fraser Valley flood of that year; driftwood demolished more than half of the longer fixed span. Repairing the bridge was often a problem, since South Vancouver voters hated taxes and wanted to keep municipal expenditures to an absolute minimum. Only two years later the bridge was declared unsafe for heavy traffic. Not more than one team of horses and one wagon were allowed on the bridge at any one time. Later, for automobile traffic, a speed limit of 3 mph (about 5 km/hour) was posted—not much better than walking pace.

There are interesting photographs preserved from a court case in 1918–22 involving this bridge. In November 1916 a jitney operating as a bus from the Ladner Ferry, apparently travelling at the excessive speed of 10–15 mph (16–24 km/h), crashed into the river when the swing span was opened, killing nine people, including one woman, Annie Evans, and injuring her oldest daughter. Annie's husband, Arthur Evans, sued the Township of Richmond and the Corporation of the District of South Vancouver, as owners of the bridge, for negligence in its operation.

The case went to the Supreme Court of BC, the BC Court of Appeal, and eventually to the Privy Council in London, England. Up until 1949 the final Canadian court of appeal was in London, not Ottawa. The family was finally awarded $5,000, plus costs amounting to about $900 "for their costs thereof incurred in England." The photographs, reproduced here, were used in the explanation to the courts of what had happened.

Over the years a number of serious accidents occurred, perhaps inevitable on such a rickety structure. And the bridge was closed many times over its life. It was replaced by the Knight Street Bridge, one major city block east, in 1974, and the old bridge was removed two years later.

Two of the photographs used in the 1918–22 court case: *Above, top*, the south fixed span, and *above*, the north swing span, here open, showing the flimsy gates used to stop traffic.

Above. This 1949 map shows the Fraser Street Bridge connecting Vancouver's Fraser Street (originally Fraser Avenue and before that North Arm Road), to Richmond's No. 5 Road. The latter led due south to Woodward's Landing, where the ferry to Ladner docked. The map shows *Mitchell Island* now connecting the original Mitchell Island (on the east side) to Twigg Island (under the word *Mitchell*, on the west side.) The two were joined in 1926. Eburne Island is depicted as a separate island; it too has been connected to Mitchell, and its westernmost tip supports one of the piers of the Canada Line North Arm SkyTrain Bridge. The Marpole Bridge and BCER Bridge are also shown.

Left. The Fraser Street Bridge after one of the more dramatic mishaps during its lifetime. On 23 June 1966 the top of an overheight barge contacted the underside of the 45-m-long southern centre span of the bridge and, with what one survivor described as "a big, crackling, crunchy noise," completely took it out, dumping seven people, including six boys and their bikes, into the river. Luckily they were quickly rescued by a nearby dredge tender.

Knight Street Bridge

The Knight Street Bridge was the result of many years of campaigning by Richmond for a replacement for the ancient Fraser Street Bridge. The Knight Street Bridge was opened on 15 January 1974. Like its predecessor the Fraser Street Bridge, it is really two bridges: a six-lane bridge between Vancouver and Mitchell Island, and a longer four-lane bridge from Mitchell Island to Richmond. It cost $12 million, with another $3 million for approach roadways, and was paid for by the provincial government.

The new bridge used a construction technique from Germany never before used in North America that allowed engineers to cantilever a span across the river without using falsework supports, infamous in British Columbia after one collapsed during the construction of the Second Narrows Bridge in 1958 (see page 18).

Right. The Knight Street Bridge soon after it opened. This is the south span from Mitchell Island (in the foreground). The road terminates at Westminster Highway, in the distance. Highway 91 (the East-West Connector) was not built until 1989.

Below. The Knight Street Bridge from River Road in Richmond. It is a cast-in-place segmental cantilever bridge. The main span was the longest in the world of this design when it was built.

CNR Lulu Island Bridge

After the Canadian Northern Pacific Railway (CNoPR) transcontinental line reached Vancouver in 1915, the company built a line on Lulu Island (Richmond) with the intention of serving the canneries at Steveston and building docks there. The railway intended to build a bridge across the North Arm of the Fraser (see map *overleaf*) but instead reached an agreement with BCER to use its bridge at the eastern tip of Queensborough (see page 117). The line was completed in 1916, but the bridge proved to be not strong enough to carry steam locomotives. The functionally isolated line was in any case closed in 1918 after a fire in the peat destroyed a trestle, the by now financially strapped company being unable to afford the rebuilding required.

In the late 1920s Canadian National Railway (CNR), CNoPR's successor, decided to revive service to Lulu Island and in 1930 began construction of a steel through-truss swing bridge near the location of the original proposed bridge. It was completed in November 1931. The railway then graded and laid 23 km of track on Lulu Island. The bridge remains today, and, as the photos demonstrate, is a quite spectacular if relatively unknown structure.

Below. The large swing span of the CNR Lulu Island Bridge sits open. It is opened and closed remotely. This telephoto image from River Road shows Mount Baker looming behind the bridge in the background.

Right. A picturesque view of the bridge, taken with an infrared camera, which renders the green leaves white.

Right, bottom. This map, which seems to date from around 1914–15, shows a bridge—or is it a proposed bridge?—across the North Arm of the *Fraser*, connecting a line along the south edge of Lulu Island (marked *C.N.P.Ry.*) to the company's lines in New Westminster. This line in fact connected to New Westminster via the BCER bridge at the northern tip of the island, after an agreement with the interurban company in 1917. In 1918 the eastern part of this line was rendered useless by a fire in the underlying peat. It was not until 1931 that the railway—by then the Canadian National Railway—built a bridge farther west on the North Arm, the bridge photographed on these pages, to provide its own access to Lulu. This map incorporated a number of proposed or even speculative features such as another bridge at the tip of Lulu Island, and a dock area along *Annacis Channel*, which had been proposed in the boom times of 1912 but never got off the drawing board. A street grid system on *Annacis Is* is also shown, but no development took place on Annacis until the 1950s (see page 69). Notably (though not shown on this portion), the map also showed a Second Narrows Bridge, despite one not existing until 1925 (see page 13). Clearly one cannot believe everything one sees on a map, as they are often used as a promotional tool, although this one was just a street map.

Above. What turned out to be a very long CN freight train slowly rumbles across the bridge on 4 May 2021. The entire bridge with approach trestles is 1,280 m long; the swing span is 73 m long.

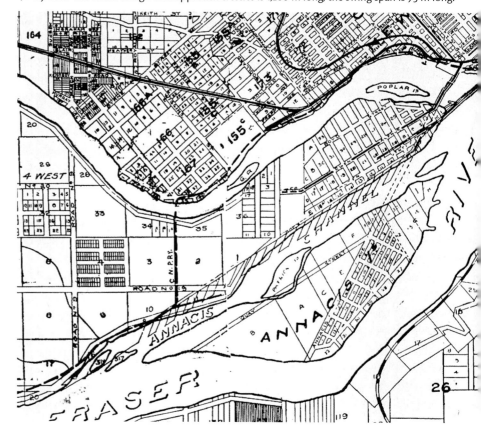

Three Queensborough Bridges

Two years after the first bridge had been built to Lulu Island, another was built at the other end of the island. This was the Lulu Island Bridge, or first Queensborough Bridge, which opened on 30 November 1891. It was a wooden bridge with a swing span and was the work of a group of New Westminster businessmen, including Alexander Ewen, who owned land on the eastern tip of Lulu Island. Ewen's name is remembered in the name of the main street of the Queensborough district.

The first bridge was constantly battered by loose barges and the like. From 1901 to 1903 the bridge was closed for repairs, with a replacement ferry being used instead.

A new bridge was planned, though it took a long time to materialize because there was a shortage of funds to build it. A new bridge, the second Queensborough Bridge, opened in 1909, at a cost of $76,000, aided by financial assistance from the BC Electric Company, which wanted to run tracks across it.

The bridge had planks of wood laid beside the rails to create a surface road traffic could use. After 1960, when the third Queensborough Bridge opened, the second bridge was sold to BCER and reverted to rails only. BC Electric became BC Hydro in 1961, and in 1988 the BCER railway system was sold to private interests and became the Southern Railway of British Columbia, now marketed as SRY Rail Link; it is this company's trains that are seen today both on this bridge (*overleaf*) and on the Annacis Bridge on the other side of eastern Lulu Island (see page 71).

As traffic built, the opening of the swing span became more and more of a nuisance, and talks aimed at building a new bridge began in the early 1940s. It was not until 1957 that a decision had been made on the location of the bridge, this time downriver from the old, and construction could begin.

Opened on 26 August 1960 as a toll bridge, it led only to Ewen Avenue (which connected to Westminster Highway), for the Alex Fraser Bridge and its connector, Highway 91A, would not appear on the scene for another 26 years.

The bridge had been paid for by the City of New Westminster (it was approved by a referendum in December 1957), and so the tolls were collected by that city. However, by 1964 the provincial government's BC Toll Highways and Bridges Authority had removed the tolls from all other toll bridges in the province, leaving the Queensborough Bridge still collecting its municipal tolls.

Then, in a surprise move, Premier W.A.C. Bennett and his entourage showed up at the toll booths at midnight on 19 November 1966 to pay a last toll. Tolls were removed as of that date and time. New Westminster's remaining debt of $3 million was wiped clean as a Canadian centennial celebration gesture.

Above, top. The first Queensborough Bridge, opened in 1891 as the second bridge to Lulu Island, was a wooden structure almost missed by this only surviving photo.

Above, centre. The Second Queensborough Bridge, opened in 1909, carried both railway and road traffic. Here, in 1955, cars line up while the swing span is open. It was the increase in traffic that led to the building of the third bridge in 1960.

Right, bottom. The now rail-only second Queensborough Bridge, also known as the BCER Lulu Island Bridge or just the Lulu Island Bridge, though this could be confused with the CNR bridge (*opposite*).

Above. On 28 November 2020, a set of five Southern Railway of BC (Rail Link) locomotives cross the second Queensborough Bridge after delivering freight to Annacis Island.

Right. The lead locomotives of the same train are on the southern approach trestle, passing one of the residential developments that have recently sprung up. What a great view of the trains the residents have!

Below. Detail of the structure of the bridge, which, except for the swing span itself, was a wooden creation.

Above. The swing span is open in this view looking north.

Queensborough Bridge during
construction – Sept. 12, 1959

Two aerial photographs taken during the construction of the third Queensborough Bridge: *Above.* 12 September 1959; the bridge piers are nearing completion. *Below, left.* 11 March 1960; the bridge deck is being laid. The bridge opened for traffic on 26 August 1960.

Right. Another aerial photo, taken in September 1960, shows the completed project. Note the toll booths, which remained until 1964, operated by the City of New Westminster, and the junction of the road from the bridge at Ewen Avenue in Queensborough. The road now turns sharply west at about where the toll booths were, and connects with the Alex Fraser Bridge as well as Highway 91, the East-West Connector.

Queensborough Bridge during
construction – March 11, 1960.

Above. The southern approach pillars shown here were built on top of 15-m-long fir poles driven down to firm sand. The surface sediments proved too unstable to support the weight on their own. It seems incredible that fir poles could support such massive concrete pillars.

Below. This little bridge next to the south approach carries a rail line repositioned from the side of Ewen Avenue in 1982.

Above. This 1960 map shows the bridge connection to *Ewen Ave*. Also shown are the second Queensborough Bridge and the first Derwent Avenue Bridge to Annacis Island.

Left. In recent years the City of New Westminster has received revenue from a tall electronic billboard high above the bridge. Here it makes an interesting stick-insect-like silhouette directly against the sun.

Above. An aerial photo of the bridge taken in July 2018.

Below, left. The third Queensborough Bridge is an arch bridge, as can be seen from this view from the south riverbank.

Below, top, and *below, bottom*. A ferry service from New Westminster Quay to Queensborough has been added following the residential development of the eastern tip of Lulu Island and has proved quite popular, avoiding, as it does, the rather circuitous route via the bridge. After a pilot season in 2017, regular service began in May 2018.

Middle Arm of the Fraser

There are four bridges in the Middle Arm of the Fraser River, between Lulu Island and Sea Island in Richmond. In addition, there was the Middle Arm portion of the Marpole Bridge, the first across this stretch of the river (see page 100).

Moray Channel Bridge and Airport Connector Bridge

Built at the same time and opened on the same day in 1957 as the Oak Street Bridge, the Moray Channel Bridge, or Moray Bridge, crosses the channel named after a sergeant in the Royal Engineers (in BC 1858–63), Jonathan Moray, later New Westminster police chief.

The Moray Channel Bridge opened on 1 July 1957, replacing the aging Middle Arm part of the Marpole Bridge, which had been the only link to Sea Island and, later, Vancouver Airport, since 1889. It was increasing traffic to the airport that finally made planners realize a new bridge was needed.

Like its predecessor, the Moray would suffer from barge collisions over the years. The Moray, again like its predecessor, is a swing-span bridge—one that, from time to time, would jam. It was electrically operated and the fault was in the electrical system. It highlighted the need for more than one access bridge to Sea Island—a need that was finally satisfied in 1975 with the opening of the Arthur Laing Bridge.

Since then the Moray has been doubled and made into a one-way bridge after the opening of the adjacent Airport Connector Bridge (or Sea Island Connector Bridge) in August 2001, which was built with higher clearances and no swing span.

Above. In this aerial shot from a plane landing at Vancouver International Airport in May 2018, the 2009 Middle Arm SkyTrain bridge is in the foreground, with the Richmond Night Market right behind it. In the middle distance is the 2001 Airport Connector Bridge, carrying westbound traffic to the airport, and behind that the 1957 Moray Channel Bridge, carrying airport traffic eastbound. In the distance the 1969 Dinsmore Bridge and the 1993 No. 2 Road Bridge are visible. The green area and some of the adjacent Night Market parking lot were Duck Island until reclamation and spoil dumping made it part of Lulu Island. Just in front of the SkyTrain bridge was No. 3 Road and the path of the Middle Arm part of the Marpole Bridge, demolished in 1965–66.

Above, left. The Moray Channel Bridge, with the Airport Connector behind it.

Left. The Airport Connector.

Above. The Airport Connector viewed from under the bridge, a photo converted to black and white.

Middle Arm SkyTrain Bridge

The third of the transit-only bridges in Metro Vancouver crosses the Middle Arm, carrying SkyTrain on its branch to the airport. It is a minimalist-designed rather slim and elegant box-girder prestressed-concrete bridge. It opened in August 2009 along with the North Arm SkyTrain Bridge and the entire Canada Line.

Right. Under the Middle Arm SkyTrain Bridge, opened in 2009, looking from Sea Island to Lulu Island. Just to the left of the bridge on the far shore is the point where the Middle Arm part of the Marpole Bridge (see page 101) reached Duck Island, leading onto No. 3 Road. Duck Island is now part of Lulu Island. To the right is the parking lot for the Richmond Night Market.

Below. The narrow, elegant form of the bridge is apparent in this photo.

Right, bottom. A SkyTrain comes off the bridge heading for the airport.

Dinsmore Bridge

Undoubtedly high in the rankings for the Lower Mainland's most unglamorous bridge design is the Dinsmore Bridge, connecting the south shore of Sea Island across the Middle Arm of the Fraser to the rest of Richmond.

The two-lane bridge was opened on 15 August 1969 and, having been funded by the federal government, also named Pont Dinsmore. It was named after John Dinsmore, who operated a fish cannery on an island between 1894 and 1913 where the bridge crosses. The island, named after him, was connected by fill to Sea Island in 1952 and, with its bridge, disappeared.

No. 2 Road Bridge

To address the fact that the 1975 Arthur Laing Bridge only really serviced the airport—except for the congested two-lane Dinsmore, which was essentially inadequate traffic-wise from the day it opened—the City of Richmond (with a little help from the provincial government) funded the four-lane No. 2 Road Bridge, which opened on a Sunday, 11 July 1993, for a "fun-run" before opening for traffic that afternoon. Finally there was a connection from Vancouver to Richmond across Sea Island capable of dealing with heavy traffic.

The 560-m-long No. 2 Road Bridge—surely someone could have thought of a better name?—is technically described as a sequential box-girder, prestressed and post-tensioned structure, with 10 separate spans sitting on 217 prestressed-concrete piles driven into the Fraser's silt.

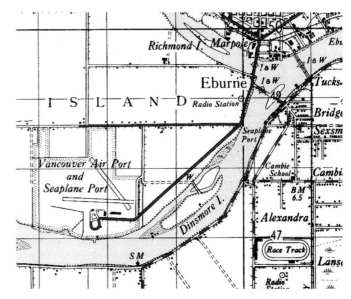

Above, top. This 1949 map shows *Dinsmore I.* and the narrow bridge that provided access to it—the original Dinsmore Bridge.

Above. This aerial view from 1944 shows the original bridge to the island. In the background is Burkeville, a wartime community established for workers in a Boeing aircraft factory there.

Below. The Dinsmore Bridge today.

Above. The massive but short piers of the No. 2 Road Bridge. Note the shock absorbers between the pier tops and the concrete box girder of the span.

Left. Even the concrete piles of the underside of the Dinsmore Bridge can be made to look artistic. The linear bridge deck supports are reflected in the water.

Above. The gardens and ponds surrounding the Richmond Olympic Oval, built for the 2010 Olympics, are enhanced by this winding footbridge.

Pitt & Coquitlam Rivers

Pitt River

The Pitt River, a major tributary of the Lower Fraser, was first bridged by the Canadian Pacific Railway as part of its transcontinental line to Vancouver, at first terminating at Port Moody, the whole being completed in 1885. The line between Port Moody and Yale was contracted in 1882 to railway builder Andrew Onderdonk.

The Pitt River Bridge, like most of the first bridges on the CPR line, was hastily constructed on site with locally cut wood, the aim being to get trains running to provide some revenue to the financially strapped railway. This bridge was completed in 1883. The last spike of the Port Moody–Yale section was driven at Nicomen, 50 km to the

Above. The first, wooden, Pitt River railway bridge, completed in 1883, was a significant structure despite its construction material. The CPR was no stranger to massive wooden bridges, though most tended to be somewhat higher than longer.

Below. The replacement steel bridge, still single-tracked, built in 1907. This wonderfully ethereal though unfortunately low-quality image shows a train headed westbound into Vancouver in late 1912 or 1913, just before construction on its replacement began, although the photograph shows some evidence of what might be beginning construction work.

east, on 22 January 1884, and the first through train from Port Moody to Yale ran the next day.

It was not long before the wooden bridge was replaced by a steel one. In 1907 a single-track steel-truss bridge—one that was destined to have a long history—was built at the same location as the first one. This steel bridge was replaced after only seven years by a double-track bridge, in 1913–14, as part of the railway's plan to double-track most of its line in the Lower Fraser Valley. The 1907 bridge was purchased by the provincial government and reconstructed as a road bridge

about 450 m upstream (see page 132). The construction of the 1914 CPR bridge is well documented because the chief engineer, Miller Beekman Heebner, was an amateur photographer and took a number of photographs of his handiwork. In addition the main contractor, the Foundation Company, also documented its work, and Heebner kept these photos too. Some are shown here. It is immediately apparent that this was quite a complex project, because there was a need to maintain rail access over the river during the construction period. This was, after all, Canadian Pacific's only route into Vancouver.

Left. The 1907 single-track bridge is at left in this view from the west bank of the river. A temporary trestle-type bridge has been built at right to maintain a connection while the bridge is replaced. The wooden structure at centre is a floating caisson, which was sunk into the riverbed and pumped dry where new or extended concrete supporting piers were constructed.

Below. This is a view from the east bank of the river and is one of only two that were dated: 10 June 1913. The part of the 1907 bridge in shallower water, without steel trusses, is being dismantled; this after the substitute trestle has been built at left to bypass it, complete with its own temporary swing span. A lot of work has gone in to maintaining the rail connection over the river during construction. In the foreground is one of the new wider concrete piers to support the double-track new bridge. The plume coming from the work site reminds us that most mechanized equipment at this time was powered by boiled water—steam.

Left. A photo of the construction work, looking west, taken from one of the crane structures seen in other photos. The old bridge is at right, a caisson is at centre, and the temporary diversion bridge is at left. In the distance the area that is now the Canadian Pacific's large yard in Port Coquitlam can be seen. This photo is dated 30 July 1913.

Below. A massive pile of bridge-decking wood is in the foreground of this image taken from the west bank looking east. A rather primitive-looking crane is used to move the wood. At left, a train is about to cross the river on the old bridge, while the temporary bridge is at centre. A number of the crane-like structures, referred to as cone towers, can be seen.

Above. The swing spans of both the 1907 bridge and the temporary diversion bridge are open in this photo. A caisson is at centre right. CPR was authorized to use the diversionary bridge—at very low speeds—in July 1913.

Below. The single-track 1907 bridge is being dismantled. It would be transported just 450 m upstream to be repurposed as a road bridge. Three spans, including the swing span, would much later (1957) be transported downstream to Mitchell Island to be repurposed once again, this time as a road and rail bridge (see page 110), and three would become rail bridges on the Pacific Great Eastern Railway (see page 165).

Above. The year the new rail bridge was complete, World War I began, and the government, afraid that fifth-column saboteurs might try to blow up critical rail bridges, posted armed guards on many of them. Note that one of the guards has brought his dog with him. See also photos on pages 170, 177 and 279.

Right, *below* and *below, bottom.* The solid-looking 1914 bridge today: the western approach, showing the double track; an eastbound train about to cross; and another eastbound train with the locomotive about to cross the swing span.

Above. Reflections of the Pitt River Railway Bridge, 29 March 2021. The road bridge is visible behind.

Above. Led by a reversed locomotive with two railway workers as lookouts, a long freight train with four locomotives at its head travels east across the Pitt River Railway Bridge on 23 August 2020. Train movements like this are quite frequent, as the CPR has yards on both sides of the river.

In January 1913 the provincial government decided to build a road bridge across the Pitt River to replace a ferry. It was initially intended to carry both a railway and a road, the railway being a proposed line (independent of the CPR) between Mission Junction and Vancouver. The railway company was to lease the bridge from the government. The railway appears to have been the Burrard, Westminster & Boundary Railway and Navigation Company, which had been granted a charter in 1907 and seems to have intended to build an electric tramway. Certainly, in 1913–14 there were a number of ads in newspapers for lots in Port Coquitlam that mention the "upcoming electric tramway and general traffic bridge" over the Pitt River. With the decline of potential traffic because of the start of World War I, the railway idea was dropped, but the road bridge went ahead.

Since the CPR was building its new bridge, the government managed to purchase the old bridge and reconstruct it, thus saving money. The old bridge was only 450 m away, so floating the spans into position on newly built piers was a relatively easy job; indeed, the entire bridge was completed in only nine months.

This bridge required single-lane traffic for trucks because it was quite narrow. It lasted—in this location—until 1957, when it was replaced by a two-lane bridge, which in turn was twinned in 1978, with each bridge being used for one-way traffic. Both of these bridges had swing spans, which snarled traffic when they opened, and it was not uncommon for the south span to get stuck! By the turn of the 21st century suburban residential development in Maple Ridge and Pitt Meadows had turned these bridges into a commuting nightmare.

Below, across both pages. The completed first Pitt River road bridge, built with spans from the railway bridge and opened in 1915. Note the ferry landing at right.

Right. The new bridge was worth having your photo taken with. Here a well-dressed lady poses with the newly repurposed structure. Compare this photo with the one in the bridge's later location (page 111).

In 2009, as part of its $3 billion Gateway Program, the BC government built a new, higher, seven-lane cable-stayed bridge in the space between the twin bridges. This was part of the North Fraser Perimeter Road and was partly funded by the federal government. It opened in 2009, the same year as the Golden Ears Bridge (see page 97).

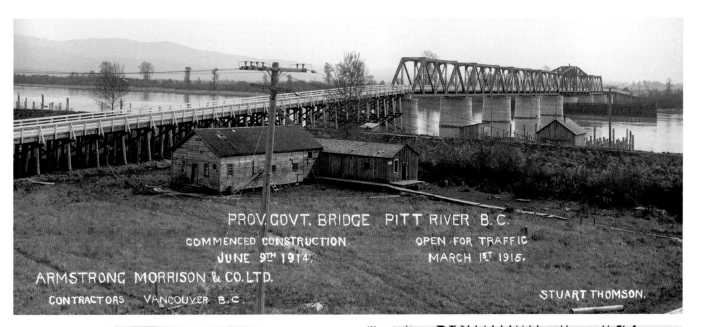

PROV. GOVT. BRIDGE PITT RIVER B.C.
COMMENCED CONSTRUCTION.   OPEN FOR TRAFFIC
JUNE 9TH 1914,   MARCH 1ST 1915,
ARMSTRONG MORRISON & CO. LTD.
CONTRACTORS   VANCOUVER B.C.   STUART THOMSON,

Above, top. The contractor for the new bridge had this photo taken to document its work—and no doubt obtain more contracts. Note the bridge has been built higher than before. The intent was to avoid much of the swing-span opening for the majority of smaller marine traffic.

Above. The ferry and landing before the bridge was built. A ferry is mid-stream, and the 1907 railway bridge swing span is open.

Above, right. This map from 1915 shows the location of the *ferry* and the CPR track. The road to the ferry in Pitt Meadows, Ferryslip Road, remains.

Above. Three bridges, 1978–2009. The railway bridge, built in 1914, is farthest from the camera. The eastbound twin road bridge was built in 1957, and the twin westbound bridge, nearest the camera, opened in 1978. They are 360 m long.

Left. The 2009 cable-stayed bridge is under construction between the twin bridges in 2008. Note the traffic signals for counterflow lanes on the older bridge.

Below. The cable-stayed road bridge today, photographed from immediately below the bridge on the east bank using a very wide-angle (12 mm) lens. Containing distortion in the image of the (more or less) straight-line cables is difficult here.

Above. The art of the bridge. This photo of the railway and road bridges together has been processed to give an impressionistic look.

Below. The view north up the Pitt River framed by the bridge.

Below. The bridges from the west bank to the south.

Above. This photo of the east piers of the Pitt River Bridge has been processed to look like a cyanotype, a blue-tinged effect invented in 1842 and used for art prints. The process was also used to create architectural drawings—blueprints—for 150 years.

Above. These bridges cross the Coquitlam River. This is the Port Coquitlam Kings Bridge on Kingsway Avenue, a photo taken in 1931 as cars decorated for a May Day parade cross the bridge, which was built in 1922. A double-track through-truss railway bridge is behind it, which was installed at the same time following the destruction of the previous bridge in a flood in 1921, shown *below, bottom*. Today, a flat beam-type bridge has been built next to the truss to provide a third track across the river.

Right. The steel-truss wooden-deck Kings Bridge in 1922, just after its completion. The railway bridge is visible at left. The photo is from the 1921–22 annual report of the BC Department of Public Works. This bridge has been replaced by a flat-concrete-beam bridge of the modern functional but unexciting design.

Far right. One of the frequent CPR freight trains crosses the Coquitlam River Railway Bridge westbound.

Below. The scene after the 1921 flood destroyed the railway bridge (on the left) and part of a wooden-truss road bridge on Kingsway Avenue.

Above and *left.* The Lougheed Highway truss bridge, built in 1949, with another parallel bridge of flat-concrete-beam design being added in 1975. The Lougheed Highway in this location was part of the Dewdney Trunk Road before being incorporated into the new Lougheed Highway in the 1940s. The 1949 truss bridge has been slated for replacement for several years and will, like many bridges of its design and age, doubtless be gone soon.

The Red Bridge, which crosses the Coquitlam River farther south, connects Port Coquitlam to the north–south section of the Lougheed Highway. The original bridge was closed in 1924 and was replaced in 1926 with this wooden-truss bridge (*below*), painted red. It collapsed in 1982, and a one-lane Bailey bridge was installed as a temporary measure, but it was not until 1996 that a new, permanent bridge was completed. It has red painted railings (*right*) to respect the original name.

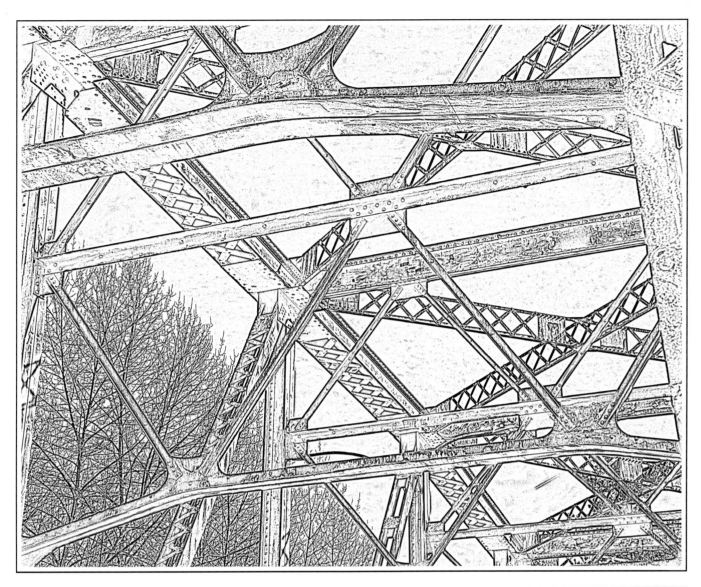

Above. The complex truss structure of the 1949 Lougheed Highway Bridge has here been rendered as a black-and-white sketch, presenting an interesting pattern of steel.

Right. The large Canadian Pacific yards in Port Coquitlam have long been an obstacle to north–south travel. In 2010 a 580-m-long cable-stayed bridge was completed called the Coast Meridian Overpass. It connects Coast Meridian Road in the south to Lougheed Highway in the north.

South of the Fraser

There are many bridges over the smaller rivers of the Lower Mainland south of the Fraser. They are not as spectacular as the Fraser's Port Mann or Alex Fraser but just as essential.

The longest must be the 800-m-long BNSF Railway trestle at the mouth of the Serpentine River in South Surrey. It originates from the 1909 rerouting of the then Great Northern Railway from its path through Hazelmere and parallel to today's Highway 15 to one through White Rock and Crescent Beach and along the edge of the North Delta bluff to the New Westminster Bridge. The trestle essentially allows the railway to take a shortcut across the low land of Mud Bay, part of Boundary Bay. For most of its life it was a traditional wooden trestle but was upgraded to a concrete structure in 2017.

The same railway line crosses the mouth of the Nicomekl River just 2.5 km farther south; this is a swing span to allow sailboats out from a marina on the river just beyond.

This is the river accessed in 1824 by James McMillan of the Hudson's Bay Company as a shortcut on his way to the Fraser River, portaging to the small Salmon River and emerging onto the Fraser at a place that three years later would be established as a trading post for the company—Fort Langley.

Both the Serpentine and the Nicomekl Rivers were used by the Indigenous peoples (Nicomekl is a Halq'emeylem name meaning "path to take") and by early settler-farmers to supply their farms. The low-lying lands south of the Fraser are very fertile but subject to flooding, and in addition to dikes the rivers here have dam structures to aid in land reclamation and prevent high tides from flooding the land upstream. One, on the Nicomekl, is also used as a bridge. The dams on the Nicomekl and Serpentine were constructed after 1911, when Surrey banned navigation of the rivers beyond them; road and rail took over from rivers.

Above. The morning Amtrak train from Seattle to Vancouver crosses the Mud Bay Trestle, at this time (August 2009) a wooden structure. The bridge actually crosses the estuary of the Serpentine River but is usually known as the Mud Bay Trestle or Mud Bay Bridge.

Below. A BNSF freight train is silhouetted as it heads south across the Mud Bay Trestle against a murky sunset on 26 December 2009.

Above. The morning Amtrak makes its way north over the now concrete Mud Bay Trestle on 27 October 2017, nicely reflected in the still waters of the bay. A telephoto lens appears to compress the train's length.

Left, centre. The cut-off piles of the previous wooden trestle are visible under the much-more-massive concrete structure.

Left, bottom. A BNSF freight train travels north across the trestle in an August heat haze in 2019. Here a telephoto lens has compressed the piers of the trestle again so much as to give an altogether different effect.

Below. The railbed on top of the trestle, like on many bridges, has inner rails. These are to try to prevent the train from moving laterally and falling off the bridge surface in case of a simple derailment.

Above, top. An unusually short BNSF train crosses the Nicomekl Railway Bridge at Crescent Beach; its length suggests it was likely engaged in track maintenance. Originally bridged by the Great Northern Railway in 1909, the crossing has been upgraded several times since. The wooden trestle parts of this bridge were replaced at the same time as the Mud Bay Trestle.

Above. The sun is setting behind the Nicomekl Railway Bridge highlighting the North Shore mountains in this view from the river.

Right. This Great Northern Railway planning map from about 1907 or 1908 shows the origin of both the Nicomekl and Serpentine–Mud Bay railway crossings. The new line is routed around the South Surrey peninsula, and even a very long bridge right across Boundary Bay has been considered—feasible, perhaps, because of the very shallow water here, with the easier pathway along the edge of the bay winning out. This map still does not show the final path across the Serpentine, which was slightly farther west than shown but in turn requiring the long trestle shown on the previous page.

Left. The first bridge in South Surrey was this one that carried the Semiahmoo Trail (an early trail originally used by Indigenous peoples and utilized as a trade route by settlers) over the Nicomekl River. It was built in 1873; this photograph is from 1880. Part of this early bridge was a lift span, necessary because of the steamers that plied the river as far inland as what is now 184th Street in Hazelmere. The building at left was the customs house. Elgin, where this bridge was built, was designated as a port of entry for Canada. The location of the customs house was such that it could control both land and water traffic.

Left; right, top; and *right, centre.* In addition to the wooden trestle bridge built in 1939 that carries King George Boulevard across the Nicomekl (*below, centre*) there was a Bailey bridge, installed in 1986, to increase capacity from two lanes to three. Intended as a temporary measure, the bridges were not replaced until 2022, 36 years later. These photos were taken in July 2020 when replacement work seemed imminent and a design contract had been let. The Bailey bridge had a weight restriction (*inset*): even the local buses had to change lanes to use the adjacent trestle bridge when travelling northbound. *Above* and *right, centre.* Both bridges can be seen.
Below. The 1939 King George Boulevard bridge across the Nicomekl.

Below. The Nicomekl River Dam, built to prevent flooding at high tide and first installed about 1912.
Inset. A much-travelled one-way road utilizes the dam to cross the river.

Above. The King George Boulevard Bridge over the Serpentine River, with the Serpentine Dam at left.

Above. The 168th Street bridge over the Nicomekl at 48th Avenue, with Mt. Baker in the background. The bridge is a 1940s design similar to those on page 175.

Above. Perhaps the bridge with the steepest grade in the province is the 152nd Street Nicomekl Bridge, opened in 1982, filling a gap that had existed since 1941 when an older bridge was closed. It is slated to be twinned by 2024.

Above. When the King George Boulevard bridge at Bear Creek (actually here Mahood Creek) was rebuilt and widened in 2019–20 to allow for a rapid-transit corridor, these Coast Salish designs were incorporated, thus making this typical modern flat-concrete structure a little brighter than normal.

Above. The 1961 Nicomekl River Highway 99 bridge undergoes seismic retrofitting in May 2022. King George Boulevard crosses the freeway in the background.

Above. Three bridges are at this location at the eastern end of the Langley Bypass. All cross the Nicomekl River. In the distance is the Fraser Highway Bridge, which replaced an older bridge. In the foreground is the Old Yale Road Bridge, taking the original road up the Fraser Valley across the river. The photo was taken from the 208th Street Causeway Bridge, completed in 1985 to eliminate flooding on that road.

Above. It is hard to imagine that much of the urban area of Surrey was once forested. This photo shows a roughly constructed trestle built to transport timber by horse-drawn sled, about 1900. The photo was likely taken near today's Surrey Lake, the location of lower land, thus necessitating this trestle to keep the skidway (the horses are pulling a sled, not a wheeled cart) level and thus allowing heavier horse-drawn loads. Here a sled loaded with shingle bolts is posed for a photograph. Note the surrounding recently logged landscape.

The building of the Deas Island Throughway (now Highway 99) south to the US border after completion of the tunnel in 1959 (see page 58), took until 1962 and required the construction of several major bridges, including one over the Serpentine River (1962, *above, right*) and one over the Nicomekl (1961, *above, left*). But although the freeway was officially declared open on 30 May 1962, there was still a gap where it crossed the Great Northern (now BNSF) railway line, built in 1909 (see page 140). Here there were off-ramps, the rail line was crossed, and then there were on-ramps (still there today—one

is shown *below*) up again to the freeway. The off- and on-ramps were retired after a bridge was constructed across the line in 1965, the massive steel twin bridges shown *left*, which finally completed the freeway.

Below. A new rail line to Roberts Bank, opened in 1970, followed the line of an earlier railway, the Victoria Terminal Railway, for much of its length, but a new bridge was required to carry it as it curved over Highway 99. Here a coal train returning to the Elk River mining region is about to cross that bridge (at extreme left), in this view that shows the now cut-off and somewhat overgrown remnant of a local road in the foreground.

Above. This 450-m-long bridge, at Cloverdale, was originally built in 1973 and twinned in 2005. It was named in honour of Constable Roger Pierlet, a police officer killed nearby in the line of duty in 1974. The 23-year-old, on his last shift before getting married, was gunned down by a passenger in a car he had pulled over for erratic driving. This is one of eight overpasses, all significant feats of engineering, constructed to carry traffic over the 72-km-long Roberts Bank railway,

which was built by the Pacific Great Eastern Railway (now British Columbia Railway) in 1969–70 to connect the Roberts Bank coal and container ports to existing track in the Fraser Valley near Fort Langley. Most overpasses were the result of a coordinated effort between governments at all levels and the railway companies. The last, Mufford Crescent Overpass in Langley, was completed in September 2014. *Below.* The King George Boulevard rail overpass, completed in 1986.

There are several pedestrian bridges over Highway 1 that are photographically and aesthetically pleasing. The three-span Tynehead Overpass (*right, centre*), shown in black and white, was completed in 2011 and connects Tynehead Regional Park to Fraser Heights, on the north side of the freeway. The Salton Pedestrian Bridge in Abbotsford (*right*) is similarly constructed, and also straddles Highway 1. It was completed in 2018. Both are arch bridges, with a lightweight tubular arch and the bridge deck suspended underneath.

Left. This rather surprising wood suspension footbridge, built in 1975 when Langley was a lot smaller, takes pedestrians over the Nicomekl River in Nicomekl Park in Langley. Slated for removal, it will likely be replaced with a typically standard but much less interesting steel structure like the one already installed at 208th Street nearby, shown *right*.

Above. A bridge built specifically for horses in Campbell Valley Regional Park. The trail connects with stables on 208th Street.

Above. This footbridge across the Little Campbell River in Campbell Valley Regional Park in Langley has a certain geometric form to it making it aesthetically satisfying. Here it is photographed in black and white, which has the effect of concentrating the eye on its shape.

Below. A misty morning at the Campbell River footbridge near the river's mouth at Semiahmoo Bay. The bridge was built in 1985 to connect the Semiahmoo Indian Reserve on the left bank to Surrey, on the right bank. Just beyond this bridge, where the river enters the bay, is the Great Northern/BNSF railway bridge.

North Shore

Vancouver's North Shore is built on mountainsides, and as a consequence needs many bridges to cross a multitude of streams. Because of the steep terrain, the seemingly tranquil streams flowing down the mountainside can from time to time suddenly turn into monstrous torrents. The situation gets worse from east to west, and many of the bridges of Highway 99, the Sea to Sky Highway north up Howe Sound, now have structures built to channel the water flow and filter out debris before it damages a bridge. For debris torrents are the biggest danger to mountain bridges. The presence of residential areas such as in West Vancouver and Lions Bay makes them even more dangerous.

The first Upper Levels Highway, which in West Vancouver was mainly a two-lane road, was completed in the mid-1950s, but the connection to the new Second Narrows Bridge (opened in 1960) was not made until 1962, with the completion of the "Cut" (down to a bridge over Lynn Creek), and a crossing at Mackay Creek, the latter today so wooded as to be virtually invisible from the road. It included an elegant reinforced-concrete arch bridge across the Capilano River.

A new four-lane Upper Levels Highway was completed in 1975 and included some spectacular new bridges such as that over Nelson Creek above Fisherman's Cove in West Vancouver. The highway has been upgraded and improved over the years since then, eliminating at-grade intersections. Notably, the Mosquito Creek Upper Levels Highway Bridge was doubled, the construction taking place in conjunction with the last interchange at nearby Westview in 1997. The latter famously removed the last traffic light between Horseshoe Bay and Hope.

More recently the bridge over Lynn Creek, at the bottom of the Cut, has had several other crossings added to it to accommodate a wider highway and on-ramps there. And the original truss bridge, built in 1960, has itself been renovated, in the process changing colour from orange to "Lions Gate Green," supposedly the same colour as its namesake bridge. The whole stretch of highway has been upgraded to include better access to the Second Narrows Bridge.

The Nelson Creek Upper Levels Highway Bridge, under construction in 1973, a photo from the 1973–74 annual report of the Department of Highways (*above, top*); as it appeared about 1980, complete with author and young son (*left*); and today (*below*), its vertical grandeur now somewhat masked by trees.

Above. The first Nelson Creek (old) Upper Levels Highway Bridge, built in the late 1950s. Railings of this type are common in bridges of that era. The bridge still exists, now as part of a hiking trail.

Above. The bridge from the road, almost not recognizable as a bridge unless one looks at right angles to the southwest when crossing to the stunning view down to Fisherman's Cove and Eagle Harbour.

Right. A contrast: another bridge over Nelson Creek, this one more like a culvert well below the Upper Levels at Cranley Drive, in a residential area. But the seemingly tame stream belies the torrents possible here.

Above. The Capilano River Upper Levels Highway Bridge under construction in 1961. The flat road surface is supported by a reinforced-concrete arch below, making a structure perhaps more interesting from below than above.

Right. The underside of the bridge today, a study in perspective. The photo has been converted to black and white to emphasize the pattern of curves and lines.

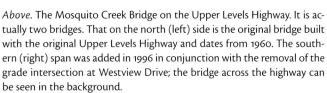

Above. The Mosquito Creek Bridge on the Upper Levels Highway. It is actually two bridges. That on the north (left) side is the original bridge built with the original Upper Levels Highway and dates from 1960. The southern (right) span was added in 1996 in conjunction with the removal of the grade intersection at Westview Drive; the bridge across the highway can be seen in the background.

Right, top. The 1960 steel Lynn Creek Bridge, still in its original orange, is shown on 9 October 2019 as the new Mountain Highway on-ramp bridge is built beside it.

Right, centre. The bridge is renovated and repainted green, the new ramp completed, in this view from the same location taken on 15 September 2021.

Above. The double steel span of the 1960 Lynn Creek Upper Levels Highway Bridge, photographed in black and white. Part of the new bridge is at top right.

Below. The adjacent 2019-built Keith Road bridge over Lynn Creek. Note the simple I-beam construction. On the older truss bridge the beams are at 90 degrees, only for stiffening of the roadbed; here they take the weight.

Left. The Upper Levels Highway temporarily uses the new bridge to curve around the 1960 steel double-truss bridge while it undergoes repair and restoration. The new Mountain Highway on-ramp bridge is at right. The photo was taken on 29 March 2021, from a new Mountain Highway Upper Levels overpass bridge.

The battle with occasionally rampant creeks also affects bridges on Marine Drive, the first east-to-west road in West Vancouver. Even before West Vancouver became a municipality in its own right, breaking off from the District of North Vancouver in 1912, there was a bridge over the Capilano River. As can be seen from the succession of bridges shown on these pages, some did not last long.

The first "permanent" Marine Drive Bridge across the Capilano was completed and opened in August 1915. West Vancouver council had been sold on the idea of a solid, concrete structure to provide "a permanent fixture not affected by storm" by a British engineering company, Naylor Brothers. Indeed, the bridge was rather elegant, with detailed slender arch forms. The company also posted a surety bond to guarantee the bridge's performance—for one year. Unfortunately a flood on 31 December the following year—four months after the surety had run out—caused partial collapse of the bridge deck, and two years after that another flood undermined a bridge abutment, making the bridge impassable. This caused problems for a while, since all freight for the municipality came in via the North Vancouver Ferry and over this bridge; the little West Vancouver Ferry was only for passengers (see page 10).

It was not until 1930 that a more substantial bridge was opened, this time a steel through-truss. The bridge opened as the final act of building Marine Drive right through to Horseshoe Bay—which of course required a number of other bridges—that had been agreed to by the municipality and the provincial government as part of the deal allowing the government-owned Pacific Great Eastern Railway to close its line from North Vancouver to Whytecliff in 1928.

On 26 November 1949 the western approach of the steel bridge was washed out by a storm, although the steel span and its piers withstood the onslaught. The provincial government declared a local state of emergency, and the Royal

Canadian Engineers were brought in to build a temporary Bailey bridge. In the meantime, the West Vancouver Ferry was pressed into service again.

Increasing traffic led to the doubling of the 1930 bridge in 1956 with a flat beam-type bridge immediately south of it (which then carried eastbound traffic), and the truss bridge was replaced with a new modern structure in 2010, first moving the 1930 bridge a few metres to the north to maintain traffic flow during construction.

Early Capilano River bridges: about 1898, *far left*, and 1905, *left*. These bridges are of the simplest truss design, with the 1905 bridge being a king or A-frame truss, a popular design for many early bridges in British Columbia, though very few survive today.

Left. In December 1916, just four months after the contractor's performance surety bond expired, disaster befell the 1915 finely detailed concrete Capilano River Marine Drive bridge, which had been sold as a "permanent fixture," much better than wooden bridges of any design. In fact most of the damage was done to a wooden trestle abutment. As can be seen here, most of the bridge remained intact.

Left. The 1930 steel-truss bridge was replaced in 2010 with a flat reinforced-concrete and steel I-beam bridge similar to the initial twin span, at right, built in 1956. To maintain traffic flow, the old bridge was first moved upstream a few metres and a new bridge was built adjacent to the other flat span, the old bridge being demolished when the process was complete.

Two Temporary Bridge Plans to Thwart Temperamental River

WEST VANCOUVER will be temporarily linked with the city again, by one or other of two proposed Bailey Bridge routes across the temperamental Capilano River, by Sunday noon. Artist's conception shows Route 1 — Bailey Bridge from the east bank to a gravel road up the old river bed to a point opposite Clyde Drive, whence a second Bailey Bridge will link the west bank. Alternate Route 2, depending on the river, will parallel the main span with two Bailey Bridges and a short gravel roadbed between.

Above. This annotated aerial photo appeared in the *Vancouver Sun* on 3 December 1949, showing the proposed alignments for temporary Bailey bridges and gravel connecting roads to bypass the Capilano Marine Drive Bridge, which has lost its westernmost span.

On 1 January 1914 service began on what was intended to be the southern portion of the Pacific Great Eastern Railway; regular passenger service to Whytecliff (Horseshoe Bay) began on 21 August that year. The difficult terrain farther north up Howe Sound, together with the financial difficulties the railway was in, partly caused by the beginning of World War I, led to the "temporary" suspension of construction, leaving a gap between Horseshoe Bay and Squamish. The railway was connected to Vancouver only by tug-pulled barges. The gap was finally filled in by the government of W.A.C. Bennett in 1956. The line along Howe Sound required over 800 tonnes of dynamite and boring four tunnels, along with numerous bridges. Much of the line was, and remains, a maintenance problem.

Above. About 1920 a Pacific Great Eastern gas passenger car crosses a bridge near West Bay. The passenger service between North Vancouver and Whytecliff used these economical gas cars most of the time. The service was shut down in 1928, but the line was reopened in 1956, much to the horror of adjacent West Vancouver residents.

Above. The view from under today's Capilano River Marine Drive Bridge, actually two bridges. The span on the right was built in 1960 or 1961 to help cope with increased traffic, and the span on the left replaced the 1930 steel truss in 2010.

Below. A narrow single-track log bridge across the Seymour River in 1919.

Left. The Vancouver Harbour Commissioners Terminal Railway was built in 1928–29 to service the lands at the eastern end of Vancouver Harbour and ran from the Vancouver docks on the south side of the harbour across the (first) Second Narrows Bridge, opened in 1925 (see page 13) to connect with the Pacific Great Eastern Railway lines serving the western part of the docks via a new tunnel under the foot of Lonsdale in North Vancouver. The cut-and-cover tunnel was officially opened on 24 April 1929 by Viscount Willingdon, Governor General of Canada. This photo shows some of the inaugural ceremonies that day. The tunnel is still used today.

Below, centre. The Pacific Great Eastern Railway bridge across the Capilano River is seen in a telephoto image taken from Stanley Park. A CNR train is crossing the bridge westbound. Park Royal Cineplex is prominent in the background.

Left. The streetcar was responsible for opening up large areas of North Vancouver. Here a streetcar poses on a wood-pile bridge over Hastings Creek, on Lynn Valley Road just east of Mountain Highway during May 1910, the inaugural month of service on this route, which terminated at the foot of Lonsdale Avenue where the ferry from Vancouver docked.

Above and *left*. The North Shore was once a major logging area. Its proximity to the harbour made it relatively easy to extract logs. The Capilano Timber Company built a logging railway beginning in 1917 from the waterfront at what is now the foot of Pemberton Avenue, north up the Capilano valley for about 25 km, together with many branches and feeder lines. This, not surprisingly, required many trestle bridges. Two are shown here: Bridge 4 (*above*), which was located close to where the Cleveland Dam now stands, now in Capilano River Regional Park. It used 90-foot-long piles and at the time of its construction in 1918 was the highest pile-trestle bridge in British Columbia. At *left* is Houlgate Trestle under construction in May 1918, which gives a good idea of the scale of the work required. The trestle carried the logging railway over Houlgate Creek, a Capilano tributary also now in Capilano River Regional Park.

Above. In complete contrast to the logging trestle bridges are the massive but low modern Lynn Creek railway bridges, which replaced earlier truss bridges. There are multiple tracks on these bridges, so they need to be particularly strong.

This page and opposite. Sometimes an old bridge can surprise. This is the railway bridge across the Seymour River near its outlet to Vancouver Harbour, photographed in March 2021. The single-track bridge, built by Canadian National Railway about 1960 to service an industrial area on the east side of the river, appears to have seen its best days a long time ago, but its decay, rust and peeling paint, generously aided by some old graffiti, have created some colourful abstract-type designs lending themselves to artistic photos.

Capilano Canyon Suspension Bridge, often referred to as just the Capilano Suspension Bridge, has been promoted as a scenic tourist attraction in Metro Vancouver for more than 70 years. The original bridge was installed in 1889 by George Grant Mackay, a Scottish engineer and land developer who had purchased land on either side of the Capilano River. His bridge was made of cedar planks and hemp ropes tied to a huge buried cedar log and was constructed with the help of Squamish Nation chief August Jack Khahtsahlano and a team of horses. The hemp rope was replaced with wire cable in 1903. In 1914 the property was purchased by Edward Mahon, a real estate developer in North Vancouver (after whom Mahon Avenue is named). In 1953 the bridge was purchased by Rae Mitchell, who began promoting the bridge as a tourist attraction worldwide. In 1956 he completely rebuilt the bridge in five days, encasing the wire cables in many tonnes of concrete on either side. Since 1983 the bridge has been owned by Nancy Stibbard, Rae Mitchell's daughter. Additional features such as a treetop walk—consisting of seven footbridges suspended from Douglas firs—and a suspended cliff walk have been added, and the bridge continues to attract well over a million tourists each year.

Right. Capilano Canyon Suspension Bridge.

Above. An undated colour postcard of the Capilano Suspension Bridge.

Below. The Lynn Canyon Suspension Bridge in its early days.

Right. Another of the North Shore's canyons, that of Lynn Creek, has a suspension bridge. It was originally opened in 1912 as a similar private tourist attraction, though it is not as high and is more prone to movement. The bridge was taken over by the District of North Vancouver the following year as part of its newly created Lynn Valley Park, and the bridge became freely accessible.

Above. Just east of Lynn Creek is the Seymour River. This suspension bridge was built in 2018 to connect trails across it.

Sea to Sky

The steep glacially carved sides of Howe Sound have presented problems to builders of both the Pacific Great Eastern Railway, which built a connection between North Vancouver and Squamish in 1956, and the road, now Highway 99—the Sea to Sky Highway. For many years the railway used to run "speeders," tiny rail vehicles with one person aboard, ahead of all trains to ensure that the bridges and track had not been recently washed out or overcome by a rockslide. Following the completion of the rail line up Howe Sound from North Vancouver to Prince George, an inaugural train packed with dignitaries set out from North Vancouver on 27 August 1956 only to be stopped in Howe Sound for 17 hours by a rockslide.

The danger here is debris torrents, flood waters laden with trees, rocks and the like ripped from the creek banks by fast-flowing water. The mountains above are prone to sudden rainstorms, because they rise precipitously from water level in Howe Sound, and their western slopes are very steep.

In the dark evening of 28 October 1981, following a period of heavy rains, eight people died driving into M Creek when the wooden bridge had been destroyed by a debris flow. (M Creek was Yahoo Creek, incorrectly identified by the media, but the name stuck and today is on the identifier sign by the current bridge, along with its Squamish name, Kw'pel.)

Above. M Creek Bridge, just north of Lions Bay, the day after its destruction by a debris torrent. Television crews crowd the bridge in a scene unlikely to be allowed today, given the lack of any barrier. The wooden, trestle-like structure is quite apparent. It is also easy to see how this design would trap debris. Compare with the modern bridge *overleaf*.

Below. The concrete single-span Loggers Creek Bridge today, with warning sign. This is the next bridge north after M Creek. This bridge was built in 2006.

Above. The M Creek Bridge today, rebuilt in 2008 and not particularly interesting but substantially stronger than its predecessors.

The issue has been solved by building prestressed-concrete bridges that are longer and avoid having any middle-of-the-stream piers that might trap debris, as it is the buildup of debris upstream of a bridge that can lead to its collapse. In particular, at Alberta Creek, in Lions Bay, the entire creek bed has been transformed into a concrete flume, further ensuring that the debris is carried straight down to Howe Sound rather than getting caught up on a bridge. And Charles Creek, at Strachan Point, has had a massive retention structure built just above the bridge to control debris flows and protect the bridge below.

Below. Three bridges of Alberta Creek, in Lions Bay, showing the straight flume designed to prevent debris from being hung up on the bridges. *Left*, Lower Isleview Place Bridge, Lions Bay; *centre*, Upper Isleview Place Bridge; and *right*, the railway bridge.

Left, top. The massive debris-retention structure above the Charles Creek Bridge, seen in the foreground. The bridge is in two parts, with the now protected northbound bridge still standing from 1974; the southbound bridge was built in 2005.

Left, centre, left. Highway 99 bridge over Charles Creek, from below the highway.

Left, centre, right. The railway bridge over Charles Creek, also protected by the debris-retention structure.

This page. Harvey Creek, Lions Bay.
Below, bottom. The Crosscreek Road Bridge in Lions Bay over Harvey Creek. Note the boulders lining the riverbed have been set in concrete. *Below.* The Highway 99 bridge, built in 1986, at Harvey Creek from below, showing its massive construction. Isleview Place Bridge is in the foreground. *Right.* Harvey Creek from the Crosscreek Road Bridge showing the debris-retention structure that protects all the bridges below it.

Above. This is a little private bridge over Charles Creek at Strachan Point. It, too, is protected by the massive debris-retention structure above the Highway 99 bridge.

Farther north on Howe Sound is the Woodfibre Ferry dock. Woodfibre was a pulp mill company town on the western shore of Howe Sound accessible only via the ferry from here. The settlement dates from 1912. The mill closed in 2006, but the ferry dock (two views, *above right, top*) has been retained as an emergency link (from Porteau Beach) should Highway 99 be closed. It may see service again, as Woodfibre is now proposed as a liquefied natural gas export facility.

Above. At the head of Howe Sound is Squamish, a town essentially created by the Howe Sound & Northern Railway, which in 1912 became the Pacific Great Eastern Railway (PGE). Although originally intended to connect with North Vancouver, the line along Howe Sound proved too expensive for the fledgling railway, and until 1956 freight was shipped from docks at Squamish to Vancouver. Although the long docks are not technically a bridge, they looked like one. Here, about 1920, having unloaded freight cars from a rail ferry, a train leaves the docks.

Above. A 1913 view of Newport. The town's name was changed to Squamish the following year. The bridge in the foreground is a road bridge built in 1911 across the Mamquam River—as it was called then. In 1921 a flood changed the course of the Mamquam so that this became what is now known as Mamquam Blind Channel; the river joined the Squamish River before flowing to Howe Sound. A dike was built to ensure the river retained its new channel.

Left. Squamish has two rather interesting pedestrian bridges. This is a footbridge across Highway 99 to the Squamish Nation's Stawamus Reserve. It has bridge supports representing a Coast Salish serpent and a thunderbird (both mythological creatures from local legend), designed by a local artist, Xwa lack tun or Rick Harry. The bridge was erected in 2012.

Above and *right.* The Stawamus Chief Pedestrian Overpass, opened in 2009, as part of pre-Olympic Sea to Sky upgrades. It connects parking lots and trails of the Stawamus Chief Provincial Park across busy Highway 99. *Above* is a fisheye image, which distorts and emphasizes the curves of the bridge. The imposing Stawamus Chief forms a backdrop. The fisheye lens takes in a 180-degree field of view, and so both directions of the actually relatively straight highway here are included in the photo.

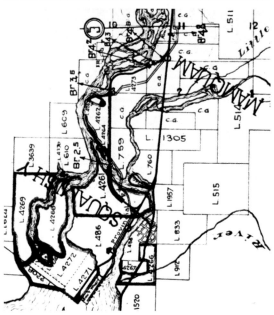

Above. The route of the PGE north of Squamish, across the Mamquam River in its original location, shown on a 1915 map.

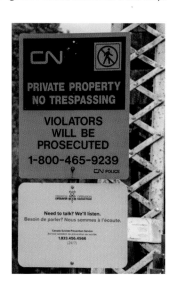

Far left. The "modern" Mamquam River Bridge, located close to the confluence of the Mamquam and Squamish Rivers. This is one span of what was originally the 1907 Canadian Pacific bridge across the Pitt River, and which was moved in 1915 to become part of the Pitt River Road Bridge (see pages 132–33). It was moved here in 1962. Another span became the PGE's Furry Creek Bridge in Howe Sound, and another went to the Pine River, near Chetwynd, when that line was being extended north.

Left, top. The front cover of a 1974 train schedule from the renamed PGE, the British Columbia Railway, featuring one of its diesel Budd cars used for passenger service between North Vancouver and Prince George. It is seen crossing the Mamquam Bridge.

Below, bottom, is another view of the Mamquam Bridge, showing a pipeline attached, and *left, bottom*, is the sign attached to the bridge to try to discourage suicides.

Far left, bottom, is the original Mamquam Bridge, 823 m long and built in 1911 for the Howe Sound & Northern. The crossing can be seen on the 1915 map, *left, centre.* After the river changed its course in 1921, an easier route presented itself that did not require such a long bridge, which is where the present bridge is located. The first train from Squamish to Lillooet ran on 20 February 1915.

Above and *right.* The Mamquam Blind Channel Bridge, completed in 1956 as part of the extension of the railway to North Vancouver. The Stawamus Chief is in the background.

Left. Cheakamus Canyon trestle in June 1925, a photo taken from the train. Both the railway and the road follow the canyon of the Cheakamus River, but the route was not an easy one. There are still many railway bridges in the canyon. On 5 August 2005 nine cars of a 144-car-long Canadian National train, pulled by seven locomotives, derailed and fell into the river from the main bridge. One car was full of 40,000 litres of sodium hydroxide (caustic soda), used as a bleach in pulp and paper mills. It killed an estimated half a million fish, mainly salmon and rainbow trout, and took six years to remediate. After investigation of the accident CN was ordered to limit its trains to 80 cars between Squamish and Clinton.

Right and *right, centre.* This nondescript modern-style bridge, built in 1981, takes Highway 99 over the delightfully named (as on the sign) *River of Golden Dreams*, properly Alta Creek, which connects Alta Lake and Green Lake. The river acquired that name in the 1930s from the Rainbow Lodge following a popular song at that time, "Down the River of Golden Dreams." Rainbow Lodge was the first retreat/resort-type facility in the Whistler area, opened in 1914 and serviced by the Pacific Great Eastern Railway. The river is a popular destination for visitors with kayaks and canoes.

Rutherford Creek Bridge, 8 km south of Pemberton on Highway 99, was built after the 2003 washout of the original bridge, along with an accompanying BC Rail bridge, on a rainy night on 18 October at about 3:45 am, claiming five victims.

One of them was 35-year-old Robert Leibel. He had a family in Prince George and was working in a gas station in Pemberton, and had decided to return to his family after his wife declined to join him; he apparently was desperate to rejoin her without waiting for payday, for he robbed the gas station and stole a truck before he left. For over a year none of the victims' bodies were found.

Then, on 13 December the following year, an excavator dredging the stream bed just downstream of the bridge site unearthed the remains of a truck, crushed flat and containing a body. DNA testing showed that the body was that of Leibel. The other four victims' bodies were never found. What happened to the victims is testament to the astonishing power of relatively minor creeks and streams when they pour down from the mountains under certain conditions.

Rutherford Creek at this location is the site of a run-of-the-river hydro power project, and as such it looks quite different compared with what it looked like in 2003. The road bridge, like many on the Sea to Sky Highway, has been replaced with a modern reinforced-concrete structure intended to make sure nothing like the 2003 incident ever happens again. The railway bridge, however, was replaced by an unusual design—one with a 31-m-long glulam wooden beam.

Above. This October 2003 aerial photo of Rutherford Creek shows the damage to the railway bridge in the foreground—the bridge has dropped from the rails, leaving them hanging in the air. Behind it (downstream) is the gap where the road bridge has been completely wiped out.

Sunshine Coast

At Powell River, on the Sunshine Coast, is a bridge that is on its second tour of duty, having been moved from Hope in 1965–66. It is the Wildwood Bridge, giving access to what since 1959 was a suburb of Powell River, Wildwood. Originally built in 1941, it carried the (old) Trans-Canada Highway across Silverhope Creek (see page 193). Wildwood grew up after 1914 when the provincial government subdivided the land there and made it available for pre-emption. Good jobs were available at the pulp mill on the other side of the river, which was at one time the largest pulp mill in the world.

The first bridge was a wooden structure built in 1916 at Cedar Street, some 500 m downstream of the current bridge. This was replaced in 1926 by another wooden-truss bridge at the same location as today's bridge, which lasted until its replacement by the Silverhope Creek bridge.

Right, top. The first bridge across Powell River, built in 1916 at today's Cedar Street, 500 m downstream of the current bridge.

Right, centre. This was the second bridge to Wildwood over Powell River, at the location of today's bridge completed in 1926. It had an 84-m wooden-truss span and a 55-m trestle. This photo appeared in the annual report of the Department of Public Works for 1926–27.

Below. The current Wildwood Bridge, shipped here and rebuilt and opened in 1966, was the rather elegant bridge that was originally built in 1941 to carry the Trans-Canada Highway across Silverhope Creek near Hope (see photo page 193). Unfortunately, when the bridge was moved, it lost the classic stone- or concrete-work it was installed with in 1941. Note one of the piers of the 1926 bridge beyond it.

North Bank Lower Fraser

A dam was built at Stave Falls east of Maple Ridge in 1912, one of the early hydroelectric projects that powered the rise of the use of electricity in British Columbia. The potential of the 24-m-high falls for power generation here had been recognized for some time before Western Canada Power Company purchased the original sponsor, the Stave Lake Electric and Power Company, and began constructing the dam in 1909. In 1910 the company built a rail line from the Canadian Pacific main line at Ruskin to service the dam site. In 1921 the power-generating system was purchased by the British Columbia Electric Company (which became BC Hydro in 1961). Another dam was built on the Alouette River in 1925 to divert more water through the Stave Falls Powerhouse, and the dam there was raised at the same time.

Another dam, the Ruskin Dam, was constructed downstream in 1930, and the new lake behind it, Hayward Lake, necessitated the rerouting of the railway line along its shore, which required some nine trestles. The powerhouse has its own steel-truss bridge for access. The lake inundated a bridge spanning the Stave River that had been built in 1908 and was the first road crossing of the Lower Stave River.

Right. The bridge carrying the railway line, built in 1910, to the Stave Falls hydroelectric facility. Today it is part of the appropriately named Railway Trail. The paddleboard is paddling on the northern extremity of Hayward Lake reservoir, formed after the 1930 construction of the Ruskin Dam downstream.

Above. One of the lost bridges of British Columbia. This quite large but nevertheless all-wood bridge was built in 1908 across the canyon of the Stave River. Known locally as the Red Bridge, it was officially opened the following year by Canadian Governor General Lord Earl Grey. This photo was taken in 1925 and shows the local Poole family proudly showing off their new car, a 1925 Dodge Touring. The bridge was located close behind the Ruskin Dam, built in 1930, and thus was flooded when Hayward Lake rose behind it.

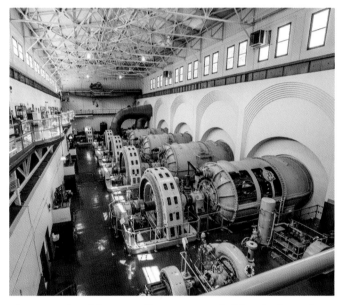

Above, top. Part of the Stave Falls Dam, across Blind Slough. The road uses the dam as a bridge.

Above. The turbines in the Stave Falls generating station.

Below. The Ruskin Dam is also used as a bridge, essentially replacing the 1908 bridge shown at *left*.

Right, bottom. This pedestrian bridge gives access to the river below the Ruskin Dam. It is suffering from erosion at either end.

Above, top. The Ruskin Dam generating station, with the steel-truss access bridge. In the distance the Stave River road bridge can just be seen.

Above. A view of the access bridge looking down from the dam.

Above. Soldiers guard the Stave River Canadian Pacific Railway Bridge in 1914. After the outbreak of World War I, the Canadian government felt that the CPR transcontinental line might be a target for saboteurs and assigned soldiers to guard strategic points, which included bridges. There are photos in this book of other bridges being guarded at the same time (see pages 130, 177 and 279). This bridge had the year before replaced an older bridge here.

Above. The bridge crossing the picturesque South Fork of the Alouette River is an unremarkable newer prestressed-concrete and steel-beam affair, but in 2021 it contained this memorial to 39-year-old Gareth Reardon, a cyclist who died here the year before after having been struck by a vehicle while riding his bike. His bike has been painted white and bolted to the bridge railings.

Below and *right.* From about 1905 into the 1920s there was much logging in the Maple Ridge area. Logs had to be extracted from the slopes, and this was one example of the lengths to which companies, in this case Abernethy & Lougheed Logging Company (Allco), would go to build logging railway lines. Here a long train of logs is hauled across a trestle built across the Alouette River. The wooden truss (*right*) is just to the left of the panorama *below*. Abernethy & Lougheed had seven logging locomotives to haul logs to a dump into the Fraser River at Kanaka Creek.

Mission Bridges

The Mission Railway Bridge was the second bridge to be built over the Fraser River in the Lower Mainland, being completed in 1891, two years after the Marpole Bridge (see page 100), but it was the first railway bridge. It was competitively necessary, to connect the Canadian Pacific with Northern Pacific lines at Sumas and thence to Seattle. The same year a competing railway, the New Westminster Southern, was opened from a point opposite New Westminster to Blaine.

This first bridge was a wood truss. It was replaced in 1903–10 (an extended construction period) by one made of steel, the present bridge. A plea was made to the CPR by the people of Mission to have the bridge deck planked so that road traffic could also use it, but the railway refused, not giving in until 1927. Road traffic was only allowed in one direction at a time, since the bridge was not wide enough, and was often held up by trains. And the southern approaches, being low-lying, were sometimes flooded in the spring.

On 7 June 1948, during the great Fraser Valley flood of that year, high water lifted the fixed span on the south side off of its piers and dropped it into the river. It was retrieved with barges and tugboats and the bridge put back

Above. The first Mission Railway Bridge, a wooden structure completed in 1891, also shown *right, top centre*, under construction.

Below. The second Mission Railway Bridge, completed in 1910.

Right, centre. The second bridge was adapted for use by road traffic in 1927 and was used by such until the new road bridge opened in 1972. At the southern end, shown here, traffic would make a sharp turn onto the road into Matsqui Village. The road is still there, but the bridge deck has reverted to rails only.

into operation within a month. On 24 July 1955 erosion of one of the piers caused a span to collapse, but this time it was over a year before the bridge was able to be put back into operation. A temporary ferry substituted for the bridge during this period.

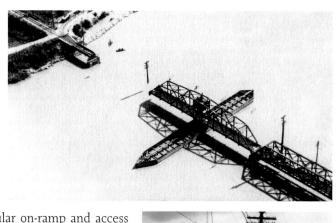

A road bridge, which took three years to build, was opened in 1972. It was high enough to avoid flooding with its long, elevated approach road, and connected to Abbotsford by the four-lane Highway 11.

The Mission Road Bridge was built between 1969 and 1972 and has 19 piers, nine of which are in the water, with the rest supporting the approaches, which include large fills on both sides and even a tunnel to accommodate a circular on-ramp and access road. The bridge was officially opened in July 1973 by Premier Dave Barrett.

Left, top. The south-side span missing from the Mission Railway Bridge in June 1948.

Left, centre right. The missing span of the bridge in July 1955, complete with bent rail.

Left, centre left. The Mission Road Bridge under construction.

Left, bottom. A classical black-and-white image showing the Mission Railway Bridge today.

Above. The Mission Road Bridge is reflected in the waters of the Fraser River in September 2012.

Right. The misty, ethereal and vaguely abstract rendering of the bridge is the result of intentional camera movement (ICM).

Left and *below*. In the forest of the mountain slope some 18 km north-northwest of Mission is Cascade Falls, in a regional park of the same name. The path to the falls includes several footbridges, of which the most ambitious is this chain-link suspension bridge, literally hung from anchor points on either side of a gorge. It offers an effective yet inexpensive way of providing durable access to the falls viewing point.

The Lougheed Highway (Highway 7) was completed as far east as Harrison in 1941 as a paved highway, and in 1953 it was extended to a junction with Highway 1 at Hope. But a rougher road existed by the 1920s and included two bridges that crossed Nicomen Slough twice, at Dewdney and Deroche. They were replaced in 1958 and 1957, respectively, with these now unusual bridges, Deroche (*above*) and Dewdney (*left*). They are relatively simple pile-and-trestle bridges, but they have certainly stood the test of time.

Morris Valley Road, which runs from Highway 7 near Harrison Mills to the Hemlock Valley ski area (which opened in 1969 and is now Sasquatch Mountain Resort), crosses the Chehalis River on this single-lane wooden-truss bridge, built in 1950. Like so many of these bridges, it is now deemed inadequate for the traffic and not worth rebuilding in its present form. Instead, a modern two-lane—and a sidewalk for pedestrians and cyclists—prestressed-concrete beam structure is being built alongside the old bridge and is slated to replace it in fall 2022. The photos on this page document the wooden bridge and show the new one rising beside it (see also pages 9 and 320).

Above, top. The 1950 bridge. The new bridge is under construction to the right in this 16 September 2021 photo.
Above, left. Both bridges on 15 June 2022. The new bridge now spans the river.
Right, centre. A fisheye view of the old bridge.
Left. An intersection of wooden beams on the old bridge—this time taken with a normal lens.

The first bridge over the Harrison River at Harrison Mills was the Canadian Pacific Railway bridge, built about 1884 when the line in the Lower Fraser Valley was built by CPR contractor Andrew Onderdonk to its terminus at Port Moody. This wooden bridge was replaced in 1913 by the present double-tracked concrete-pier and steel-beam structure. It is seen under construction at *left*. A year later, Canada was at war, and the government placed guards on all the major CPR bridges (see also pages 130, 170 and 279). The Harrison contingent is shown, smartly at attention, *above*. Today, the 1913 structure remains in use and is seen *below* with a Canadian National freight crossing it about 10 am on 16 September 2021. The train is nicely reflected in the still waters of Harrison Lake. The CNR train is headed east on CPR track as part of a reciprocal agreement between the two railways that allows one-way traffic north up the Fraser Canyon on the west (CP) side and south on the east (CN) side, an efficient arrangement for both companies as trains can follow closer on the mainly single track in the canyon than they could if opposing trains had to pass. The split and rejoin occurs at the first possible crossing of the Fraser, at Mission.

Fraser Valley East

For centuries the biggest feature of the eastern part of the Lower Fraser Valley was Sumas Lake, a huge but quite shallow expanse of water whose main reputation seemed to be producing hordes of mosquitoes, to which a number of early surveys, including the 1857–62 US–Canada Northwest Boundary Survey, refer. In 1875–94 the Chilliwack River, which before 1875 flowed north to the Fraser (just west of downtown Chilliwack), was diverted by log jams into Sumas Lake, compounding the flooding during an exceptional flood in 1894.

In 1919 a plan was drawn up by the province's new Land Settlement Board, which had been set up to provide land for soldiers returning from World War I, to drain Sumas Lake and reclaim the fertile farmland beneath it. Work began the following year. The Vedder Canal was dug to divert the Chilliwack River from the lake, instead directing it north into the Fraser, joining the Sumas River (which originally drained Sumas Lake but reversed seasonally) at the north tip of Sumas Mountain. In addition, the Sumas Drainage Canal was dug down the centre of the draining lake to connect with the Sumas River, joining the canal just before it gets to the Fraser. In 1923 pumping began, and by 1924 the lake was dry. Sumas Prairie, as the drained area is known, remains criss-crossed with drainage canals and ditches, all requiring bridges big and small to carry the service roads.

Above. The Sumas Drainage Canal, seen looking south from No. 5 Road Bridge. Sumas Prairie, the drained Sumas Lake, is either side.

Right. The first bridge across the Vedder Canal, completed in 1924. It is where the bridge over the Trans-Canada Highway is now.

Below. The 1924 bridge was replaced in 1950 with this one, and twinned in 1961 (*right, bottom*) for the Trans-Canada freeway.

Above. The Vancouver, Victoria & Eastern Railway (VV&E) a Great Northern Railway–controlled company, built a line from Cloverdale to Cannor, near Chilliwack, in 1912–14 to meet the Canadian Northern Pacific Railway (now CNR) transcontinental line then being built into Vancouver, wanting to connect with a VV&E line from Princeton over the Hope Mountains (which did not proceed because of an agreement reached with the Kettle Valley Railway, a Canadian Pacific Railway subsidiary). Part of this line required a trestle along the north shore of Sumas Lake, now the Sumas River, since the lake abutted the steep side of Sumas Mountain. Despite being abandoned in 1919, the remnants of this trestle are still visible over a hundred years later. This photo was taken in 2018.

Vedder Bridge

The Chilliwack River, which downstream of the Vedder Bridge was called Vedder Creek until about 1908 and then Vedder River (though both names are used), has a history of destroying bridges when it floods. If you look at a topographic map like Google Terrain, it is not hard to see why: at Vedder Crossing the river passes through two mountain masses, which although appearing like a good spot for a bridge, creates a restriction that would increase the flow and height of the river at times of flood.

It should also be noted that the bridge here was, before the draining of Sumas Lake, the only route west to Vancouver, joining the Trans-Provincial Highway, which ran south of the lake, about 8 km to the west.

No fewer than nine bridges have spanned the river at Vedder Crossing, though this count includes the use of a logging railway bridge planked as an emergency crossing twice when the road bridge had gone. The railway bridge itself, built in 1924, makes ten.

Left, centre. Keith Wilson Bridge over the Vedder Canal, linking Chilliwack and Abbotsford. This bridge was built in 1998 and replaced an Acrow panel bridge (*left, bottom*), a modern successor to the Bailey bridge, erected by military engineers from CFB Chilliwack in November 1986, who built it in a few days as an exercise. The bridge was 183 m long and had seven spans. It was hardly a field exercise, for tubular steel piles filled with concrete had been previously placed by a civilian contractor. A bridge was required in a hurry to provide an alternative route for slow-moving farm vehicles and the like so that they did not have to use the Trans-Canada Highway, which was undergoing upgrading to true freeway standards. The photo of the soldiers working on the Acrow bridge appeared on the front page of the *Chilliwack Progress* on 29 November 1986.

These date as follows: 1879; 1891; 1895; 1910; a temporary bridge in March 1918; 10 July 1918, closed to heavy traffic in December 1930; the 1924 railway bridge planked in February and March 1931 for temporary use by heavier traffic; 18 August 1931; the railway bridge used for road traffic again in August 1941 while repairs were done on the 1931 bridge; July 1948 (though it had a 1947 date on the concrete abutment; work was held up till the following year); and October 2017 (the present bridge). Few places can match such a list!

There was also a makeshift ferry operated by a local Indigenous chief for a while between when the first bridge washed away and 1891. So in total there have been 11 crossings!

The first bridge (1879) was a rudimentary affair built by Indigenous peoples. The second (1891) was also built by

Above. A horse and buggy are posed beside the 1891 bridge.

Left. This photo of the 1895 bridge has been digitally altered to produce a posterized, ethereal look, creating a pleasing but quite different image from the original. It is thus an image produced purely for artistic reasons rather than being the historical record of the original.

Indigenous peoples, and received a $200 contribution towards costs from the provincial government; it only lasted four years, irrevocably damaged by high water flows in the 1894 flood that affected much of the Fraser Valley. The third bridge (1895) had piling driven down to bedrock and concrete abutments. This was, initially, a toll bridge.

This bridge was destroyed in November 1909 when the river created a new channel and flowed into Sumas Lake to the west instead of going north to the Fraser.

The following year the fourth bridge was built. Because of the lessons of the previous months, it was much more substantial, using 114 tonnes of cement shipped specially from Victoria in its foundations. Though intended to survive the worst the river could throw against it, this bridge did not last long; in December 1917 the bridge was once again damaged beyond repair by a raging river.

This time a temporary bridge (No. 5) was hastily constructed, opening in March 1918, while another permanent

bridge (No. 6) was built, about 250 m upstream from the previous bridges (and where all future bridges would be built). On 9 June 1918, before the new permanent bridge was even complete, the temporary bridge was rendered unusable by more flooding. However, this time the permanent bridge was nearly complete, opening a month later.

In December 1924 a heavy snowfall followed by heavy rain and mild temperatures caused more flooding, accompanied by considerable quantities of tree debris. This time the bridge survived.

By 1930 the bridge had deteriorated to the point where it was restricted to one-way light traffic only, and once again a new bridge was planned. In the meantime, another alternative was now possible, for in 1924 the Campbell River Timber Company (which was logging the area to the south to feed its mill at White Rock) had built a logging railway bridge at this location. The decision was thus made to plank the railway bridge (thus becoming bridge No. 7) for use by all

road traffic (though it was still one-way) until a new bridge was ready, which it was on 18 August 1931. However, this new bridge—No. 8—was a disappointment to the local people, for it was a wooden span considered too narrow for vehicles of that time. The bridge had been paid for by the provincial government, which had chosen the cheapest possible design as an economy measure when it faced declining revenues because of the onset of the Great Depression. But it would have to do.

In a way, this bridge lasted longer than might have been expected, for it was not until 1948 that it would be replaced, although between August and December 1941 it had to be repaired, and the railway bridge was used once again as a temporary crossing while the repairs were being effected.

By 1946, after World War II restrictions had been eased, a decision was made to replace the 1931 wooden bridge, and it was demolished to make way for a new one in February 1947. Yet again the railway bridge was pressed into service as a temporary crossing, though by this time it was nearing the end of its life and required 24-hour supervision. Guards were placed at either end to guide motorists over the one-way bridge. The steel for the new bridge, in the meantime, had not arrived, partly owing to postwar shortages compounded by a steelworkers' strike in Vancouver. The delay lasted until the following year. Finally, in July 1948 the new bridge, No. 9, opened for traffic.

It was not too soon, for less than three years later, in May 1951, the railway bridge collapsed and fell into the river.

Above. The abutments of the 1910 bridge remain, today used by supports for a water-gauging cable operated by the federal government's Water Survey of Canada.

Below. On 27 August 1912 Thomas Wilby, a British travel writer, and his driver, Jack Haney, set off from Halifax to cross Canada by "the All-Red Route," that is, without entering the US on the way. The All-Red Route referred to a route around the world via the countries of the British Empire. The car was a 1912 Reo, and Wilby had persuaded the Reo Motor Car Company that this would be great advertising. In fact their travels were not entirely by car, as the car had been loaded onto a train for the 1,500 km from Sault Ste. Marie to Winnipeg. Wilby and Haney arrived in Port Alberni on 18 October 1912, having at least demonstrated the rising viability of the car for long-distance travel. Wilby wrote a book about his exploits, *A Motor Tour through Canada*, which was published in 1914. This photo shows the Reo and entourage on the 1910 Vedder Bridge, on the only route west at the time. Wilby is standing in the car; Haney is at left. The car in front was a guide car provided by the New Westminster Automobile Club.

It was just as well that the new road bridge proved strong and reliable now that the "backup" was gone. However, the 1948 bridge deteriorated over time, and several times repairs had to be made when vehicles crashed into it. By 2011 it was clear a new bridge was essential, and the City of Chilliwack began planning for a new one, negotiating with both provincial and federal governments for funding. In April 2016 a new bridge design was chosen and the contractor selected.

Bridge No. 10, the present bridge, built adjacent to the older bridge, was completed in August 2017 and officially opened in October that year. Built on land beside the river, the bridge was placed into position using an innovative method never tried before with this type of bridge—a steel arch. This type of bridge does not have the strength to be cantilevered by itself, so as it was cantilevered out over the river (the term used was "launched"), it was supported by a "kingpost" and cable system that held up the "launched" end until it reached its pre-built pier. This was a claimed world "first" for this type of bridge. In November 2017 the old bridge was dismantled using a similar method in reverse.

Below. Climax locomotive *No. 2* of Vedder Logging, which had taken over operations in the Chilliwack area in 1934, crosses a temporary trestle bridge in the area southwest of Cultus Lake in 1936. Many rough logging railway bridges were built in British Columbia, and they were abandoned along with the grade once the area had been logged out.

Right, top. This 1927 photo shows the 1924 logging railway bridge at left and the 1918 road bridge (No. 6) at right, with the approach trestles neatly crossing each other in the foreground. The railway bridge is a through-truss with a king truss (the triangles) added nearest the camera. This bridge was planked in March 1931 (thus becoming bridge No. 7) when the road bridge was found to have become unsafe, and vehicles used the railway bridge until 18 August 1931, when a new road bridge (No. 8) opened.

Right, bottom. Bridge No. 9 under construction in 1948. Although slated to open the year before, its foundations lay unused until the following year because of a shortage of steel, and a steelworkers' strike delayed the delivery of the superstructure. This bridge lasted until 2017, when it was replaced by the present one. Note the 1924 logging railway bridge in the background.

Above. The new steel-arch bridge is complete in this 2017 photo from bridge builder Emil Anderson Group. The photo also shows (nearest the camera) the 1948 truss bridge it replaced. The innovative "launch" of the new bridge was made into a spectacle, with the public invited, in April that year.

Left. A City of Chilliwack webcam captured the final hours of the 1948 bridge in November 2017 as an excavator ripped up the steel for scrap. It was "delaunched" using the same method as the new one's construction, in reverse, by supporting one end while the bridge truss was slid onto the south river bank.

Left, above and *overleaf*. An elegant arch bridge such as the 2017 one is ideal for photography. The photo at *left,* rendered in black and white to emphasize the lines and curves of the bridge, is taken with a 15 mm fisheye lens, and the one *above* is taken with an 8 mm fisheye lens, both very wide angle but somewhat distorting the arch or the road in order to get everything in; and *overleaf,* the scenic location creates an unusually composed but very satisfying landscape.

Agassiz-Rosedale Bridge

A rudimentary ferry across the Fraser River at Rosedale was in place as early as 1896. Highway 9, from Agassiz and Highway 7, on the north side of the Fraser, to Yale Road in Rosedale, on the south, opened in 1953, using the ferry for its river connection. The ferry was replaced by the bridge three years later. When the Chilliwack section of the Trans-Canada Highway opened in 1961, Highway 9 was extended south to meet it.

The Agassiz-Rosedale Bridge, a steel cantilever truss structure, was formally opened to traffic on 31 October 1956, with the Minister of Highways, Phil Gaglardi, presiding over the ceremony, as he always did. He had planned the bridge, built for the government's BC Toll Highways and Bridges Authority, and the bridge tolls were intended to pay for the bridge. As it happened, all tolls were removed province-wide as part of a policy change in 1964.

Above. MV *Agassiz*, built in 1931, leaves the dock on the Agassiz side of the river in this 1930s postcard view. Mount Cheam is in the background.

Below. MV *Agassiz* unloads vehicles on the Rosedale side c. 1949. When the bridge was built in 1956, the vessel was transferred to the new Albion service between Fort Langley and Maple Ridge, being renamed MV *T'Lagunna* (see page 97).

Left. The British Columbia Electric Railway (BCER) built an interurban line in 1910 from New Westminster to Chilliwack to serve the Fraser Valley. Here a single interurban car crosses a later-built bridge over the Vedder River some 5.6 km downstream from the Vedder Bridge. The line passed to BC Hydro in 1962 and is now part of the Southern Railway of BC system. This photo was taken in 1949, a year before passenger service was withdrawn.

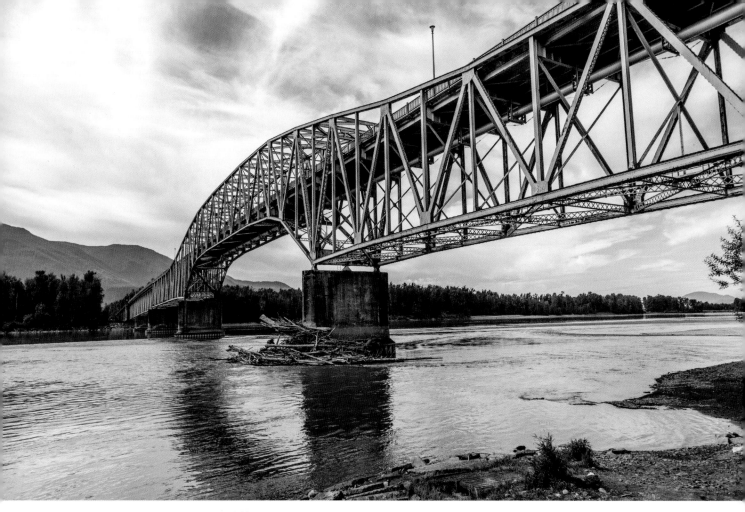

Above. The Agassiz-Rosedale Bridge is a very long bridge. Including its approaches, which have a steel stringer (beam) structure on the north side to avoid possible flooding, it is 2.6 km long. The length of the main cantilever truss over the river is 600 m. This length makes for a spectacular structure. Here, viewed from the north side, the bridge towers above the photographer. Note the forest debris piled up against the concrete pier.

Far left, bottom, and *left.* Two infrared images of the Agassiz-Rosedale Bridge, which tend to emphasize the immensity of the structure.

Above. This is a view through the steel trusses of the bridge from the south side. The abundant receding steel beams and cross supports create a dramatic, almost abstract pattern. This is a south-side approach span, technically a Warren through-truss; the main span (the curved part) is a polygonal Warren through-truss. How the graffiti gang manage to get to some parts of this bridge, like, it seems, all bridges, is a mystery.

Hope

Hope, at the eastern end of the Lower Fraser Valley, has a very interesting bridge, one over the Fraser that was originally built as a combined rail and road bridge but now just carries the road—in fact the Trans-Canada Highway. It was built by the Kettle Valley Railway (KVR) to connect its tortuous line down the Coquihalla Valley and through the Quintette (or Othello) Tunnels (see page 194) with the Canadian Pacific Railway's main line to Vancouver on the west bank of the Fraser.

Through an agreement with—and payment from—the provincial government, a road was integrated into the bridge, running on top of the trusses through which the railway ran. That replaced the previous private ferry service here, which had begun in the 1880s. The bridge was completed in March 1915 for rail traffic and in the fall that year for road vehicles. The new bridge was the largest bridge on the entire KVR. When the Coquihalla subdivision closed in 1962, the bridge was sold to the government for $1 and remained as a road bridge only.

Below. A rather scenic 1941 view of the Hope Bridge, sometimes called the Hope-Fraser Bridge. The railway track can be seen on the lower deck, while a car of the period crosses eastward towards Hope on the top road deck.

Above. The Hope Bridge seen from the rail level today. The roadway above was widened in 1995–96, accommodated by the fitting of triangular supports attached to the truss structure beneath, and these are also used to strengthen the structure inside the truss, shown at *right*.

Right. The uniform receding form of the main trusses of the bridge makes for a great photograph; here the view has been rendered in black and white to emphasize the pattern of steel. A similar, though not the same, colour version of this image is shown on the half-title page.

Above, top. The merge point of the railway and the road on the Hope Bridge can still be seen clearly on the east side of the river, despite changes in the road supports. The rail bridge, now unused, would make a great pedestrian and cycle path.

Above. This is the top of the Hope Bridge today, widened in 1995–96, with a walkway on the north side. This is the view from the west side looking east.

Below and *right, bottom*. The rather spectacular Enbridge Natural Gas Pipeline bridge crosses the Fraser River just downstream from Hope. The pipeline and the bridge were built in 1971. It is a suspension bridge, with the pipeline hanging from numerous cables attached to the two main suspension cables.

Above. A scenic view of the Coquihalla River in Hope, with the Canadian National Railway Bridge in the distance. The CNR line runs down the east side of the Fraser Canyon.

Above. Until its demise in 2011 this bridge over the Coquihalla River in Hope was used by filmmakers, including for the Sylvester Stallone–starring *Rambo* series. Properly the Kawkawa Bridge, it was known locally as the Rambo Bridge. It was replaced by a modern steel-pile and reinforced-concrete beam bridge (*inset*) of little interest to filmmakers.

Above. The beautiful bridge over Silverhope Creek, near Hope, which was built in 1941 and dismantled and rebuilt in 1965–66 as the Wildwood Bridge at Powell River (see page 167). This photo appeared in the annual report of the Department of Public Works in 1966. Twin modern bridges were built over Silverhope Creek in 1985 to carry the Trans-Canada Highway when it was upgraded to freeway standards.

Below. The Canadian National Railway Bridge over Silverhope Creek makes a beautiful photo with the mountains behind. A pipeline bridge can be seen in the background. There are a total of five bridges over this creek within 350 m of each other here. The CPR train is going west (this is the end locomotive) on the CNR line, which here is part of the Fraser Canyon line-sharing agreement between the two companies.

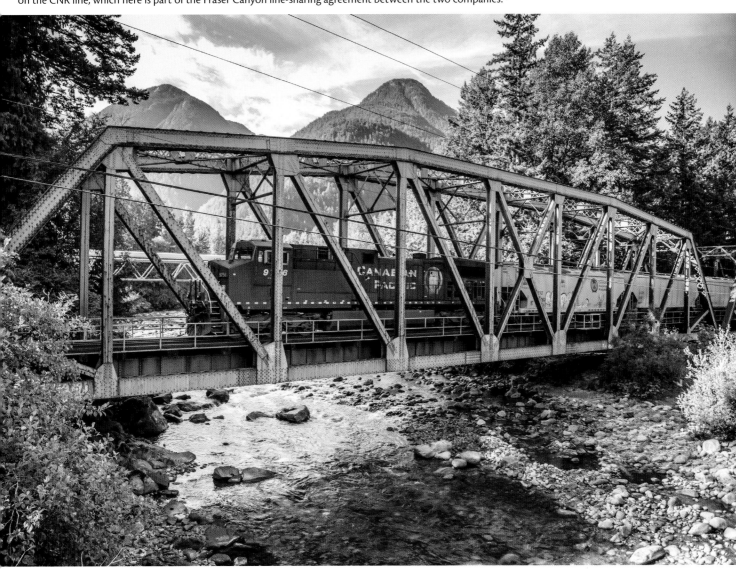

Coquihalla

A few kilometres beyond Hope lie the Quintette Tunnels, also known as the Othello Tunnels, cut by the Kettle Valley Railway (KVR) in 1915–16 to connect its line down the Coquihalla Valley with the CPR main line at Hope, across the Hope Bridge (see page 190).

The entire line had been conceived as an alternative route from the CPR main line to the coast and to connect the mining areas of southeastern British Columbia to Vancouver to stem the trade south across the border by the CPR's arch-rival, the Great Northern Railway (GNR). But any line to the southern coast that did not use the Fraser Canyon—which was difficult enough as it was—faced the barrier of the Hope Mountains. The only possible route was down the Coquihalla, but near the river's confluence with the Fraser at Hope it ran through the very narrow 90-m-deep Coquihalla Gorge with no possible room for a railway. The solution was a series of tunnels.

The KVR was a CPR subsidiary, and was built under the direction of that railway's Andrew McCulloch, who was used to onerous engineering challenges, and who was responsible for the many difficult bridges and trestles on the rest of the line, one long considered the most difficult ever built. So the tunnels were, to him, a response to yet another challenge. In 1909 James Hill, the GNR's feisty president, had announced that his railway would build a 13-km-long tunnel that would have been the longest in North America at the time. This proposal was withdrawn when, in the failing economic conditions before World War I, the KVR and the GNR reached an agreement to share the KVR's line down the Coquihalla and the line from Princeton north to Brookmere, at the top of the Coquihalla Valley, which had been built by the GNR's subsidiary the Vancouver, Victoria & Eastern (VV&E). At Hope, the GNR would join the Canadian Northern main line as far as Cannor, where it again reached its own line across the northern margins of Sumas Lake (see page 179).

To begin the tunnelling work at Quintette, men had to descend ladders on the canyon sides, lay charges, and then quickly run back up the ladder to get out of the way of the blast. There were four tunnels—they look like five because of an open side on one—connected by two bridges across the river. The tunnels opened for regular traffic, with the line, on 31 July 1916. After many years, when the cost of maintaining it exceeded the revenue, the Coquihalla line was officially closed in 1962. The tunnels were opened as a provincial park in 1986.

Right, top. A 1920 photo showing the bridge between two tunnels.

Right, bottom. The original bridge structure can be seen under the wooden trail bridge built on top when the area became a park.

Far right, top. The view from a tunnel across a bridge.

Far right, bottom. View from the trail bridge atop the original railway bridge into a tunnel. These photos give a good idea of the difficulty of building these tunnels.

Left. Early construction of the Quintette Tunnels: ladders down into the gorge used to lay charges to begin to excavate a tunnel. That was a long way to climb in a hurry to escape the explosion.

Above. This 1925 photo shows the open side of one tunnel and the bridge and tunnel beyond. Both ends of this tunnel (called #3 and #4 on park maps) had a bridge crossing the river.

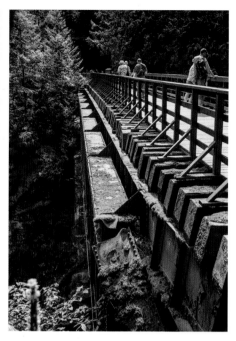

Above, left and centre. In the 1950s the CPR strengthened parts of the tunnels with concrete liners and cribbing.
Above, right. The top of part of the original steel bridge can be seen at the side of the narrower modern wood trail bridge.

Above and *right*. The most spectacular of the KVR bridges in the Coquihalla Valley was the Ladner Creek Trestle, 28 km north of Hope. *Right* is the curved falsework in place during the construction of the bridge in 1915. The bridge was fabricated and erected by the Canadian Bridge Company for the Kettle Valley Railway. It had the sharpest curve of any of the 234 curves on the Coquihalla part of the line. The bridge was set on fire in May 2018, caused, it was believed, by a cigarette butt, but the steel structure under the wooden bridge deck survived. Here (*above*) is the bridge after the fire. Today the Ladner Creek Bridge is a modern steel-and-concrete structure carrying the Coquihalla Highway across the creek near the old railway bridge.

The Coquihalla Highway, Highway 5, built in the run-up to Expo 86 in Vancouver in 1984–86, used the railbed of the KVR for some of its route. Begun in 1979 after much lobbying from the Merritt Board of Trade and including a caravan of vehicles down the abandoned KVR grade, the project moved slowly until fast-tracked in 1984 to be ready for Expo. From 1986 to 2008 the highway was tolled, with toll booths at the summit. The new highway required some 38 bridges and overpasses, including 18 major bridges over the creeks feeding the Coquihalla River. Between Coquihalla

Above. Dry Gulch Bridge, a steel-arch span, on the Coquihalla Highway in 1986, soon after the bridge's completion. It is one of the most dramatic bridges on the route, though from the highway it hardly seems like a bridge at all. Below it lies the ruins of a Kettle Valley Railway wooden-frame trestle. The latter was blown up on 28 September 1969 by Canadian Forces as a training exercise. In November 1959 the Coquihalla subdivision of the KVR had been closed after being severely damaged by slides and washouts, and never reopened. Soon after, freight destined for the coast was routed north to Golden and thence on the CPR main line to the coast, a longer way round but less subject to disruption by nature. Ironically, the steel for the construction of this highway bridge was one of the last destination loads for the KVR before it closed. The steel was delivered to Brodie, the nearest remaining point on the railway to the bridge, some 25 km away, and then trucked from there. In a way this photo really embodies the battle of road and rail for transportation supremacy, with road winning out.

Pass and Ladner Creek the highway was located higher up the valley side than the railbed had been, in order to avoid snowslides in the winter; these are still a major issue.

The second phase of the project, Merritt to Kamloops, was completed in 1987, and the third phase, the Coquihalla Connector, linked the highway to the Okanagan Valley at Peachland, and was completed in 1990.

Right. The Great Bear Snowshed on the Coquihalla Highway. Maybe not really a bridge in the sense used in this book (but it is a bridge for snow!) the snowshed is nevertheless an important part of the highway, helping to keep it open in winter.

Five bridges and whole sections of road on the Coquihalla Highway were washed away in the storm of mid-November 2021 (see page 9).

Middle Fraser

Some 44 km north of Hope, and 21 km north of Yale, where the Fraser Canyon begins, is a beautiful old bridge with a provincial park around it. This is the Alexandra Bridge, built in 1926. It was not the first bridge at this location, however.

The original road bridge here was built in 1861 by Joseph Trutch, a British surveyor who would in 1864 become Commissioner of Public Works for the Colony of British Columbia, and in 1871 British Columbia's first Lieutenant Governor.

The idea for a suspension bridge is attributed to Trutch seeing and being impressed with a similar bridge over the Niagara River a few years before.

There had been a flat-bottomed punt ferry in this location since 1858, but a bridge was required as a vital link in the Cariboo Road then being built—some of it by Trutch on contract to the government—to connect the coast with the goldfields of Barkerville and area.

This bridge was the first permanent crossing of the Fraser River. In true British Empire style Trutch named the bridge after Princess Alexandra, wife of Queen Victoria's eldest son and the future King Edward VII.

The bridge was strengthened with new foundations by the Royal Engineers in 1863. Trutch's bridge-building contract allowed him to collect tolls from the bridge for many years.

This bridge was damaged to the point of being unusable in May 1894 by the major flood of that year. The bridge deck was overtopped despite being 90 m above the normal water level. Its remains were dismantled in 1912 when the Canadian Northern Railway built its line through the canyon. The Cariboo Road itself had been virtually unused since contractor Andrew Onderdonk built the Canadian Pacific Railway in the canyon in 1884, destroying much of the road in the process.

With a rising demand from automobile traffic, the road was rebuilt in the mid-1920s and with it a new bridge, opening in 1926, built on the footings of the 1863 structure. During construction, an aerial basket ferry was used to cross the river. The 1926 bridge is still there today, in Alexandra Bridge Provincial Park, created in 1984. This bridge remained in service until 1962, when a new, higher, truss-arch span bridge was opened about 2 km downstream as part of improvements to the Trans-Canada Highway.

Below. Joseph Trutch's Alexandra Bridge. The toll house is on the left (west) side. The extent of the 1894 flood can be appreciated from this photo, as it can be seen how much the river had to rise to overtop the bridge deck.

Left, top. The 1926 Alexandra Bridge, photographed in 1944. Note the massive concrete piers and the wooden bridge deck. The latter was replaced with steel mesh (see photo *overleaf*), as were many bridges in the province.

Above, top. One of the suspension cable anchors on the 1926 bridge.

Above, centre. The decorative end of the 1962 Alexandra Bridge celebrates the salmon, for which the Fraser River has been an essential pathway.

Above. The rather prosaic road deck on the 1962 bridge. This is a 2012 photo; the railings have more recently been replaced and the bridge deck resurfaced.

Left. The 1962 Alexandra Bridge. This 488-m-long bridge, at the time of its construction, was the second-largest steel-arch span in the world, with an arch of 245 m. This photo shows it well.

Despite its age and size, the 1926 Alexandra Bridge makes an imposing sight to the traveller. This is the view from the east side.

The highway through the Fraser Canyon was significantly upgraded in the 1960s, producing such bridges as the Alexandra and Nine Mile Canyon (Ainslie Creek), north of Boston Bar (see page 205). A number of locations were so difficult that the only solution was tunnels. Seven tunnels were bored in the Fraser Canyon in the early 1960s. The longest, the 638-m-long China Bar Tunnel, opened on 1 May 1962, was at the time the most expensive section of highway in the province, costing $5 million, then a fortune.

Right, top. Just above the Alexandra Bridge, this is the original Cariboo Highway in the mid-1860s. It gives a good idea of the engineering challenges posed by the canyon. Trestles and bridges allow the road to overhang the canyon sides.

Above. Inside the Alexandra Tunnel, built in 1964.

Right. The Ferrabee Tunnel, also opened in 1964.

Below. The Yale Tunnel, completed in 1963.

Above. The Spuzzum Creek CPR bridge about 1895, in the process of having its wooden-truss span replaced by a steel one. The modern Trans-Canada Bridge crosses the creek right beside it. Spuzzum Creek is about 15 km north of Yale.

Above. Hell's Gate is a sudden narrowing of the Fraser, making the river flow faster. It was named by explorer Simon Fraser (after whom the river is named) in 1808 when he travelled the river from today's Prince George to Vancouver. A rockslide triggered by the construction of the Canadian Northern Pacific Railway (now CNR) in 1914 increased the flow of the river to the point that salmon could no longer migrate upstream; this is considered by some experts to have changed the salmon fishery on the river forever. The Hell's Gate Airtram, a popular tourist attraction, crosses the river here, descending to a terminal next to a small suspension bridge. Both can be seen in this photo. It was constructed in 1970 by a Swiss company and opened in July 1971.

Farther north are the communities of Boston Bar and North Bend, the latter, on the west side of the river, a division point for the Canadian Pacific. Between them, from 1940 to 1986, was an unusual aerial ferry that was able to carry cars, but only one at a time. Despite that, by the time it closed it had carried over 2 million vehicles—one at a time, over 46 years—and 6 million passengers. It was the only road access to North Bend, and, when a bridge replaced it, that community gained better emergency services protection, not to mention lower insurance rates.

The ferry was replaced by the Cog Harrington Bridge, a steel-truss span named after a Fraser River pioneer. A much more efficient way to cross the river, but not remotely as exciting!

Left. The Boston Bar–North Bend Aerial Ferry, in mid-air with a single car and its occupants.

Right. During a flood in 1948 the aerial ferry nearly became a cable ferry. The ferry had to be shut down for a few days because debris from the river was snagging on the bottom of the aerial cage.

Left. The North Bend Aerial Ferry is now on display at a roadside park/ open-air museum in Boston Bar.

Right. The aerial ferry sometimes carried a horse and cart.

Below. The Cog Harrington Bridge, which replaced the aerial ferry in 1986.

Some 9 km south of Lytton are the Cisco (or Siska) Bridges, one CPR and one CNR. There are two bridges here because they are at the point in the canyon, there being room for only one railway on each side of the canyon, that the Canadian Northern Pacific builders were forced to change sides of the river because CPR had already claimed the best route, crossing the river here in the process.

The first bridge, the CPR bridge, was built in 1884. It was prefabricated in Britain and shipped to Canada in pieces in 1883. It was then assembled by the San Francisco Bridge Company on contract to the CPR. It was at the time one of the longest cantilever spans in North America. This bridge was judged unsuitable for increasingly heavy freight trains in 1910 and was replaced that year by the current bridge. The first bridge was disassembled and moved to Vancouver Island, where it was used on the Esquimalt & Nanaimo Railway (E&N), to replace a wooden span across the Niagara Creek Canyon, where it can still be seen today (see page 298).

Above. The first Cisco Bridge, completed in June 1884. This photo, showing an empty ballast train, was taken in 1886. The CPR Cisco Bridge was the first railway bridge across the Fraser, and the second of any kind, after the Alexandra Bridge.

Above. This beautiful photo of the Ainslie Creek (Nine Mile Canyon) road and rail bridges together was taken by railfan Owen Laukkanen on 30 November 2016 from a viewpoint above a short tunnel that the long container train has just exited westbound. The rear locomotive seen here is remotely controlled from the leading locomotive. The arch of the Trans-Canada bridge towers above the railway bridge.

Right. The Cisco Bridges in 2017. The CPR bridge is the black bridge in the foreground, and the CNR bridge is the orange one in the distance.

Below. The CNR bridge in a 1930 photo, with the CPR track in the foreground, about to lead onto the that railway's bridge.

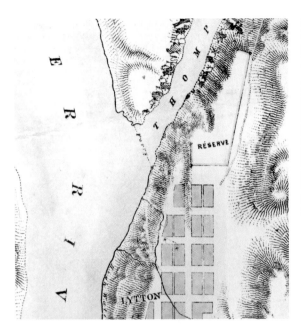

At Lytton, the confluence of two rivers, the Fraser and the Thompson, necessitates bridges. Here the road to Lillooet continues north with the Fraser, so there is a road bridge over the Thompson, and the CNR line crosses the Thompson simply to be on the other side of the river to the first-built CPR. *Above, top, left,* is an 1860 Royal Engineers map intended to show the new layout of Lytton, but it also notes a ferry crossing the Thompson. Lillooet was an important way station on the route to the goldfields, and a significant centre in its own right, and so the first wagon road included a bridge across the Thompson here (*above, top, right*). The later Canadian Northern bridge (*above, left*) had its railbed destroyed in the 30 June 2021 wildfire that wiped out the village of Lytton. This bridge crosses the river next to the modern road bridge (Chief David Spintlum Bridge, *above, right*), built in 2001. The piers of an earlier bridge can be seen below it.

Right. The reaction ferry at Lytton, and, *left,* the array of cables that allow it to stay in the right position when crossing (see *opposite page, top*).

Above. The Lytton reaction ferry in mid-river. A reaction ferry is a cable ferry that uses the reaction of an angled vessel to propel itself across the river but is prevented from simply going downstream by overhead cables. The principle is the same as that used by a sailboat to tack into the wind. Note that in this photo, which is taken more or less at right angles to the river, the ferry is viewed at an angle. The cables keep the vessel at the appropriate angle, though it is possible to do this using a rudder. Note also the attached small power boat. This is a safety measure, so that passengers might be rescued should the ferry break loose from its cables and float downstream. This happened once before, in 1979; passengers were rescued by boats downstream at Boston Bar. Operated under contract to the BC Ministry of Transportation, the ferry is toll-free, runs on demand, and carries a maximum of two cars or one small bus (the local school bus). The Fraser River flows quite fast here, ideal for a reaction ferry.

North of Lytton is Lillooet, an important Indigenous settlement. It was one of the main centres for the Fraser Canyon gold rush of 1858–59—the one that led James Douglas, afraid of being overwhelmed by American miners, to create the Colony of British Columbia.

Initially, the river was crossed using a rudimentary reaction ferry, which operated from 1860 and 1888, replaced in 1889 by a wooden-truss bridge. This was in turn replaced in 1913 by a steel suspension bridge with a single-lane wooden deck with a wooden pony truss on either side of the deck for stiffening. This bridge was restored as a tourist attraction in 2003 and now carries only pedestrians. In 1981 the suspension bridge—now known as the Lillooet Old Bridge—was superseded by a new bridge 3 km downstream, the usual modern featureless concrete-and-steel structure.

It does have a more exciting name, however. This new bridge was the subject of a naming competition. Local resident Renee Chipman won with the name "Bridge of the 23 Camels." This name celebrates the importation of 23 two-humped Bactrian camels from Asia about 1858; since the terrain and climate were similar to the camels' natural habitat, it was thought they might be ideal for use as pack animals in these gold rush days. The experiment was not successful, and the camels were released into the wild, where they seemed to thrive for a while; the last one died in 1896. But no other bridge in BC celebrates camels!

Right. The Lillooet reaction ferry.

Above. The town of Lillooet, sitting on a bench above the Fraser River in this view looking south. The 1913 suspension bridge is in the foreground.

The Old Bridge (built in 1913), Lillooet.
Above. The view from the east side with the railway bridge in the background.
Left; right, top; below; and *below, bottom.* Details of the suspension system.
Right, bottom. The bridge deck showing the wooden pony truss at its sides.

Above. The railway bridge at Polley, just upstream from the Lillooet Old Bridge.

Just upstream from the Old Bridge is the railway bridge at Polley (which is a railway point name). This was built by the Pacific Great Eastern Railway (PGE) in 1931 to replace a deteriorating wooden one further downstream, near the mouth of the Seton River. A decision was made to build the new bridge some 5 km upstream, which would allow the line to be routed through Lillooet, and a 9-km re-routing line was laid for this purpose.

The old 814-m-long wooden railway bridge had been built in 1915 along with the line itself—the first train from Squamish to (near) Lillooet arrived on 20 February 1915. The 1915 bridge was disposed of in grandiose fashion in 1931—it was blown up.

Above. The railway bridge at Polley as seen through the pony-truss beams and the suspension cables of the 1913 Lillooet Old Bridge.

Left. The first PGE bridge across the Fraser near the mouth of the Seton River. Although over 800 m long, the entire structure was made of wood.

Below. Once the Polley bridge was complete in August 1931, the 1915 bridge was no longer required and was blown up. A sad end for a magnificent bridge. Note the brave soul on the bridge at far left.

Above. North of Pavilion there was a ferry at a place called Low Bar, about 35 km north of Lillooet. It was also a reaction ferry, as can be seen from the pontoons and aerial cables. This photo was taken in the 1890s.

Above. There was, until the early 1950s, an aerial ferry at Pavilion, about 10 km north of Lillooet. It was reputed to be not only the smallest ferry in BC maintained at public expense but the smallest ferry in the world, with a capacity of just two people. The source of power was the passengers' muscles! As can just be made out from this photo, the ferry was only just above the surface of the river, but the road down to the ferry was reported to be a "nightmare." This grainy image is from a January 1952 newspaper.

Below. This wooden-truss bridge, built in 1957, carries Highway 40, the Lillooet-Pioneer Road, across Bridge River some 7 km north of Lillooet. The road connects with Gold Bridge and Bralorne, former gold-mining towns, over 100 km away. Bridge River is a tributary of the Fraser, which it meets just downstream of this bridge. The photo was taken from Highway 99, high on the opposite bank.

North on the Fraser

Between Williams Lake and Lillooet, the Fraser passes through another rugged canyon, making roads, let alone bridges, difficult. Another reaction ferry, at Big Bar, 60 km north of Lillooet and some 72 km west of Clinton, services ranchers and Indigenous settlements along a dirt road. It carries a maximum of only two cars. When the water on the Fraser here is low, or icy, an aerial tramway is put into operation, though this is only for passengers.

About 45 km north of Big Bar is an unexpected suspension bridge, built principally for the use of local ranchers over a hundred years ago. This is the Churn Creek Bridge, usually referred to as the Gang Ranch Bridge, since it connects two parts of that ranch, which was created in the 1860s. At one time this ranch covered an astonishing 1.6 million ha, or 16,000 km².

Farther up the Fraser, carrying the highway to Bella Coola from Williams Lake (Highway 20) across the river is the Chilcotin Bridge, sometimes referred to as the Chimney Creek Bridge or Sheep Creek Bridge. The current bridge opened in 1961. Near this location there was a large Indigenous village at Chimney Creek (8 km north of the current bridge), where the current slackened, allowing log rafts to be used to cross the river.

At Chimney Creek an early ferry at first consisted of a large freight-carrying canoe, and later a small scow, both of which had to be rowed across the river. Because of the scow's small size, horses, unhitched from their wagons, were made to swim, being towed by the ferry!

This arrangement was becoming untenable by the turn of the 20th century, and the settlers in the area petitioned the provincial government for a bridge. Unusually for that time, the government agreed, and a site was chosen downstream, at the site of the present bridge. A wooden suspension bridge opened in 1904. For two years materials were shipped by rail to Ashcroft and then hauled north by horse teams pulling wagons in the summer and sleighs in the winter. The stone footings, made of granite blocks, were so well built that they can still be seen today. The suspension cables, in a bit of trickery that would not be tolerated today, were supplied by a company belonging to a new premier of BC, Edward Prior, which bid *after* he had viewed all the other bids. His company mysteriously just underbid all of them! It did cost Prior his job, however; censured, he resigned after only eight months in office.

The bridge, despite an innovative design—a low suspension cable and counterweight, intended to cut down on bridge deck movement—tended to sway a lot, to the extent that animals sometimes balked at crossing. Holding pens were built at either end of the bridge because only a small number of animals could be persuaded to cross the bridge at one time. Later, only one car would cross at a time.

This bridge lasted for nearly 60 years despite its shortcomings. It was replaced in 1961 with the present steel-arch

Above, top. The Big Bar reaction ferry in the 1920s.

Above, centre. The Big Bar reaction ferry today.

Above, bottom. The Churn Creek Bridge, built in 1908 and rebuilt in 2000. It connects two parts of the Gang Ranch, one of the largest ranches in Canada, and for this reason is often referred to as the Gang Ranch Bridge.

Above. Scenic British Columbia at its best: the Chilcotin Bridge and the Fraser River, viewed from halfway up Sheep Creek Hill on the western bank. Note the piers and abutment of the 1904 bridge.
Below. The bridge's intricate shadow cast on the Fraser.

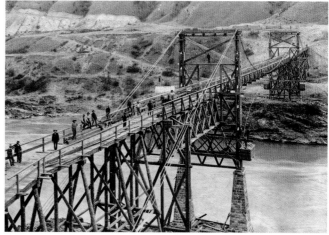

Above. The 1904 bridge under construction. It was then called the Chimney Creek Bridge despite being some distance south of the creek of that name. The trail up Sheep Creek Hill is in the background.

Right. The original granite block piers of the 1904 bridge are still standing in July 2021.

Abstract art from the Chilcotin Bridge. *Above*. The decayed remains of a plaque attached to the western end of the bridge shows an astonishing array of subtle colours and patterns. *Right*. Patterns of rust on the complex structure of the bridge's steel arch and its shadows in the background.

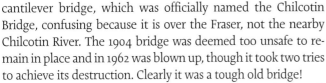

cantilever bridge, which was officially named the Chilcotin Bridge, confusing because it is over the Fraser, not the nearby Chilcotin River. The 1904 bridge was deemed too unsafe to remain in place and in 1962 was blown up, though it took two tries to achieve its destruction. Clearly it was a tough old bridge!

The Chilcotin River joins the Fraser 34 km south of the Chilcotin Bridge. Some 15 km up that river is Farwell Canyon, touted as British Columbia's Grand Canyon. While the Farwell Canyon Bridge is not that spectacular itself, the surrounding scenery certainly is. The gravel service road on both sides takes multiple hairpin bends to descend to the river before repeating the pattern uphill on the other side. At the bottom is the bridge, crossing the Chilcotin River. There have been three bridges here. The first was built in the early 1900s and was a simple wooden structure, impossibly low to the water for its location in a steep-sided gorge. Predictably, this bridge was soon swept away in a flood. The second bridge, a much higher wooden-trestle and steel-beam structure, lasted until 2006, when it caught fire and was destroyed. The third and present bridge is a prestressed-concrete beam atop strong steel pilings.

The next bridge north on the Fraser has a special story. It is the Rudy Johnson Bridge, some 20 km north of Williams Lake, once billed as Canada's biggest do-it-yourself project. Johnson had a ranch that stretched along the west bank of the Fraser, across the river from Williams Lake. When going to or from Williams Lake, he could use the Soda Creek ferry to the north, where there had been a crossing since the late 1800s, but this was an old and unreliable scow with a capacity of two cars. Indeed, Johnson's wife once fell off this ferry and nearly drowned. Or he could use the Chilcotin Bridge, 26 km south. Both then required that he drive an equivalent

Above. The first Farwell Canyon Bridge was a low wooden-truss bridge destined to not survive long across a river as turbulent as the Chilcotin.

Below. The modern bridge built after the second bridge was destroyed by fire in 2006. Functional, of course, but not very picturesque compared with the second bridge, *above, right*.

Above. Cariboo photographer Chris Harris took this photo of a logging truck crossing the second Farwell Canyon Bridge across the Chilcotin River in the stunning Farwell Canyon a few weeks before its destruction by fire in 2006.

distance once more on the west bank over poor roads. So Johnson resolved to build his own bridge, not from scratch, but by moving an existing bridge and reassembling it.

In 1968 Johnson found just the bridge he was looking for, in Alaska. At Soldotna, on the Kenai Peninsula near Anchorage, the highways department replaced a steel-arch truss bridge with a more modern flat concrete-and-steel structure and was prepared to sell the old one. Johnson purchased the bridge, dis-

Left. Rudy Johnson's bridge in its original location at Soldotna, Alaska.

Below. The completed Rudy Johnson Bridge. The provincial government purchased the bridge in 1978, 10 years after it was installed here.

assembled into 3,300 pieces, for $40,000, and had it shipped by barge and rail to a suitable site 22 km north of Williams Lake. There he used an innovative trick to place the bridge in position. He borrowed a system of cables called skylines from the logging industry and using a method quite similar to the king-post-and-cable method that was later used for the 2017 Vedder River Bridge (see page 182). He had to reassemble the bridge half at a time because there was not enough room in the gorge to assemble the whole bridge. The first half was slid out above the river and sat halfway across, held up by cables while the other half was assembled—a process that took 10 days. Then the whole bridge was pulled right across the river to sit on concrete abutments pre-built to fit.

Below, right. The bridge halfway across the river during its assembly.

Johnson recouped some of his investment by charging logging trucks to cross, though cars were free. It was the only privately owned toll bridge on the Fraser. Ten years later, in 1978, the provincial government purchased his bridge and removed all tolls.

A hundred kilometres north of Williams Lake is Quesnel, where there is a 260-m-long five-span wooden-truss bridge over the Fraser, which was completed in 1929 to replace a reaction ferry that had been operating since 1911. It became a pedestrian bridge in 1971 with the completion of the nearby modern-style Moffat road bridge that year and was restored in 2010. Amazingly, this bridge is the longest wooden-truss pedestrian bridge in the world.

Below. The Quesnel reaction ferry, which operated between 1911 and 1929.

Above. The Old Fraser Bridge at Quesnel, photographed in 2021, and *above, top,* a fisheye view.

Right. Another of Quesnel's bridges, this one a two-span steel-truss bridge carrying Highway 97 across the Quesnel River just before its confluence with the Fraser. The bridge was built in 1961.

The PGE/BCR/CNR railway bridge across the Quesnel River into Quesnel. This photo was taken on 2 July 2021, and the water flowing under the bridge in the middle foreground is not the Quesnel River at all, but a flooded road. The actual river can be seen beyond it. Nevertheless, with its wildflowers in the foreground it makes for a scenic image.

Above. The Quesnel Dam Bridge, a photo taken when the bridge had just been completed, on 5 July 1923. The dam, thrown up in 1897 across the Quesnel River to aid in placer gold mining, was blown up in 1920. The little town of Quesnel Dam, about 73 km southeast of Quesnel, became known as Likely (after a local prospector, John Likely), and this bridge was built to provide access to the settlement. Shallow water allowed multiple piers and the cheapest method of bridging, the king truss, the A-frame-like structures. This type of bridge was quite common at one time (albeit as a single span) but most have now disappeared.

The Fraser Valley north of Lillooet is also the route of the Pacific Great Eastern Railway (PGE), after 1972 called the British Columbia Railway, and after 2004 part of Canadian National. Coming from Squamish, it crossed the Fraser at Lillooet (see page 208) and back again at Prince George (page 220), but required many bridges on its way, some quite spectacular. A few are shown here.

The PGE acquired its charter in 1912 and slowly built northward towards its goal—Prince George—over the next decade. In 1922 the railway, which the government had taken over in 1918 after it got into financial difficulty, stopped construction just shy of a long and expensive bridge that would have been required to cross the Cottonwood River, a Fraser tributary just north of Quesnel. The track only went as far as Quesnel for the next 30 years, when the government decided it should be extended to Prince George, and even beyond, so as to "open up the north." It would reach as far north as Fort Nelson in 1971.

The immediate problem at the beginning of the 1950s was how to cross the Cottonwood Canyon. The solution was a completely different route. A PGE surveyor, Charlie Crysdale, enlisted the help of an Alberta trapper and mink rancher, W.O. Greening, who knew the area well, and found a much easier route over the Cottonwood and Ahbau Creek, its northern arm. The first train rolled over both new bridges on 1 November 1952 headed for Prince George.

Prince George had a railway much earlier than this, however, for it was on the route of the Grand Trunk Pacific

Above. The PGE's Fifty One Creek Bridge, near Clinton, photographed by railway photographer Dave Wilkie in August 1975. This high steel structure replaced an original wooden trestle.

Above. The railway bridge high above the Cottonwood River, between Quesnel and Prince George. This route over the Cottonwood was the third to reach the survey phase, and the cost of the first surveyed bridges was one of the major contributors to the decision to cancel continuing the line to Prince George in 1922. This bridge was built in 1952.

Left and *below.* Deep Creek Bridge, about 27 km north of Williams Lake. At 95 m, this bridge is not only the highest bridge on the entire route of the railway, and the highest railway bridge in British Columbia, but when it was built in 1921, it was the highest railway bridge in the British Empire! Considering the size of the British Empire at that time, that is quite a feat. It is also quite long, at 365 m. Deep Creek is properly Hawks Creek, but this official name has never seemed to stick.

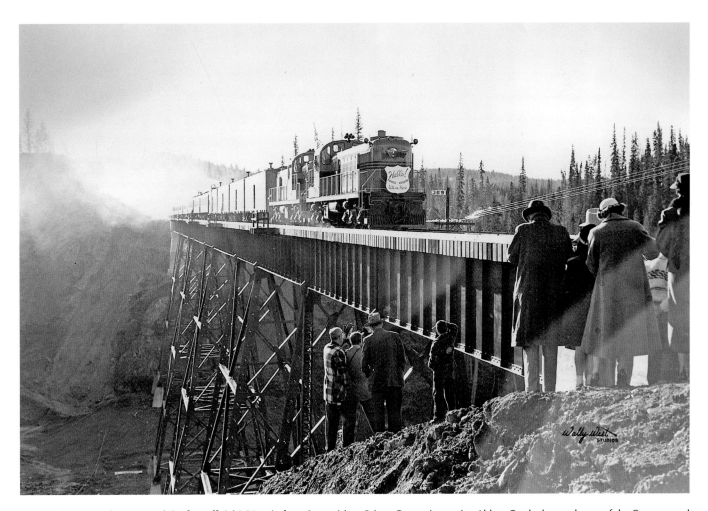

Above. It is 1 November 1952, and the first official PGE train from Squamish to Prince George is crossing Ahbau Creek, the north arm of the Cottonwood River, north of Quesnel. The train is en route to Prince George, where it would officially celebrate the line's opening some 30 years after the line between Quesnel and Prince George was cancelled. The train is headed by a pair of new diesel locomotives. The PGE was one of the pioneer railroads of North America with its use of diesel locomotives for widespread use on its line. The header board on the locomotive reads "Hello! Prince George, We're Here." Given the time it took to reach the city, it was no wonder the PGE was popularly derided as "Prince George Eventually," although that name was popular because of the leisurely manner the railway operated.

(GTPR), which arrived in Prince George—then called Fort George—from the east in 1914.

Construction of a bridge over the Fraser here began in 1913. The first bridge completed was a temporary bridge, and rails were laid over it on 27 January 1914. The following day the bridge was destroyed by an ice jam. It was quickly rebuilt, and work began on a permanent bridge beside it, which was completed in record time; the first train ran over the permanent bridge on 12 June that year. It was the fourth crossing of the Fraser River (after Alexandra, Cisco, and New Westminster). At 810 m long, it was, and remains, the longest railway bridge in British Columbia.

The GTPR had expected to share the costs of the bridge with the provincial government in return for allowing road traffic to use the bridge, replacing a ferry downstream that had been operational since 1911. However, after all the materials had been ordered, the province refused to pay because the price had gone up following a decision to change the bridge design. The railway had at first intended to only build a simple flat bridge on piles over half of the bridge west

Above. The Grand Trunk Pacific Railway steel-truss bridge across the Fraser at Prince George nears completion in the photo, dated 21 May 1914. The temporary bridge that was built first can be seen at left. It was this bridge that was destroyed by an ice jam the day after it was built. This is a view from the west side; the opening span was on the east side and does not appear to have been erected yet.

Above. The first train over the permanent bridge at Prince George, 12 June 1914. Note the steel brackets outside the truss, ready to carry a roadway. Vehicle use of the bridge continued until 1987.

Below. The bridge today. The roadways on either side of the bridge remain but are only used occasionally by railway maintenance crews. The photo was taken on 2 July 2021, during a period of unusually high water.

of a small island, first called Railway Island and later Goat Island. (This island subsequently migrated downstream and now sits about 100 m south of the bridge.) The ice conditions in the river had convinced the engineer in charge of construction that such a bridge would never last.

The GTPR went ahead and built a bridge with narrow roadways on either side, outside of the railway trusses. The province only settled and paid the railway in 1918 after GTPR refused to pay for sewers in Prince Rupert until the bridge was paid for. Cars and pedestrians used the bridge until 1987, when the modern concrete-and-steel Yellowhead (Highway 16) bridge was completed just south of the railway.

On 7 April 1914 the track across British Columbia was connected with track being laid eastward from Prince Rupert. A last spike ceremony took place near Fort Fraser, 137 km west of Prince George. The railway was completed at the very beginning of World War I, which diverted many of the settlers it had hoped to attract to its lands on either side of its tracks, and it rapidly got into financial difficulties. When GTPR defaulted on federal government loans in 1919, it was taken over and made a constituent part of Canadian National Railways in 1920.

Right. A view east across the bridge inside the trusses vividly illustrates its status as the longest railway bridge (810 m) in British Columbia.

Above. A view of the Prince George Railway Bridge from the western end shows the roadways outside the trusses used by the general public until 1987. The lack of current use can be seen from the vegetation growing through the steel-mesh road deck.

Above. The bridge was a direct-lift bridge, which avoided the use of tall towers that have cables to lift the span between them. Instead it used an ingenious system of counterweights directly attached to the truss span via parallelogram-shaped arms, seen well in the photo *right, top*. To open the bridge, the arm rotates to lift the span up. The counterweights are sitting on top of the adjacent trusses. Here one of two steamboats used by railway contractor Foley, Welch & Stewart, SS *Conveyor* or SS *Operator,* passes under the open bridge for the first time in late 1914. Use of the rivers by steamboats was in decline when the bridge was built, and the lift span, included to allow their passage, never saw much traffic. It seems that it was last raised in 1921. In 1954 the bridge was officially declared to be a fixed span rather than a lift span.

Above. The lift arms of the railway bridge are seen quite starkly in this photo taken after sunset from the east bank.

Other Prince George bridges:

Above, right. The first, wooden-truss bridge across the Nechako River, a photo taken on 16 December 1917. It illustrates the problems there can be with ice, here level with the bottom of the bridge. The image comes from the annual report of the BC Department of Public Works for 1918–19.

Right, centre. The Simon Fraser Bridge carries Highway 97 from the south across the Fraser into Prince George. It was built in 1963 and twinned in 2009. This is a view from under the two bridges, with the steel trusses of the 1963 bridge at right and the steel beams of the 2009 bridge at left.

Right, bottom. A few kilometres north of Prince George is the Canfor Northwood Pulp Mill, built in 1964–65, and close to it is this substantial privately owned four-span steel through-truss bridge across the Fraser, built at the same time. At left is the unpaved Beaver Forest Service Road, while at right is a disused railway line. This line connected the pulp mill to the CNR main line and was not used after that railway absorbed BC Rail in 2004, which gave it easier access via the west bank north from Prince George. The pulp mill has had its own railway since its inception and still has its own locomotive. There are about 60,000 km of forest service roads in British Columbia, reflecting the significance of the lumber industry to the economy.

The Northwest

Arguably the most famous historical bridge in British Columbia was that built across the Bulkley River at Hagwilget, an Indigenous settlement just north of New Hazelton. There have been four bridges here, with the first dating from 1856, before Euro-Canadian settlement in the area. It was built by the local Gitksan-Wet'suwet'en people with poles, planks and cedar ropes, using only axes and knives as tools. This first bridge had a load capacity of about 225 kg. Loaded pack animals were led across the bridge one at a time. It was basically a cantilever design.

This bridge was rebuilt about 1880 to take advantage of something that had fortuitously arrived on the scene as part of an unrelated project—the Collins Overland Telegraph. The idea of this project was to lay a telegraph cable to Europe across Bering Strait, where it would remain on land for the majority of its route. The line had reached New Westminster in 1865 (where it was famously first used to receive the news of US President Abraham Lincoln's assassination) and had continued north, reaching Fort Stager, near Kispiox, by the summer of 1866. At this point news was received of the successful completion of an undersea transatlantic telegraph cable. Since this was the fifth time a cable had been laid, and the previous four had broken quickly thereafter, work continued on the Collins line until the following year, when the realization that the transatlantic cable was permanent led to orders to cease work.

Above. The second Hagwilget Bridge, built with cable from the abandoned Collins Overland Telegraph about 1880.
Below, left. The first bridge, built of poles and ropes.
Below, centre. A view of the second bridge at crossing level. It may not have looked very elegant, but it worked!
Below, right. Curves and lines. The third bridge above the second bridge in the canyon soon after the third was built, about 1912.

The northernmost part of the line now went no-where and was abandoned. The Gitksan-Wet'suwet'en used this cable they found lying in the woods to strengthen and modify their bridge, giving it a different appearance in the process. This second bridge was a combination of suspension and cantilever in design. It is said that when the bridge was completed, it was tested by sending women loaded with packs across it while the men were below with long poles ready to prop up the walkway if necessary!

The bridge served the local people well and was modified over the years to improve its strength, but it was replaced by a suspension bridge at the top of the canyon of more conventional design in 1912. This one looked remarkably similar to the one built across the Fraser in 1861 by Joseph Trutch (see page 198) though it was, like its predecessors, a footbridge only. This bridge, in turn, was replaced in 1931 by a third bridge, built by the provincial government. This was a steel suspension single-lane bridge that carried a road (now Highway 62). This bridge was upgraded in 1990 to increase its load capacity but otherwise remains today. At 80 m above the water, it is one of the highest suspension bridges in North America. Over 450 tonnes of steel cable and nearly 10 km of thick wire rope were used to construct the bridge—quite a difference from the woven cedar ropes used for the first one!

Above. The Hagwilget Canyon Bridge.

Left. The Hagwilget Canyon Bridge and the Bulkley Valley. Just after passing under the bridge, the river makes a sharp turn on its way to the Skeena River, of which it is a tributary. The author's son views the gorge in this 1996 photo.

Below. The reaction ferry at Kitwanga, on the Skeena River 35 km west of Hazelton, in 1946. The ferry has now been replaced by a bridge. It carries the Dease Lake Highway (Highway 37) north from Highway 16. The photo comes from the 1946–47 Department of Public Works annual report.

Above. These bridges cross the Khyex River where it empties into the Skeena, 45 km east of Prince Rupert. The modern arch bridge at left, built in 1972, contrasts with the GTPR bridge built in 1911, the year the first 160 km of track east of Prince Rupert opened.

Above and *right*. Sometimes Google Street View cameras just happen to be in the right place at the right time. Here one has captured a CN locomotive between spans on the Lakelse Avenue railway bridge in Terrace. The photo, *right*, also shows in the background the road bridge for Highway 16, built in 1976. The railway bridge here was built in 1954 next to the existing road bridge as part of a branch line south from the CNR main line on the north bank of the Skeena across that river to the new town of Kitimat, created by Alcan to produce aluminum. The photo, *right*, shows the railway bridge under construction. *Left*, from a Department of Public Works annual report, is the road bridge, completed in 1924 and officially opened the following year; it is now known as the Old Skeena Bridge. *Below*, the road bridge under construction in 1924. Before the bridge there was a ferry. The photo *above, centre*, shows a new reaction ferry just before its launch in 1923.

Grand Trunk Pacific Railway bridges under construction.

Above, left, top. The high steel trestle at Porphyry Creek during construction in 1912. The creek is about 50 km north of Smithers and flows into the Bulkley River.

Above, right, top. Another high steel GTPR trestle, this one near Hazelton, also about 1912.

Above, right. The photo of an unidentified bridge on the GTPR route shows the way steel beams were placed, one at a time, to construct these bridges over shallow but wide valleys. The railway was almost obsessively concerned with maintaining a low grade, which it considered vital for economic operation. However, this strategy also contributed significantly to costs and was one of the reasons the company bankrupted itself a few years later.

Above, left, centre. The railway changed sides of the river at Skeena Crossing, about 23 km west of Hazelton. Here the significant steel structure is under construction in June 1912, two months after the GTPR lost its president, Charles Hays, who went down with the *Titanic*.

Left. The Skeena Crossing Bridge today, still in excellent shape.

Left. Some 12 km south of Smithers, the railway crosses the Telkwa River on this steel-truss bridge, another of the railway's substantial bridges. It was built in 1912.

Above. A GTPR train crosses the Telkwa railway bridge about 1914.

Below. The Francois Lake Ferry in 1918. Here it is attached to a raft capable of transporting livestock—here horses— but it also operated independently.

Above. The reaction ferry at Usk, near Terrace, across the Skeena River, in 1923, about the time the ferry began to be operated by the government. Before that, starting in 1913, a small skiff was used, which was extremely treacherous in winter. The modern ferry services about 25 people living at Usk, on the north side of the Skeena, and is supplanted by an aerial ferry for passengers only, which travels between two steel towers when the river is too icy or water is too low.

Above. One of the problems with wooden bridges is illustrated by this photo of the Nechako River Bridge at Vanderhoof, on fire, 23 July 1980.

Left. The newly built Nechako Bridge at Fort Fraser, shown in the BC Department of Public Works annual report for 1918–19.

Right. Some 20 km south of Burns Lake is Francois Lake, running west–east for 100 km. To reach communities south of it, and, in modern times, provide logging trucks access to Highway 16, a ferry was required. It crosses more or less in the middle of the lake, saving a 100 km drive on unpaved roads to go around it. A power ferry of sorts has operated here at least since 1914. In 1983 the *Omineca Princess* was put into operation. It carries 34 vehicles and 200 passengers. An increase in commercial traffic led to the construction of the current ferry, the *Francois Forester,* which can carry 52 vehicles and 145 passengers. Here the *Francois Forester* prepares to leave its Southbank terminal for the 15-minute run across the lake. The *Omineca Princess* is docked at right.

Below. This amazing Ministry of Transportation photo, taken in August 2018, shows the *Francois Forester* against a background filled with forest fires. The ferry proved to be a vital link for firefighters and evacuees at that time, switching to round-the-clock service.

The North

The two most important roads in the north of British Columbia are the Hart Highway, now Highway 97, from Prince George to Dawson Creek; and the Alaska Highway (or Alcan Highway), now Highway 97, from Dawson Creek to the Yukon boundary near Watson Lake. The Hart Highway was begun under BC Premier John Hart in 1945 and opened in 1952. It connected at Dawson Creek with the Alaska Highway, which had been built in 1942, during World War II, by the US Army Corps of Engineers to provide a land route to Alaska after the Japanese had attacked the Aleutian Islands. At that time the Alaska Highway connected with roads in Alberta (and supplies to build it were brought in by Northern Alberta Railways). Hart's road provided a BC connection soon after the Alaska Highway opened to the public in 1948.

Both roads, of course, had many bridges, though in the case of the Alaska Highway many were initially quite roughly built, at first just good enough to carry tough army vehicles. Speed of construction was essential, and many were at first floating pontoon bridges, and others were just temporary log bridges (termed pioneer bridges), with upgraded replacement bridges being constructed soon after. The US Public Roads Administration (PRA) took over engineering responsibilities after the initial army trailblazing, replacing 133 bridges over the whole highway.

One exception was a suspension bridge built over the Peace River at Taylor, just south of Fort St. John, replacing a ferry. Here there were problems obtaining a footing for the north bank abutment, which supported the north span of the bridge and anchored its cables. Late on 15 October 1957 the bridge was closed after subsidence on the north bank became apparent. It was clear the bridge was going to collapse, which it did the following morning, watched by hundreds of spectators alerted to the coming spectacle. One enterprising photographer had set up a movie camera in anticipation of the collapse and recorded what is perhaps the only live footage of a major bridge "naturally" collapsing (rather than having been blown up) anywhere in Canada.

Traffic was diverted a week later to a ferry, but three weeks after that, the river froze, and a railway bridge 5 km upstream, which had just been completed to extend the Pacific Great Eastern (PGE) railway northward (see photo, page 232) was used for road traffic temporarily. The railway bridge was equipped with railings and one-way traffic strictly controlled. To reach the railway bridge, another temporary bridge was required, over the Pine River, which empties into the Peace here. This was initially a crude wooden trestle that was later replaced with a Bailey bridge. This arrangement persisted for nearly three years until the modern road bridge at Taylor opened in 1960.

A similar suspension bridge to the one at Taylor was built by the US Army over the Liard River, on the Alaska Highway 500 km to the north; it still stands. This bridge is noteworthy in

Above, top. The Peace River Suspension Bridge, officially opened on 30 August 1943 as part of the Alaska Highway. Previous crossings of the river here had only been by boat, an ice bridge in the winter or, from the early 1920s, a cable ferry. The bridge collapsed on 16 October 1957 (*above*).

Below. The Liard River Suspension Bridge, built by the PRA in 1944 using steel salvaged from the Tacoma Narrows Bridge.

that it was built from steel salvaged from the Tacoma Narrows Bridge, the famous "Galloping Gertie" bridge that destroyed itself by oscillating and twisting in a windstorm on 7 November 1940, only four months after it opened.

Above, top left. At an undisclosed location—perhaps for security reasons—is one of the many floating pontoon bridges built by the US Army to establish a usable road link to Alaska in a hurry in 1942.

Above, top. Here a second-generation bridge is photographed next to a pontoon bridge it would replace. This image was produced as a postcard for US troops, presumably so they could show the folks at home what they were doing up north. This one was used by an army truck driver to show the kind of truck he was driving—a "ten-ton diesel."

Above. Bridges over the Kiskatinaw River, a tributary of the Peace River, 20 km south of Taylor in 1943. The pioneer bridge, built by the US Army, is the low wooden trestle. The higher bridge under construction is a three-span wooden-truss structure, which, when completed, was the first wooden curved bridge in Canada. Built by the PRA, it had to be curved to accommodate a steep change in grade on the west end and the need to land at a notch in the cliff on the east end. The piers had to be enclosed for 10 days to keep the temperature high enough to prevent the concrete from freezing. The Alaska Highway here was rerouted in 1978, and a new bridge built, bypassing about 10 km of highway and this bridge. It is now called the Historic Kiskatinaw Bridge and retained as a tourist attraction.

Left, centre, and *left, bottom.* The Sikanni Chief River Bridge, about 150 km north of Fort St. John on the Alaska Highway. *Left, centre,* is the pioneer bridge, built in 1942, replacing a floating pontoon bridge. It was noteworthy at the time for being built by a Black regiment of the US Army (regiments were segregated at the time) in only three days, an almost unbelievable feat. *Left, bottom,* is a higher replacement bridge built by the PRA the following year. It was the first permanent bridge to be built on the Alaska Highway. The older bridge can be seen below. This was also a postcard, now in colour.

Above. The bridge and curved trestle across the Peace River near Taylor are shown on 3 October 1958 as one of the three inaugural trains on the Pacific Great Eastern Railway extension to Fort St. John crosses northbound. The structure has been fitted with guardrails because it was being used as a temporary road bridge following the collapse of the suspension bridge. The bridge carried both trains and road traffic from October 1957 until January 1960, when the new road bridge was opened. Because the first road bridge was some distance away from the rail bridge, another temporary bridge had to be built across the Pine River, which flows into the Peace between the two bridges. The complete railway bridge and trestle were almost a kilometre long.

Below, left. On 20 October 1979 the PGE trestle burned down, leading to a temporary bridge being built over the Pine River to allow trucks to bridge the gap for the railway; it linked sidings at Teko to the Alaska Highway. The temporary bridge was later upgraded to a semi-permanent structure, shown here, with 110 m of Acrow deck. Note the steel ice breakers in front of the bridge piers. The burned trestle was replaced by a fill, reducing the length of the bridge structure to 866 m.

Below, right. Some other Alaska Highway bridges are quite substantial. This is the bridge over the Muskwa River, a tributary of the Fort Nelson River, built by the PRA in 1944. It crosses the river about 2 km south of Fort Nelson.

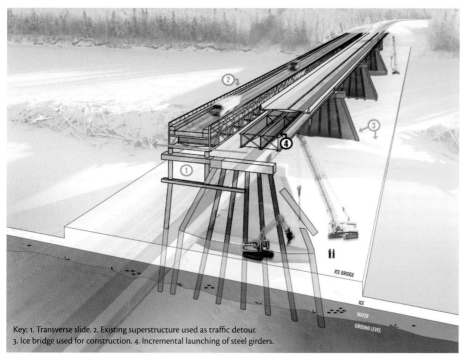

Key: 1. Transverse slide. 2. Existing superstructure used as traffic detour. 3. Ice bridge used for construction. 4. Incremental launching of steel girders.

The Liard Highway runs from a junction with the Alaska Highway (Highway 97) 28 km northwest of Fort Nelson to the BC–NWT border, where it continues north as NWT Hwy 7. It was constructed between 1975 and 1982 and opened to traffic in 1984 with the completion of the first Fort Nelson River Bridge. The road was designated BC Highway 77 in 1986 and was paved to the NWT border by 2018.

The first bridge only had funding for the foundations and piers, so a temporary Acrow bridge (steel truss with wooden deck) was installed. To build a new, two-lane bridge deck, the contractor, McElhanney, devised an innovative solution to allow traffic flow to continue during the building period. This involved constructing temporary bridge piers next to the bridge and then sliding the Acrow deck across to reveal the foundations and piers completed in 1984, on which the new deck was to sit. The new bridge was completed in 2017.

Left. A McElhanney graphic showing how the new bridge deck was built.

Above. The 2017 Fort Nelson River Bridge deck on the 1984 piers.

Below. The temporary Acrow bridge deck on the 1984 piers, as completed that year.

Above. A hovercraft, marketed as a Hoverlift Ferry, built by an Alberta company, Hoverlift Systems, was used for a while at the Fort Nelson River crossing of the Liard Highway in 1979. It continued until an ice bridge could be used from mid-December. Operated again in 1980, it supported, apart from regular users, continued construction of the Liard Highway north of the river. Here, in this BC Ministry of Transportation photo, the ferry is being readied for a test on Mesachie Lake, near Lake Cowichan, in late 1978. The vessel broke into sections for transport by road.

Above. The steel-truss bridge across the Parsnip River on Highway 97, built in 1953. It was replaced in late 2019 by a modern flat-type bridge to remove the last low overhead along this road. A supply boat is in the foreground. This is the river ascended by Alexander Mackenzie in 1793 during his trek to reach the Pacific Coast from Canada.

Above. The Bell-Irving River Bridge, named after a Canadian war hero of World War I, on Highway 37, the Stewart-Cassiar Highway, 250 km north of its junction with Highway 16. This is the second crossing of that river going north. The steel through-truss bridge was built in 1967.

Above. A pipeline bridge across the Peace River at Taylor, just south of Fort St. John, can be seen from the 1960 Alaska Highway bridge, in the foreground.

Above. Hudson's Hope Suspension Bridge, about 6 km from the village of Hudson's Hope on what is now Highway 29 at a narrowing of the Peace River. It was completed in 1964, replacing a ferry. It was part of the development of the region in conjunction with the building of the nearby W.A.C. Bennett Dam, completed in 1968. It was one of the first suspension bridges to be built using prestressed precast concrete, both for the towers and the bridge deck.

Left. The Tumbler Ridge branch line of the British Columbia Railway (BCR) opened in 1983 to connect coal mines to the port at Prince Rupert. The line had steep grades, eleven bridges, and five tunnels, two of which were very long, required because it crossed mountains of the Continental Divide. Unusually, the line was electrified from Tumbler Ridge to the BCR main line, because it was thought that the 9-km-long Table Tunnel and the 6-km-long Wolverine Tunnel would make fumes from normal diesel locomotives toxic to train crews. BCR purchased six electric locomotives to run on this line. After several closings and openings of the coal mines, and it being shown that diesel fumes in the tunnels could be managed, the line now uses normal diesel locomotives. BCR was taken over by Canadian National Railways in 2004. Here a coal train headed by two electric locomotives exits the Wolverine Tunnel on 18 September 1987, immediately crossing one of the eleven bridges. The photo was taken by railfan Marty Bernard.

Opening the Tumbler Ridge coal mines also required six road bridges to be built in 1983–84 to allow a road called the Northeast Development Road to connect them with Chetwynd, 80 km to the north.

Left. Sometimes road bridges that look simple from the road have quite complex structures underneath, especially where the stream to be bridged has a deep valley or gorge. This is the case at the West Twin Creek Bridge, on Highway 16 125 km east of Prince George. The bridge was completed in 1969 and has a heating system in the bridge deck, necessary because of the grade and the curve. The road descends steeply to this bridge. Highway 16 from Prince George to the Yellowhead Pass at the BC–Alberta boundary was constructed in 1968–69, and this bridge was built in 1968.

Below. Blackman Road Bridge, a classic wooden-truss bridge over the Fraser River just off Highway 16 1 km west of Tête Jaune Cache. With Mica Mountain in the background it makes a truly scenic photograph. It was built in 1953 and seems not heavily used, so it perhaps stands a reasonable chance of surviving for some time.

Above. The Moose River Bridge built in 1971 on Highway 16 between Tête Jaune Cache and Jasper, with the piers of the original Canadian Northern Pacific Railway bridge seen at left (see *overleaf*). The modern CNR bridge, now two bridges to accommodate double track, can be seen in the distance.

In 1913–15, the Canadian Northern Railway (in BC called the Canadian Northern Pacific Railway, CNoPR), in the process of building the third transcontinental line to Vancouver, laid track through the Yellowhead Pass to Tête Jaune Cache before heading south to Kamloops. This part of the line paralleled the Grand Trunk Pacific Railway (GTPR), on its way to Prince Rupert via Prince George—track that had been laid in 1911–12. Whereas the GTPR had very high standards for its line construction (in particular the maintenance of as low grades as possible), the CNoPR, late to the game and nearly running out of money, wanted to keep construction costs as low as it could possibly get away with. Thus, when both railways became bankrupt and were nationalized, becoming Canadian National Railways, rationalization allowed for only one path through the Rocky Mountains, and the superior GTPR one was chosen. That of CNoPR was used in part by various attempts at road building, including the modern road. In three places the old CNoPR bridge piers can still be seen: in one case, across the Upper Fraser, shown *above*, adjacent to the road bridge, and in another (*previous page*), over the Moose River, a tributary of the Fraser, just 100 m or so away from the road bridge. The first automobile trip through Yellowhead Pass occurred in 1922, but the "road" and bridges used were abandoned railbeds and even live line. The modern road, Highway 16, completed here in 1968, was officially opened by Premier W.A.C. Bennett in 1970 as the Yellowhead Inter-provincial Highway and was fully hard-topped by 1973. The road bridge here was built in 1971.

Left. The reaction ferry at McLure, and *left, bottom*, the reaction ferry at Little Fort. Both cross the North Thompson River near Highway 5 between Kamloops and Tête Jaune Cache. Little Fort also has an aerial tramway for low-water or icy periods. Note, in both photos, the rescue boat attached.

Below. Abandoned railway bridge piers over the Moose River west of the Yellowhead Pass. A Canadian National train crosses the modern bridge in the background.

North Thompson Valley bridges:

Left, top. The wide steel-truss bridge over the Barriere River, a North Thompson tributary, built in 1957.

Right. The Gosnell Bridge, built in 1971, over the North Thompson.

Left, centre. The modern highway bridge, built in 1972, over the Fraser at the intersection of Highways 5 and 16 at Tête Jaune Cache. Minor repairs are underway.

Right. This amazing trestle bridge carried the Canadian National Railway line over Lyon Creek, beside the North Thompson River some 11 km north of Avola. It was later filled in.

Below. This beautiful view is of the CNR bridge over the North Thompson at Irvine, about 12 km north of Vavenby. Note the steep valley sides beyond the bridge.

Kamloops Colours and More

Kamloops sits at the confluence of the North and South Thompson Rivers and has a number of interesting bridges. Two are railway bridges, both Canadian National (CNR), one over each river. Canadian Pacific's track is confined to the south bank of the Thompson and South Thompson and so requires no bridges here. Four are road bridges, including one that carries Highway 5 from Tête Jaune Cache over the South Thompson. Historically, four Kamloops bridges have been named after a colour—white, black, blue and red.

The oldest surviving original bridge is the railway bridge over the North Thompson, built by the Canadian Northern Pacific Railway in 1914—Canada's first lifting bridge. The oldest road bridge is the Red Bridge, over the South Thompson, built in 1887, just after the CPR arrived. Before the first bridge a ferry system of sorts was operated by local Indigenous peoples consisting of a rowboat pulling a barge.

Above. In a somewhat more idyllic setting than it is today, this old postcard shows the 1914 Canadian Northern Pacific Railway (now CNR) bridge over the North Thompson at Kamloops. It is a lift span, with the towers at centre raising the middle span vertically.

Above. The 488-m-long Overlanders Bridge over the Thompson River, opened in 1961, with the piers of the previous 1925 bridge behind it. Behind that (not visible here) are the remains of the first bridge (*right, centre*), opened in 1901 and later dubbed the White Bridge after it was painted that colour. It led to the development of a large irrigation project on the north shore known as BC Fruitlands after the company that planned it. The cut piles of this bridge (shown *below*) are still visible at low water, 600 m downstream of the modern bridge. The second bridge (*above*), a mainly steel structure, replaced it in 1925; it became known as the Black Bridge. It was replaced in 1961 but stood for a decade; when it was finally demolished in 1973, two of

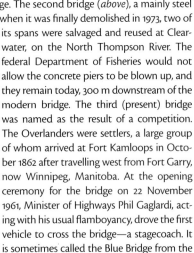

its spans were salvaged and reused at Clearwater, on the North Thompson River. The federal Department of Fisheries would not allow the concrete piers to be blown up, and they remain today, 300 m downstream of the modern bridge. The third (present) bridge was named as the result of a competition. The Overlanders were settlers, a large group of whom arrived at Fort Kamloops in October 1862 after travelling west from Fort Garry, now Winnipeg, Manitoba. At the opening ceremony for the bridge on 22 November 1961, Minister of Highways Phil Gaglardi, acting with his usual flamboyancy, drove the first vehicle to cross the bridge—a stagecoach. It is sometimes called the Blue Bridge from the colour of its steel understructure.

Left. Three bridges of the Thompson River at Kamloops are shown in this still-icy March 2022 photo by geographer Ken Favrholdt. The cut wooden piles of the 1901 bridge are in the foreground; behind it are the concrete piers of the 1925 bridge, and beyond that, the 1961 Overlanders Bridge.

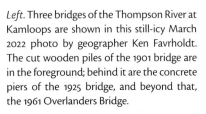

Above. The CNR bridge across the South Thompson River at Kamloops was built in 1926 to allow CN trains access to the CPR station. Today it is used by Rocky Mountaineer trains to load and unload their passengers, who typically spend a night in Kamloops hotels as part of their tour from Vancouver to Jasper. The bridge has a central swing span, which is rarely opened. This photo shows the dilemma sometimes faced by photographers, and one that is easily overcome by painters. The river was almost devoid of ripples when the above photo was taken, giving a wonderful reflection of the swing truss, but by the time the tourist steam train crossed (*below, left*), just minutes later, the wind had picked up just enough to destroy any reflection. While it would have been nice to photograph the train and the ripples together, it was not to be. If the camera had been on a tripod, a blended multiple exposure might have worked.

Above. Before the Kamloops Heritage Railway gained access to the CPR station and the CNR bridge, the Rocky Mountaineer arrived to unload its passengers. Despite appearances, here it is reversing, back across the bridge to wait overnight at CNR facilities on the north bank.

Above. Ex-CNR steam locomotive *2141*, built in 1912 for the CNoPR, heads a Kamloops Heritage Railway train north across the 1926 bridge in the evening light of a late-August day in 2017.

Above. Detail of the Red Bridge and its reflection in the river.

Below. The south approach trestle of the Red Bridge.

Left. The unusual pedestrian suspension bridge on 3rd Avenue over the CPR tracks was built in 1993. In 2005 CPR added a sign on the bridge to commemorate the role of Chinese workers in building the line in BC. Trains sometimes stop here for extended periods, so this bridge allows people to cross even when that happens. This photo was taken in September 2020; the bridge was repainted the following year and is now dark grey, with the yellow cables remaining.

Above. The Red Bridge, officially named the Government Bridge, across the South Thompson River at Kamloops. Bridges here got their name from the red colour of the Douglas fir with which they were built. This photo, complete with a nice reflection, shows the complex wooden structure of the current bridge, which has been restored and strengthened several times to prolong its life. It was built in 1936 by 26 men in five months. When the Highway 5 bridge was built in 1969 a little further upstream, the government intended to tear the Red Bridge down, but with the mayor and public sentiment against it, the bridge was instead restored.

The first bridge here (*left, centre*) was constructed in 1887 as a direct consequence of the increase in population brought about by the arrival of the Canadian Pacific Railway. It was replaced in 1912 with a second, higher bridge (*left, bottom*) to accommodate steamers then plying between Kamloops and Shuswap Lake. One of its piers was destroyed in a fire in 1931, and the bridge was condemned. However, likely because of the lack of funds during the Great Depression, the existing bridge was patched up the following year and remained in use for another four years before it was replaced by the third and present bridge, which has lasted for over 86 years—an amazing lifespan for a large wooden bridge. Not surprisingly, there are very few wooden bridges of this size left in Canada.

Thompson-Nicola

For most of its journey from Kamloops Lake at Savona to its confluence with the Fraser at Lytton, the Thompson River flows in a canyon that has proved difficult for both railways and roads. In its efforts to find a route not pre-empted by the CPR, the CNoPR had to cross the river several times, and at Black Canyon this involved both a bridge and a tunnel immediately before it.

One bridge, at Walhachin, has an unusual raison d'être. It was built in 1911 over the Thompson River, allowing access to a utopian type settlement begun in 1908 and aimed at upper-class Englishmen. The assumption had been made that this would be an excellent area for growing fruit, since the climate was similar to the Okanagan, where it had proven successful. Actually the climate was colder in winter—cold enough to kill fruit trees. In addition, the Thompson, the only possible source of water for irrigation, is deeply entrenched here, making the distribution of water from it very difficult.

Nevertheless, in the halcyon years just before World War I, the project successfully attracted settlers to this little bit of old England on the banks of the Thompson. A hotel was built in 1910, where it was mandatory to wear formal evening dress. English-style gardens were laid out. Access via the CPR,

Above. There has been a bridge across the Thompson at Savona, where the river flows from Kamloops Lake, since 1884. This is the 1993-built bridge, with the piers of a 1929 bridge (*right*) beside it.

Right. A pipe-line suspension bridge next to the Savona Bridge.

which was on the south side of the river, was not considered enough, and the government, anxious to encourage settlement, built an unusually substantial bridge for the time to allow access to the Ashcroft-to-Savona wagon road. But this bridge soon became perhaps the most under-capacity crossing in the province, for the war sounded the death knell for Walhachin. Patriotic Englishmen all, the settlers responded en masse to the call from the Mother Country, and by 1916 no farmers of military age remained. Many who had left found good jobs in Britain after the war and did not return. By 1922 the main flume was no longer bringing water to Walhachin, the last settlers moved away, and the bold English experiment reverted to grazing land.

The Walhachin Bridge.
Left. A scenic view of the Walhachin Bridge and the Thompson River from the steep road down from Highway 1. The steel-truss girders make a strong and interesting shadow pattern on the wooden bridge deck (*above, right*), while above an osprey has used the superstructure to build a large but somewhat messy nest (*right, bottom*). There is a plaque above the roadway (with further hints of bird's nest) on this bridge showing that the provincial government built it in 1911 (*above, left*). The mainly dry climate coupled with minimal use has allowed this bridge to reach over 110 years in age.

Below is a graphic illustration from the cover of a 1910 brochure promoting the Walhachin settlement.

Above, top. The 1903 provincial government–built wooden-truss Spences Bridge.

Above. A new 230-m-long steel-truss Spences Bridge, built in 1930. This was the bridge seen being dismantled at *far right, top.*

Right, top. This is the CNR, originally CNoPR, track on the west side of the Thompson Canyon just south of Spences Bridge. Two tunnels are seen, plus a concrete rockfall protection structure between them. It illustrates the extreme difficulty the railway had on account of being the second line along this route, always having to use the side of the river rejected by the CPR, whose line can be seen in the foreground.

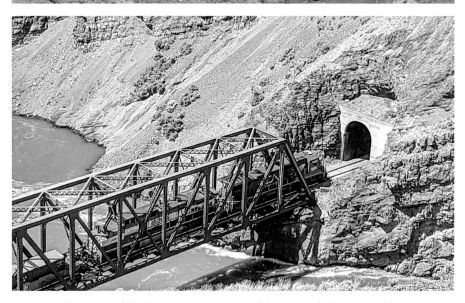

The CNoPR line also ran into difficulties at Black Canyon, where the canyon of the Thompson River narrows (*above, centre*). The CPR could get away with a 180-m-long tunnel on the east side of the river (the track with no train on it in this photo), but the CNoPR had to not only build a longer tunnel (450 m) but also cross the river at the same time. A CNR train is passing through the tunnel and over the bridge westbound in this September 2015 photo by railfan Mike Danneman. *Above, right*, a CNR train is on the bridge about to enter the tunnel in 2017 in this photo by Doug Smith. *Above, left*, the view is through the then wooden-decked bridge into the tunnel sometime in the 1930s.

Right. The 1930 Spences Bridge being dismantled in March 2015. Here the final span is removed. This was an under-deck truss, and the different heights of the piers shows where the bridge transitioned from the deck being on top of a truss to where it was directly on the piers, the higher one nearest the far bank. The bridge was closed at the end of 2013 following engineer's reports that it had become unsafe. It had been effectively replaced by a new bridge built downstream in 1962 to carry the Trans-Canada Highway over the Thompson.

Below. The Canadian Pacific Railway built a branch line from its main line at Spences Bridge to connect with coal mines at Merritt in 1907, leasing for 999 years an existing charter granted for this line to the Nicola, Kamloops & Similkameen Coal & Railway Company in 1903. The initial impetus for the line came from a 1905 strike at Vancouver Island coal mines in Nanaimo, which had endangered the railway's vital supply of coal for its steam locomotives. By 1911 the line had been connected with the Kettle Valley Railway (KVR) line from Midway to provide an alternative route to the coast should this be required. The CPR had by this time gained effective control of the KVR. This bridge, across the Nicola River, was abandoned in 1964 when the line closed—so much for the 999-year lease—but still forms a crossing for a trail and creates a scenic view for photographers. This is a 2013 photograph; the bridge was dislodged from its abutments in the flood of November 2021.

Right. Another bridge on the 1907 CPR Nicola line, now incorporated into a trail. This one is on the western side of Merritt.

South Thompson

The south branch of the Thompson River flows from the Little Shuswap Lake to Kamloops but is connected also to the much larger Shuswap Lake. Some 35 km east of Kamloops is Pritchard, where there is an unusual creosoted-wood trestle bridge that looks older than it is; it was built in 1985. The bridge it replaced was a similar, though less well protected, structure, having been built in 1920 with untreated wood.

This earlier bridge was the subject of a dispute in 1933, when one Willie Louie, a Chase merchant, invoked federal river navigation law to force the provincial government to install a lift span in the bridge so he could pass through with a riverboat that he had purchased and restored. His plan was to transport cordwood and potatoes more cheaply than by rail.

The provincial government had built the bridge at Pritchard without a lift span because it was thought at the time—1920—that the steamboat era had passed, so it would not be necessary.

What makes this story important is that Louie was a Canadian of Chinese extraction, and this happened in an era when Chinese Canadians had less rights than those of European origins.

When the bridge was replaced with the present one in 1985, it had a clearance of over 18 m for navigation—the government was taking no chances this time!

To the north lies Adams Lake, the most northerly of the Shuswap lakes system. Here there is a cable ferry, which, unlike most remaining ferries in the province, does not have a long history but was born of necessity. In 1995 the Adams Lake Indian Band was in a dispute with the government, claiming ownership of the only access bridge and road to the east side of the lake. They blockaded the road, cutting off access for about 50 families on that side of the lake. Then an arsonist torched the

Above. The 400-m-long, concrete-decked, wooden trestle bridge at Pritchard, built in 1985.

only bridge across the Adams River at the south end of the lake. The provincial government hastily arranged for a ferry, a tug-and-barge affair that initially was costing some $11,000 a week. In January and February 1996 the cost increased by $800 a night because of the need to maintain an ice-free channel across the lake.

The issue resolved itself when a permanent cable ferry began operation on 21 December 1996. The ferry's route is 850 m, compared with 90 m over the burned bridge it replaced.

Above. The current Adams Lake Cable Ferry, which replaced the 1996 ferry in 2017, departs the west side of the lake.

Right. The Squilax-Anglemont Bridge, built in 1990, carries the road to Adams Lake from the Trans-Canada Highway across the South Thompson. Note the piers of an earlier bridge. There have been three bridges here.

Left. There has been a bridge at Sicamous, over Sicamous Narrows, the connection between Mara Lake and Shuswap Lake, since the Canadian Pacific Railway built one for its transcontinental line in 1885. The first bridge was a wooden drawbridge, seen here with the rear of a freight train with an official car attached to the end.

Left, centre. The railway bridge at Sicamous Narrows opened on 10 November 1982, a double-track operator-controlled replacement for an earlier single-track, manually opened swing expansion bridge built in 1898.

Below and *below, bottom.* The R.W. Bruhn Bridge at Sicamous Narrows, named after a local businessman who was briefly Minister of Public Works in 1941. The bridge was built in 1962 and carries the Trans-Canada Highway across the Narrows. As can be seen, the bridge is not in very good shape and is only two lanes wide. In 2022 work will begin on a four-lane replacement bridge here.

Left. On the east side of Sicamous is the Eagle River, at the western outlet into the lake of the valley in which the CPR Last Spike was driven on 7 November 1885, at a place they named Craigellachie. This is the CPR bridge over the river, with an array of replacement rails in the foreground.

The Okanagan

The valley in which Okanagan Lake sits is 200 km long, running from Sicamous in the north to Osoyoos in the south. It contains some of the best fruit-growing and wine-producing areas in Canada.

In the north, 11 km east of Enderby, is the Baxter Bridge over the Shuswap River on Trinity Valley Road; it is sometimes referred to as the Trinity Bridge. Situated against a very scenic backdrop, it is a contender for the prettiest bridge in British Columbia. However, it is a single-lane, wooden-truss bridge and is, in the ominous words of the Ministry of Transportation, "nearing the end of its service life," and a replacement is being planned, with the existing bridge being entirely removed once the new one is in place. It is the same story as has been repeated throughout the province; no one seems to think that some of these old bridges might be worth saving as historical items for recreational use.

When the CPR arrived at Sicamous in 1885, it was not long before a branch line was planned southward to the Okanagan Valley, with its tremendous potential for fruit growing: livelihood for settlers and freight for the CPR. A group of local entrepreneurs chartered the Shuswap & Okanagan Railway. It was completed to Okanagan Lake at a place

Left, above, and *right.* The Baxter Bridge across the Shuswap River east of Enderby, built in 1950, is, sadly, slated for replacement and removal. *Left* is a view through the wooden truss; note the wooden bridge deck also. *Above* is a view of the idyllic scenery along the river framed by the timbers of the bridge.
Right. An infrared image of the bridge, with billowing white clouds over it. This kind of scene, with foliage that the camera renders as white, plus the clouds, which stand out against a blue sky, is ideal for black-and-white infrared photos.
Below. CPR steamboat SS *Sicamous* at Penticton wharf in 1914.

Below. This unassuming modern bridge crosses the Shuswap River at Enderby, but no fewer than four bridges preceded it. The first bridge here was built in 1893, a second in 1905, a third in 1920, a fourth in 1943, and a fifth, this one, in 1982. The latter bridge was authorized after a piece of wooden deck on the 1943 bridge popped up under a full school bus, disabling it.

Above. SS Sicamous, *a Canadian Pacific Railway steamboat now preserved as a museum on the shores of Okanagan Lake at Penticton.*

called Okanagan Landing (now in Vernon) and immediately leased to the CPR. The CPR decided to build steamers to operate on the 135-km-long lake as a more cost-efficient way of servicing the region; it was the beginning of an integrated transport network that opened the area up for fruit farming.

At the middle of the lake, at its narrowest point, sat an early mission that became Kelowna, the largest city in the region. Because of its location, going round the lake to reach the other side was a long journey, and so a ferry was essential. From 1885 there was a scow ferry propelled by rowing. In 1905 the provincial government awarded a contract for a steam ferry operating from Kelowna to Westbank, and the steamboat *Skookum*, with a barge, began service in 1906. Other steamboats followed. Traffic increased, and with the beginning of the automobile era a privately owned service was begun in 1921, with a car ferry not

very imaginatively named *Kelowna-Westbank*, a 28-m-long vessel capable of carrying 15 cars. The government took over the service in 1927. In 1939 a ferry with increased capacity took over, the MV *Pendozi*, able to carry 30 cars and 150 passengers. An additional ferry, the MV *Lequime*, was added in 1947, and a third, the MV *Lloyd-Jones*, three years later. Traffic continued to increase until, in 1958, the first bridge was opened. The retired ferries had an interesting afterlife. *Pendozi* became a clubhouse for the West Kelowna Yacht Club, the *Lequime* became a tour boat, and the *Lloyd-Jones* was cut into pieces and shipped to the coast on flatbed trucks where she was reincarnated as a BC Ferry, the *Bowen Queen* (not the newer vessel of that name today), in 1965 renamed the *Vesuvius Queen*, and in 1998 sold to a ferry company in the Dominican Republic. She was a ferry that travelled a lot!

Kelowna was the riding of Premier W.A.C. Bennett, and he was determined to provide his hometown with the bridge its citizens wanted. At first, he advanced the idea of a

suspension bridge, but the span was long enough to make the project infeasible, for the lake is very deep and the soil conditions difficult for the foundations that other bridge types would require. Instead, a floating bridge—one built on anchored pontoons—was built. It was not a completely new concept; one (the Lacey V. Murrow Memorial Bridge) had been built across Lake Washington in Seattle in 1940. The Princess Margaret Bridge, as it was officially called (the premier rejecting calls to name it after himself), was opened by its namesake on 19 July 1958. The bridge was subsequently generally known as the Okanagan Lake Bridge or sometimes the Kelowna Floating Bridge. It had a lift span near the Westbank side and had tolls until 1963.

But it had only two lanes. In 1984 the bridge deck was reconfigured to insert a third lane, used as a counterflow. But by the turn of the 21st century it had become unable to support the level of traffic, and a new bridge was planned. Despite a 10,000-signature petition in favour of a tunnel, the provincial government in 1999 decided to build a totally new floating bridge just a few metres north of the existing bridge.

Construction began in 2005. The bridge was opened by Premier Gordon Campbell and ex-premier William R. Bennett on 25 May 2008. This time Campbell named the bridge after W.A.C.'s son, who had lobbied for its construction. The bridge has a floating section and a fixed section, with two transition sections to connect them. The bridge is secured to the bottom of the lake with 12 anchors on either side.

Above. The 2008 bridge under construction in 2007.

Below. The full length of the 2008 bridge, viewed from Kelowna.

Above, top. The *Fintry Queen*, once the MV *Lequime*, and Okanagan Lake ferry. The photo was taken in 2010.

Above, centre top. A postcard view of the 1958 bridge from the Westbank side. Note the lifting section, and the toll booths in the foreground. Tolls were removed on 1 April 1963.

Above, centre bottom. The lift span of the 1958 bridge.

Above, bottom. The 2008 bridge is complete, and remnants of the 1958 bridge can be seen nearest the camera.

There were over a hundred trestles on the Kettle Valley Railway (KVR), but nowhere were they more concentrated than just south and east of Kelowna in Myra Canyon. They were built in 1914. The difficulty of finding a path for the KVR is well illustrated here in the railway's route around KLO Creek and its tributary Pooley Creek descending the east side of the Okanagan Valley on its way to the valley bottom at Penticton. Between Myra and Ruth Stations, within a distance of 10 km, the railway had 18 trestles and 2 tunnels, all on a round-the-canyon route of 9 km, compared with an as-the-crow-flies distance of about 2 km. Engineer Andrew McCulloch literally hung his trestles right around the steep canyon sides.

In 1995 the trestles, tunnels and the connecting grade were made into a trail, and many of the trestles have been rebuilt since a fire in 2003 destroyed them—all except, that is, the West Fork Canyon Creek Bridge (Myra Trestle No. 6) over Pooley Creek, which, because it was made of steel, only lost its wooden deck. This trestle is the longest and highest of the bridges in Myra Canyon, 220 m long and 55 m high. A wooden trestle was replaced in 1931–32 with steel and consists of 12 steel through-plate girder spans on steel towers.

Below. A westbound KVR train is posed for a photograph on Trestle No. 6, the West Fork Canyon (Pooley Creek) crossing, in 1916, soon after service commenced. This is the longest and highest trestle in Myra Canyon and was replaced with steel in 1931–32 (see photos *opposite page*). This was likely intended as some sort of promotional photo; railways do not often pose their trains for photos these days.

Trestles rebuilt after the fires of 2003 include No. 15 (*above*), 46 m long and 12 m high; trestle No. 11 (*below*), 132 m long and 24 m high; and trestle No. 13 (*below, bottom*), 87 m long and 15 m high. The Myra Canyon route also includes two tunnels. This one (*right*) is 114 m long and this entrance is at the highest point on the KVR, 1,274 m.

Above, top. Replacement of the largest wooden trestle in Myra Canyon took place in 1931–32. This is the trestle in West Fork Canyon, with the Canadian Bridge Company equipment working on the new bridge. Steel towers for the bridge have been built up within the old wooden trestle.

Above. The completed bridge. This was likely a promotional photo for the railway, as the train posed on the bridge has new steel cars, introduced the year before as part of a general upgrading of the railway. Because the bridge is made of steel, it survived the fires of 2003.

Right. The bridge today, part of the Myra Canyon Trail.

Left. Wooden falsework holds up the steel bridge truss for the Trout Creek Bridge, built in 1913. At 74 m, this was the highest bridge on the Kettle Valley Railway and illustrates the immense difficulties that had to be overcome to build the line; indeed, even as this bridge was under construction in May 1913, the first falsework was washed out and had to be rebuilt. The bridge was completed on 25 October 1913.

Below. The approach trestles for the Trout Creek Bridge have been completed in this photo, but the steel truss over the deepest part of the canyon has not yet been placed.

Left. The Trout Creek Bridge today forms a spectacular end to the line of the tourist-oriented Kettle Valley Steam Railway, which runs over a section of the former Kettle Valley line near Summerland. The bridge forms the railway's most easterly point. The wooden approach trestles were replaced with steel in 1927–28. It was dubbed the "Infinitesimal Bridge" as "incalculable, inestimable, great and fathomless." A bit overblown perhaps, but it was the highest structure on the KVR and the third-largest of its kind in North America when built.

Below. A train with fruit reefer cars heads north on a pile trestle across the Okanagan River at Okanagan Falls at the southern end of Skaha Lake. The trestle was built in 1931 as part of a southward extension of the KVR, which took until 1944 to reach Osoyoos—and then only lasted until 1979. Service to Okanagan Falls continued until 1984, when the rails were removed from this trestle. At *left* is the same trestle today, restored as part of the Kettle Valley Rail Trail.

Above. This rare sequence of photographs shows the process by which many trestles met their demise—by infilling. Trestles required a lot of maintenance; fills almost none. The location is on the Kettle Valley Railway approximately 3.5 km west from Penticton's lakefront station (at Mile 2.2 of the Princeton Subdivision, in railway language) in 1923. #1 was taken on 4 July; #2 on 18 July, and #3 on 9 September, with the work almost finished. #4 shows the fill being unloaded from special cars, creating much dust in the process. It couldn't have been pleasant work!

The first bridge in the southern Okanagan was built in 1861, a rudimentary one across the narrows at what became Osoyoos; it was replaced in five years later with a toll bridge. The picturesque Val Haynes Bridge, *below*, is a much later creation, built in 1956 across a canalized Okanagan River near Osoyoos. The bridge construction, however, was to an old design, using a modified A-truss called a king truss, one of the simplest for smaller bridges but now virtually all gone from the province. Indeed, this was the only one I ever found.

Similkameen

At the Copper Mountain open-pit mine some 16 km south of Princeton are two rather unusual bridges. One was built in 1972 and carries a pipeline for tailings, slurry and water across the Similkameen River. It has a span of 290 m and, at 128 m high, claims the title of the second-highest bridge in Canada. The other bridge, which carries an ore conveyor across the river, was built in 1980. It has a 404 m span and, at 175 m high, is the highest bridge in Canada. Some 1,600 tons of copper ore can cross the river using this bridge.

The valley of the Similkameen River early in the 20th century was the scene of railway rivalry. The opponents were the Canadian Pacific–sponsored Kettle Valley Railway (KVR), trying to connect the Columbia & Western Railway (a CPR subsidiary) at Midway with the CPR track at Hope; and the Vancouver, Victoria & Eastern Railway (VV&E), a subsidiary of the Great Northern (GNR), which had lines across the border in the US and was trying to connect them to the coast, more to outdo the CPR than any real sound business reason. But both railways were after the lucrative mineral trade from southeastern BC.

The VV&E line crossed the border at Chopaka, where the Similkameen River also crosses, and reached Keremeos on 10 July 1907. One of its bridges was washed out soon after, and rebuilding it, plus a slowing economy, retarded construction of the line. Nevertheless, Princeton was reached late in 1909. However, west of Princeton things got much harder, for the Cascade Mountains near Hope had to be crossed. The railway announced that it would build a 13-km-long tunnel, which would have been the longest in North America at that time.

At this point the CPR made a decision that the KVR would proceed with a line from Midway to Merritt, where a connection with the branch line to Spences Bridge and the CPR main line could be made. Its track reached Princeton, via Penticton and Myra Canyon and the Trout Creek Bridge (see pages 252–54) on 21 April 1915.

With declining economic conditions, both railways by this time had declared a truce and on 9 April 1913 came to an agreement to co-operate on the completion of the track to the coast. The VV&E would give the KVR running rights on its section from Coalmont (18 km northwest of Princeton) to Brookmere (44 km south of Merritt near the Coldwater River valley), and in return the KVR would give the VV&E running rights on its section down the Coquihalla Valley to Hope, which included passage through the Quintette (Othello) Tunnels (see page 194).

World War I intervened, and the difficulties of operating a railway in the Coquihalla, with its rockslides and enormous winter snowfalls, sunk in. The VV&E/GNR lifted its track in 1954,

Above, left. The 1972 tailings pipeline bridge.

Above, right. The 1980 ore conveyor. The rather odd-looking corrugated structures are a discontinuous cover for the conveyor belt that runs under them, not, as might first be supposed, individual ore carriers.

Above. In 1911 the VV&E dug a 324-m-long tunnel through Bromley Ridge, just west of Princeton, and then almost immediately the line required this bridge over the Tulameen River. Both remain as part of a rail trail. This is the view looking across the bridge towards the tunnel in the distance. The tunnel bears the date 1961, which was when the CPR last repaired it.

and the KVR phased out its service, finally closing in 1985. Both railways left trackbed and bridges unused in their wake, many of which have today been rehabilitated and become trails for recreational users.

Above. The view on 21 April 1915 as the KVR lays its last rail to connect with the VV&E/GNR line at Princeton. That railway has crossed the Tulameen River where the Bridge of Dreams (see *next page*) is now; that bridge can be seen as the construction train approaches it *below*, earlier the same day. *Above*, the photographer has positioned himself atop the VV&E truss bridge into Princeton. At left is the approach to a road bridge. *Right*, this road bridge is in the foreground and the VV&E Bridge in the background in this 1930s photo. *Right, top*, the view here today; Highway 3 has a new concrete bridge where the VV&E bridge was (which replaced a truss road bridge built when Highway 3 was developed as a through-road following completion of the Hope-Princeton Highway in 1949). The new highway in the Similkameen Valley followed much of the old VV&E railbed. What looks like the remains of bridge footings of the earlier bridge can be seen beside the modern bridge.

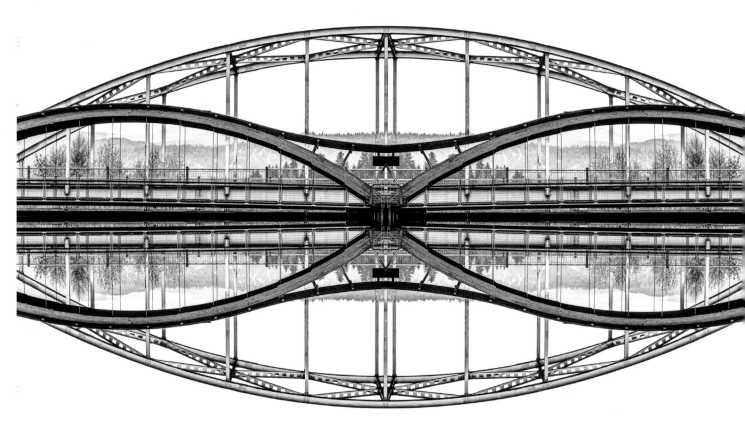

Above. While judging a competition of photographs on the theme of bridges for the Victoria Camera Club, I came across this clever composition of a double mirror effect applied to two adjacent bridges across the Tulameen River in Princeton, photographed and processed by club member James Fowler. After removing the wires, a single photo of part of the two bridges (the top left quarter) has been flipped both horizontally and vertically to create this impressive balanced image. The two bridges are the Highway 5A road bridge, built in 1963 (*below, left*), and the Bridge of Dreams (*below, right*), a covered pedestrian rail-trail bridge built in 2010 on the alignment of the Kettle Valley Railway (*previous page, bottom*).

Left. The oldest surviving bridge in Princeton, the 1930s Brown Bridge, the third bridge here over the Tulameen River.

Right, top, and *right, bottom.* The Red Bridge at Keremeos is the only survivor of five bridges built by the Great Northern Railway subsidiary Vancouver, Victoria & Eastern Railway. Work on the line began in 1907, and it reached Princeton in 1909. The last train to cross this bridge did so in 1954, and the bridge was converted to road use in 1965. The bridge trusses were covered in 1926 and painted red, hence the name. New cladding was completed in 2005. Samples of the replaced now-not-so-red cladding are attached to the bridge.

Boundary–Kootenay

Highway 3, British Columbia's southern Trans-Canada Highway, begins at Hope and runs across the southern part of the province, exiting into Alberta through the Crowsnest Pass. For this reason it is often called the Crowsnest Highway.

Much of southern BC is centred around this road and its branch Highway 3A, through Nelson and across Kootenay Lake by ferry. It was also the route of the early railways: the Columbia & Western (C&W) and the Kettle Valley Railway (KVR).

One of the most impressive Highway 3 bridges is at Rock Creek Canyon in Bridesville. It was built in 1951, and widened and strengthened in 1992. It is 91 m high and 286 m long.

Farther east on Highway 3 is Greenwood, an old copper-mining town, now the smallest incorporated city in Canada. Just north of it is a strange sight: a tunnel exposed, not now going under anything. It was originally built in 1913 for the road to pass under the C&W. The line had been built west from a connection with the CPR's Columbia & Kootenay Railway (C&K) from Nelson at Castlegar to Midway in 1899 and had crossed the river here on a trestle-and-truss bridge. In 1913 it was filled in, necessitating a tunnel for the road underneath. It was replaced with a two-lane tunnel in 1964, and the old tunnel was buried.

When the railway was abandoned in 1990, all the fill was removed, leaving the tunnel exposed. In 2000, as a millennium project, over 210 flags from all over the world were painted on the exposed tunnel, now officially the Tunnel of Flags.

Farther east again is Grand Forks. The two remaining railway bridges in Grand Forks were both part of the C&W and now

Right, top. This pleasant scene is of the bridge at Westbridge, on Highway 33, which connects Kelowna and Rock Creek, about 14 km north of Rock Creek. It replaced an earlier bridge whose footings can still be seen beside this bridge. The bridge crosses Ed James Creek, a tributary of the Kettle River. It was built in 1978.

Right, centre. Rock Creek Canyon Bridge, over another tributary of the Kettle River. It was built in 1951.

Right, bottom. The Rock Creek Canyon Bridge as first built in 1951, before its widening.

Left. The large under-truss Ingram Bridge carries Highway 3 over the Kettle River some 9 km east of Rock Creek. It was built in 1951, replacing a 1925-built one. The Kettle Valley Rail Trail runs underneath, along the river bank.

Below, centre left, and *below, centre right*. The 1913 exposed Tunnel of Flags at Greenwood. Note the date on the tunnel portal.

Below, bottom. Children play in the low water of the Kettle River under the Darrell J. Priede Bridge in Grand Forks, named after a local hero of the war in Afghanistan. Note the pipeline on the bridge. This is one of two railway bridges in Grand Forks (see *overleaf*).

Below, bottom left. A detail of the Darrell J. Priede Bridge, an array of bolts on a now paint-flaked and rusting part of the bridge.

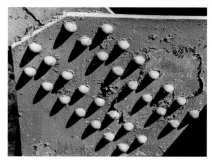

the Columbia & Western Rail Trail. The rail crossing at Kettle River Drive was once known as the Black Bridge, from its colour, but was renamed in 2011 the Darrell J. Priede Bridge in honour of a fallen local hero of the war in Afghanistan. Priede was a Canadian Army photographer who had at one time photographed this very bridge. This bridge was built in 1913. On the south side of the bridge, rails are still in place, now forming part of the Grand Forks Railway of the Interfor mill there. This company-owned railway connects with what was once a Great Northern Railway line, now the shortline Kettle Falls International Railway, which in turn connects in the US with BNSF. Both C&W bridges now also carry gas pipelines.

Above. The Highway 3 bridge over the Granby River, a Kettle River tributary, immediately east of Grand Forks. Built in 1957, it replaced a wooden structure built in 1922.

Above, right. The other Columbia & Western Railway bridge in Grand Forks, reflecting nicely in the Kettle River. The C&W crossed and recrossed the Kettle River because real estate interests in Grand Forks decided they did not want the railway tracks crossing their newly laid-out streets and threatened violence against C&W personnel should they build there. This is unusual in the real estate world; promoters usually wanted to attract railways, not keep them away. Note the pipeline once more.

Right, bottom. The Cascade Gorge Bridge over the Kettle River near Christina Lake. It replaced an unusual covered bridge (*below*) that had been constructed in 1899, at the time the C&W was first built from Castlegar as far as Grand Forks. The bridge crosses the river right beside the site of a dam built in 1901 to supply power to the region, which was closed in 1907 and dismantled in 1922.

Below. This immense wooden bridge was built over the Granby River near the smelter used to refine the ore from the Phoenix mining area to the north. Here a train of ore cars crosses the bridge. The powerhouse flume for the smelter is in the foreground.

Railway building along the boundary often required the construction of huge trestles to carry the rails over the rivers or gullies. *Above* is the Columbia & Western bridge, originally made completely of wood, across the Kettle River just to the south of Cascade, a long-gone mining town south of Christina Lake in the inverted "V" of the river valley. *Below* is the equally spectacular wooden trestle built by the Great Northern Railway over Deadman's Gulch, now Glenside Creek, on its line to Phoenix; no expense was to be spared to outdo the CPR. The trestle was 60 m high and 205 m long on a 14-degree curve.

Left, right and *right, centre.* Some 22 km northeast of Christina Lake, Highway 3 crosses over McRae Creek and the old trackbed of the C&W on the beautiful Paulson Bridge, a classic example of a bridge that hardly looks like one from a driver's point of view and yet has a much more complex support system underneath it. The 258-m-long and 84-m-high bridge was opened by then Minister of Highways "Flyin' Phil" Gaglardi in October 1962, along with an entire new section of the southern Trans-Canada from Christina Lake to Kinnaird (part of Castlegar from 1974). The previous routing of the highway was via a gravel mountain road from Cascade to Rossland.

At Trail, several bridges cross the Columbia River. The city has a classic double four-span steel-arch bridge that visually appears to be two bridges. It was completed in 1961 and replaced an earlier bridge from 1911, though this still exists, now slated for demolition. The latter, about 800 m downstream from the 1961 bridge, is a metal-truss bridge with a wooden deck and is now fenced off. Close by is a replacement pedestrian suspension bridge called (in line with the current vogue) the Columbia River Skywalk. It is 300 m long and thus one of the longest pedestrian suspension bridges in North America. The bridge carries utilities underneath. It was opened on 15 December 2016.

Bridges at Trail.

Left, top. The 1911 bridge crosses the Columbia against a dramatic background of belching chimneys.

Right, top. The double four-span 1961 bridge.

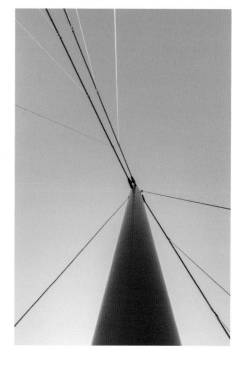

Left, centre, and *left, bottom.* The 1911 bridge, fenced off and awaiting demolition in this 2020 photo.

Right, centre, and *right, bottom.* The 2016 Columbia River Skywalk.

Far left. The 1961 Columbia bridge, showing its four spans.

Left. The 1893 railway bridge soon after completion.

Below. The two bridges in 2021, seen from the Columbia River side. Note the large osprey nest on top of the once-rail, now-road bridge, the highest bridge, nearest the camera.

Above, right and *below.* There is a huge double bridge, one rail, one road, at Waneta, on the Columbia 18 km south of Trail on Highway 22A. Since the bridges are only a few hundred metres from the US border, they are often missed by tourists travelling within BC. The bridges cross the Pend d'Oreille River where it joins the Columbia about 500 m downstream of the Waneta Dam. The first (and highest) bridge was built by the Nelson & Fort Sheppard Railway (N&FS) in 1893 as American mining promoters attempted to direct the mineral wealth of this area to the United States. It was converted to road use in 1947 when the highway was created, and another rail bridge was built right beside the other one. No one (including the BC Ministry of Transportation) seems to know why this was done, but it may be that trains were getting too heavy for the original bridge. The once-rail, now-road bridge is the oldest large bridge in British Columbia. The railway line is, as of 2019, that of the shortline St. Paul & Pacific Railroad, a subsidiary of Progressive Rail, which connects with BNSF at Chewelah, Washington.

Above. The two bridges, about 2 m apart. The current rail bridge is on the right. See also the photo on page 4.

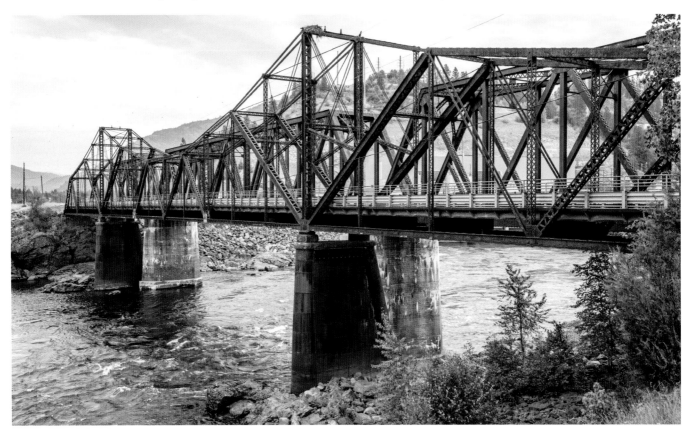

Right, top. The bridge that carries Highway 3 across the Columbia River at Castlegar, the Kinnaird Bridge, completed in 1965, has become a topic of conversation since August 2018, when a bridge in Genoa, Italy, collapsed, killing 43 people. For both bridges were designed by Riccardo Morandi, a professor of bridge design at the University of Florence. His name can be seen inscribed on the plaque at the end of the bridge, shown *far right, centre.* The bridge design dates from 1960 and features unusual V-shaped piers. However, this bridge is different from the Genoa one in many ways: it is much shorter (300 m compared with just over 1 km), and the design is different (though both have the V-shaped piers). Nonetheless the Genoa incident has caused Morandi-designed bridges around the world to be re-examined, and the Kinnaird Bridge is no different. However, inspections have concluded that the bridge is in good condition and is safe.

Right, bottom. This stunning 302-m-long arch bridge in a beautiful setting carries Highway 3A across the Kootenay River at Brilliant, near Castlegar. It was built in 1967 and replaced a much earlier suspension bridge built by Doukhobor settlers in 1913 (see *next page*).

Above. The Columbia River ferry at Castlegar from the 1929 annual report of the BC Department of Public Works. The 1935 report flagged dry rot in this vessel's hull.

Left. The bridge built across the Columbia River at Robson in 1902 as a substantive link in the CPR's Columbia & Western and Columbia & Kootenay Railway line from Nelson to Midway. It was a swing span, to allow passage for steamboats.

Below and *left.* The Brilliant Suspension Bridge was built by Doukhobors in 1913 to connect their settlement at Brilliant with a village site along the east side of the Columbia. About one hundred volunteer workers heeded the call of their leader Peter Verigin and built the bridge in eight months. The suspension bridge has a deck stiffened by pony trusses on either side of the roadway, and the deck is suspended from steel-reinforced concrete towers either side. The bridge was designed by J.R. Grant, who went on to design the Burrard Bridge in Vancouver and who was engineer for the Granville Street Bridge. Replaced in 1966 by the adjacent Highway 3 bridge, which towers above it, the bridge became derelict; only local outcry saved it from demolition. It was restored in 2009–10 and is now a historic site in a regional park. Shadows of the combined pony-truss sidewalls and the guardrails installed on restoration make an interesting pattern on the wooden bridge deck (*left*).

Above. Detail of the underside of the 1966 highway bridge at Brilliant makes a somewhat abstract pattern.

Above, top. This scenic view includes the cable ferry at Glade, across the Kootenay River about 27 km west of Nelson. This vessel is the *Glade II*, launched in January 2018 to replace an aging ferry in service since 1948. The ship was assembled on the river bank and launched by being pushed into the water by three large trucks.

Above. A pedestrian suspension bridge connecting Castlegar's Zuckerberg Island Heritage Park in the Columbia River to the city. It was constructed in 1984 by the 44th Field Engineer Squadron of the Canadian Armed Forces as a military exercise and was allowed to remain. Original wooden support towers were replaced by steel structures in 2008.

Above and *left.* The Columbia & Kootenay Railway bridge built over the Kootenay River at Taghum, 6 km west of Nelson. The first bridge, a wooden truss, was built with the line from Nelson to Midway in 1899. This was replaced by a steel bridge in 1903. The photo is taken from the Highway 3 Taghum Bridge, built in 1980–81, next to it.

Above. From a photographic point of view the light was just right for this early-morning photo aboard MV *Columbia.* The vessel is also shown at *right*, leaving Shelter Bay.

Left. The Lower Arrow Lake ferry from Needles to Fauquier in 1943.

Stretching nearly 200 km northwest and north of Castlegar are the Arrow Lakes, essentially a widening of the Columbia River, originally two lakes but now one because of higher water levels behind the Keenleyside Dam at Robson, built in the mid-1960s. Crossing the Upper Arrow Lake are two ferries—one running from Galena to Shelter Bay at the north end of the lake and one at Arrow Park, 22 km south of Nakusp. The latter is a cable ferry and the former an independently powered one. Both current ferries are relatively new, having been built on the shore of the lake at Nakusp, along with the ferries for Glade (previous page), Harrop (*opposite, bottom*), and Adams Lake (page 246). Ferry service at the head of the Upper Arrow Lake has a long history. Canadian Pacific operated a ferry from Arrowhead to Thomson's Landing, now Beaton, in 1896. It connected with a branch line to Revelstoke. The ferry was taken over by the provincial government in 1956 and the east-side terminus was relocated to Galena Bay in 1957. The west-side terminus moved to Shelter Bay in 1968 after rising lake levels behind the new dam flooded Arrowhead. A new road from Revelstoke to Shelter Bay was also built at this time. The current ferry, the MV *Columbia*, which can carry 80 cars, was built at Nakusp and launched in 2014, replacing two smaller ferries.

Below. One mountain range east from the Arrow Lakes is Slocan Lake, which had a CPR rail ferry service for many years, connecting Slocan City at the southern end of the lake with Rosebery, near the north end. This enabled trains to travel from Nelson to Nakusp. The entire train was carried on the ferry, really a barge propelled by a tug, the *Iris G.* Here the ferry is seen leaving Rosebery in 1988. Service ended in December that year with the closure of the Nakusp-to-Rosebery line.

NELSON BRIDGE OPENING

November 7th
1957
✫
Banquet
Civic Centre
NELSON, B.C.
✫
SOUVENIR
PROGRAM

At Nelson there had been a ferry across the West Arm of Kootenay Lake since 1913, providing a reliable service, though in 1936 the ferry had to be hauled out to repair extensive dry rot in the hull. By that time the ferry was so busy that a 24-hour service was maintained. The government of W.A.C. Bennett replaced the ferry in 1957 with the current "Big Orange" steel cantilever bridge, now a local landmark. A banquet was held at the bridge's official opening (*left*), which featured a turkey dinner and organ music and a speech by Phil Gaglardi, the Minister of Highways responsible for much of the road and bridge building in BC in the 1950s and 1960s. Note the ferry and ferry landings beside the new bridge in the photo on the cover of the souvenir program, and also the toll plaza at the south end. Tolls were removed in 1963. *Below, left,* is a view of the bridge from the west of Nelson and *below, right,* is a view from the bridge deck.

Below, bottom. The cable ferry across the West Arm of Kootenay Lake from Harrop to Procter, east of Nelson, makes a tranquil view at 5:30 on a July morning in 2018. A ferry has been operating here since 1925; the photo shows one built in 1949, which was displaced by a new ferry later that year.

East-to-west travel in southern British Columbia has always been an issue because of the north–south orientation of the mountain ranges. The Kootenay River flows in two such valleys, but the western one is filled by the 105-km-long Kootenay Lake, which enabled lake steamers to connect first the railways and then the roads of the region. The Columbia & Kootenay Steam Navigation Company (CKSN), founded in 1890, ran steamboats on both the Arrow Lakes and the Columbia River, and Kootenay Lake and the Kootenay River into the US. Canadian Pacific bought CKSN in 1897 to connect its railway lines down the valleys from its main line at Revelstoke. A year later, on 6 October 1898, it began service on Kootenay Lake to connect its lines at Nelson with that of its subsidiary British Columbia Southern Railway, which had just completed a line into the province from Lethbridge, Alberta, across the Crowsnest Pass to Kootenay Landing at the southern end of the lake (see map page 274). The Great Northern Railway (GN) at this time also began running steamboats on Kootenay Lake. They connected to its N&FS line to Nelson, acquired in 1899, to its Kaslo & Slocan Railway, and to Kuskonook, at the southern end of the lake, the terminus of its Bedlington & Nelson Railway to Spokane. The latter declined after a fire at the Kuskonook terminus in 1900. In 1931 a road was built up the east side of the lake, and ferries could take the much shorter route between Fraser's Landing (downstream from Balfour, today's ferry terminal) and Gray Creek. After the road was extended in 1947, ferries linked Balfour with Kootenay Bay. The Kootenay Lake route remains an important one despite completion in October 1963 of the Salmo–Creston cutoff (Highway 3). The latter route traverses Kootenay Pass through the Selkirk Mountains, the highest highway pass open year-round in Canada.

SS *Moyie* was purchased by CPR and launched at Nelson on 22 October 1898. The vessel was built in Toronto, originally intended for service on the Stikine River in northern BC to carry gold miners on their way to the Klondike, along with her sister ship the SS *Minto*, which was put into service on the Arrow Lakes. *Minto* served until 1954 and then suffered a "Viking burial"—a nice way of saying it was set on fire and sunk in the middle of the lake. *Moyie*, seen *left, centre*, calling at Kaslo in the 1930s, lasted until 1957 and had a better fate, being sold to the town of Kaslo where she was restored as a museum on the waterfront, just out of the water but still on Kootenay Lake (*left, top*, and *below*). *Moyie* is the oldest intact surviving sternwheeler in Canada.

Above. In 1931 SS *Nasookin* approaches the dock with the daily Greyhound bus seemingly precariously balanced on its bow. This steamboat was built at Nelson for the CPR in 1913 and was principally used for the run between Nelson and Kootenay Landing, known as the Crow Boat Route from its connection to the railway through Crowsnest Pass. It was retired in January 1931 when the railway line from Procter to Kootenay Landing was completed. It was purchased by the BC government in April 1931 and modified somewhat to become a ferry from Fraser's Landing to Boswell, then the northern end of a new east-side road.

Below. The present ferry, *Osprey 2000*, can carry 80 cars and 250 passengers. Here it is shown in mid-lake. The 9-km route from Balfour to Kootenay Bay is considered to be the world's longest free ferry ride.

Above. In 1947 *Nasookin* was replaced by the MV *Anscomb,* and in 1954 part of it was converted into a private house that can still be seen on the road between Nelson and Balfour. The MV *Anscomb* (*above, right*) was built for the run across Kootenay Lake in 1947. It was built in Vancouver and shipped in pieces by rail to Nelson, where it was reassembled. It ran from Balfour to Kootenay Bay for 53 years, until 2000, when it was replaced by the much larger *Osprey 2000.* Anscomb was sold but sank in 2004. The wheelhouse and captain's quarters, which were made of wood, somehow detached themselves from the rest of the ship and washed up on the beach. This part of the *Anscomb* has now been restored (*above, right centre*) and sits at the Balfour ferry terminal.

Below. The MV *Balfour* was launched in 1954 to increase capacity across the lake and still acts as an overflow ferry in the summer months but is slated for replacement by 2023. The replacement will be an all-electric-ready diesel hybrid similar to BC Ferries' new Island Class ferries.

The British Columbia Southern Railway had been granted a charter in 1894 to build a line from the Alberta boundary through Crowsnest Pass to the south end of Kootenay Lake. The company was purchased by the CPR in 1897 and the line completed the following year. For 32 years the connection to Nelson and beyond was maintained by a combination of trains and lake steamboats, with the transfer point at Kootenay Landing at the southern end of Kootenay Lake. The steamboat dock (*right, centre*) was reached via a long wooden trestle over the marshy low-lying land at the end of the lake (*below*), in the 1930s, with part of it a short bridge; the structure even had a siding on it. The steamboat dock was located on the main channel of the Kootenay River, where there would have been deeper water. *Below, bottom*. The trestle on the western side of the new bridge in 2010.

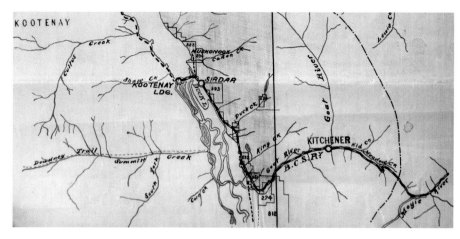

Above. The British Columbia Southern Railway line to Kootenay Landing shown on a 1901 map. The railway had enormous land grants, encompassing almost the entire eastern side of the lake, including the area shown on this map in red. This land grant was inherited by the CPR and added to vast land grants in southern BC already acquired via its Columbia & Kootenay and Columbia & Western subsidiaries. Note the dashed line up the western side of the lake, the route of the 1931 rail connection to Nelson that would put most of the lake steamers out of business.

Kootenay Landing, c. 1910.

Above and *below*. When the 55-km extension up the west side of the lake to Procter was completed in 1931, it was the final link in CPR's southern main line, an alternative route to the coast deemed essential after the closure of the main line for several weeks when the Surprise Creek Bridge collapsed (see page 284). A bridge across the Kootenay River was required, extending the existing trestle west to the far shore. This steel-truss bridge, with a centre vertical lift span, was installed. The Kootenay River railway bridge remains today. It is about 120 m long, with the lift span being 21 m long and allowing 15 m vertical clearance above high water. Here a rare daylight-running CPR freight crosses the bridge eastbound. The photos (*above*, *below* and *opposite, bottom*) were taken by railfan team Garry and Roz Miller in 2010.

Left. This postcard view shows a CPR passenger train about to leave Kootenay Landing about 1910. The steamboat is docked at left.

Left. A bridge over the Kootenay River at Wardner, 35 km east of Cranbrook, was replaced in 1928, and the BC Department of Public Works took this photo of the new bridge, at left, and the old bridge, about to be demolished, at right. Both are Pratt trusses, the new one steel, the old, wood. The new bridge was demolished in 1983.

Left. The ferry across the Kootenay River, west of Creston, is photographed in 1944. The ferry was replaced by a bridge (*below*) in 1961 as part of the realignment of Highway 3 from Salmo to Creston through Kootenay Pass, opened in 1964. The bridge is photographed here in 2020 while a major renovation was taking place.

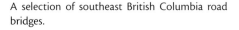

A selection of southeast British Columbia road bridges.

Right, from top:
The Walker Bridge, over the Goat River, built in 1950, about 10 km east of Creston on Highway 3; the Curzon Junction Bridge, over the Moyie River just west of Yahk on Highway 3; the Curzon Bridge over the Moyie River on Highway 3/95 at Yahk, identified as a Warren through-truss; and the Springbrook Bridge over the Kootenay River at Skookumchuck, built in 1956 and identified as a Parker through-truss.

Right, bottom. The Yahk Bridge, over the Moyie River, just east of Yahk, rendered in black and white to emphasize its curves and texture.

Above. A now almost disappeared king-truss bridge with its distinctive A-frame shape. This one was at Ymir, south of Nelson, over the Salmo River, photographed in 1924.

Right. Dutch Creek Bridge, with hoodoos behind it. Dutch Creek flows into Columbia Lake. The bridge carries Highway 93 over the creek about 2 km south of Fairmont Hot Springs. Hoodoos are weathered rocks that have been protected by harder rock on the top to create columnar formations. This steel-truss bridge was built in 1955, replacing an earlier wooden truss bridge shown here in 1944 (*above*).

Left. Galbraith's Ferry at Fort Steele, across the Kootenay River. This was one of the earliest ferries in the province. It was a form of cable ferry. The cable, seen in this 1868 photo, was used to prevent the ferry from floating downstream while it was being propelled across it. John Galbraith set up this ferry in 1864 to transport miners to a gold find at nearby Wild Horse Creek. A small settlement called Galbraith's Ferry grew up around the ferry. In 1887 a contingent of North-West Mounted Police led by Major Sam Steele arrived and created a fort here. This was in anticipation of an uprising by Indigenous peoples in the region, which never materialized. Galbraith renamed the settlement Fort Steele. When the railway arrived, Cranbrook eclipsed Fort Steele as a centre for the region. The fort was restored and is today a National Historic Site.

Rogers Pass

The road and rail route over the Selkirks between Donald and Revelstoke goes through Rogers Pass, which for the railway, with its need for a low grade, involves a number of major bridges and tunnels. At the western end sits Revelstoke. At first known as Farwell, this was where the CPR established its servicing area for locomotives and where eastbound trains changed to more powerful locomotives for the long slog uphill. One of the two crossings of the Columbia River is here, and a series of bridges, shown on these pages, have spanned the river.

The railway has always been routed through Rogers Pass, but the road—the Trans-Canada Highway—only took that route after 1962. From 1940 to 1962 the road was routed around the Big Bend of the Columbia, involving a long detour north. Before 1940 there was no road at all, and cars were ferried through Rogers Pass by rail.

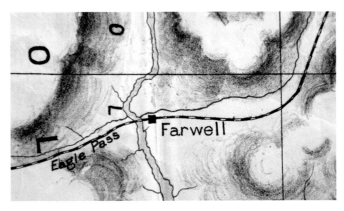

Above. This 1885 map shows the route of the CPR across the Columbia River from Farwell, a settlement created by surveyor Arthur Farwell, who worked out where the railway would have to cross the river, and, by obtaining a Crown grant of land in October 1883 there, hoped to force the CPR to buy him out. The railway, however, was by this time used to outwitting land speculators, and plotted a route around his pre-emption and built its station some distance from Farwell's settlement.

Above. The first CPR bridge at Revelstoke, a wooden structure hastily completed in 1885. The stone-filled crib piers were completed ahead of time during the previous winter, when water levels were lowest. The top level was for the railway, the bottom for a road. The bridge replaced a toll road bridge built by Gustavus Blin Wright for freight wagons. He had been a major contractor on the Old Cariboo Road in 1862 and built the Eagle Pass Wagon Road to connect with his bridge here between 1883 and 1884.

Above. This was the opening ceremony on 29 June 1940 for the Big Bend Highway and, with it, its critical link: this substantial bridge over the Columbia River at Boat Encampment. The road was the final connection in the Central Trans-Provincial Highway, precursor to the Trans-Canada, which followed the Columbia River between Revelstoke and Donald, 28 km north of Golden. The road was designated as Highway 1 the following year. The route was made redundant in 1962 with the opening of the Trans-Canada Highway through Rogers Pass, which reduced the distance between Revelstoke and Donald from 305 km to 122 km. The entire area was flooded behind the Mica Dam after it was completed in 1973, creating Kinbasket Lake, a project that was part of the 1964 Columbia River Treaty between Canada and the US. Today's BC Ministry of Transportation has no record of this bridge either being moved elsewhere or abandoned to the rising waters of the lake, and Ministry of Highways annual reports do not mention it (which suggests it was not used elsewhere), but a retired ministry employee thinks that it was moved; however, no one knows where it might have been moved to!

Above. A westbound CPR freight crosses today's Columbia Bridge at Revelstoke on 6 July 2021. This bridge opened on 23 February 1968, replacing one built in 1907.

Above. The bridge was replaced in 1907 by a steel-and-concrete structure (*left*). This bridge was double-tracked—in a way. Unusually, the rails were double laid but overlapped; this allowed trains to cross in alternating directions without having to throw a switch. The bridge had to be only slightly wider than for a single track. The CPR was implementing a policy of double-tracking as much of its line as possible at this time. A contingent of Rocky Mountain Rangers guard the 1907 bridge during World War I (*right*).

Left. The second CPR bridge, built about 1890.

Left, bottom. About 1898, one span of the 1890 bridge was raised to become a through-truss, presumably to allow for safer river navigation. Here the newly raised span is temporarily supported by dozens of poles. Again the work was done when water levels were at their lowest.

Above. Sometime between 1900 and 1906 the elevated 1890 bridge was clad to protect it from the elements, as it was a wooden bridge and approaching the end of its life. Cladding would hopefully prolong the bridge's life but came at a cost: the structure was now more susceptible to being burned by one of the steam locomotives of the day, a problem solved once and for all in 1907 by a new steel-and-concrete bridge.

Above. The Columbia Suspension Bridge at Revelstoke, built in 1961, shown here in an infrared photo.

Right. The multi-span Big Eddy (Wilson Street) road bridge, built across the Columbia in 1924. Here its intricate steelwork is rendered in black and white for dramatic impact.

When the Canadian Pacific Railway was built, the most difficult sections were those through Rogers Pass and up the valley of the Kicking Horse River between Revelstoke and the Alberta boundary. Rogers Pass required the construction of some of the most fearsome trestles and bridges anywhere at the time.

Rogers Pass had been discovered for the railway through the Selkirk Mountains in 1882, by Major Albert Bowman Rogers, after whom it is now named. It proved to be a difficult choice for a railway because of the extent of snowslides, and would require snowsheds. Indeed, even when the railway was completed in November 1885 it was abandoned until the following spring because it was overwhelmed by snow.

Going from east to west, in the direction the line was built, the route required the following major bridge structures: over Mountain Creek; over Surprise Creek (now Cut Creek); over Stoney Creek; over Cascade Creek; two bridges over Loop Brook, the site of a great loop to try to maintain a semblance of reasonable grade; plus three crossings of the Illecillewaet River immediately after. The latter four crossings were removed in 1916 by the completion of the 8-km-long Connaught Tunnel, and separation of trains in each direction was achieved in 1988 by the construction of another tunnel, the 14.66-km-long Mount Macdonald Tunnel.

Right. This 1902 map shows the route at the time of the Canadian Pacific Railway through the western approaches to *Rogers Pass*. The line has been highlighted in yellow. The multiple loops it used to manage the steep gradients have been marked in red:
A, B = first and second (*right, bottom*) crossings of Loop Brook.
C, D and E = first (*right, top*), second and third crossings of the *Illecillewaet* River. Note the further huge loop around the headwaters of the Illecillewaet at *Glacier*, with its *Hotel*. The series of high bridges are about 10 km farther east from *Rogers Pass* marked on this map.

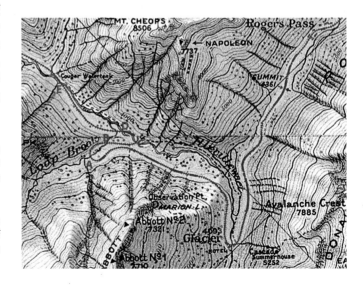

Above. The first crossing of the Illecillewaet River, a long, high trestle, at *C* on the map at *left*. This photo was taken in July 1897, with the daily *Atlantic Express* heading east with a pusher locomotive at the rear. The two long snowsheds behind the train are separated by a gap protected by snow-diversion structures on the mountain slope above. The forest, which was badly burned during the construction phase, has still not recovered.

Right. The second crossing of Loop Brook, *B* on the map. The train is the daily *Pacific Express*, headed for Vancouver. The train appears to be posing for the photograph, something a long-distance train would hardly do today.

The loops here were eliminated when the Connaught Tunnel opened in 1916 (see page 284). The modern single crossing of Loop Brook (also called Five Mile Creek) is a low, featureless girder bridge.

The Stoney Creek Bridge (*all on this page*). At 84 m high, Stoney Creek was the highest wooden bridge ever built, and at the time the second-highest bridge in North America, attracting attention from tourists and photographers worldwide. The first wooden structure was built when the line was created in 1885 (*above, top*). This was replaced in 1894 by a steel-arch bridge, shown beginning to take shape, with false-work supports underneath (*above*). The partially built steel bridge is seen being tested with the weight of six locomotives (*left, centre*), and in service later (*left, top*). A modern photo, with four diesel-electric locomotives crossing with a long freight train, is shown at *left, bottom*.

Above and *left*. Although at 47 m the Mountain Creek Bridge was not the highest of the CPR bridges in the Selkirks, it was the longest (330 m) and most impressive. In the 1890s the bridge approach trestles were filled in by sluicing (*left*). A high-pressure jet of water was used to dislodge material from a fill source site nearby and the slurry sluiced to the bridge and deposited as shown. A retaining wall has been built between the fill and the creek to help ensure the fill goes where it is required. The centre span was then replaced with steel (*below*).

The 55-m-high current bridge at Surprise Creek, now called Cut Creek, is the third in this location (*right*). The original wooden-deck truss bridge (*above*) was replaced by a steel trestle in the 1890s, and this in turn was replaced by a new bridge built slightly uphill in 1929. Just before the new bridge was completed, a locomotive caused the collapse of the east approach span of the bridge it was about to replace. This accident (*left*), on 28 January 1929, killed the two men on the locomotive and left it, and pieces of the bridge, embedded in the mountainside below. The main line was closed for several weeks. The closure led directly to the completion of a southern alternative route, creating a continuous line by connecting the track at Kootenay Landing to Procter. This included the building of the Kootenay River bridge at the southern end of Kootenay Lake, opened in January 1931 (see page 275).

Below. A 120-m-long wooden CPR bridge over the Columbia River at Donald.

Above. The Surprise Creek (now known as Cut Creek) Bridge today. This photo shows the typical steep gullies that the railway had to deal with on this stretch of the line.

In 1913, the CPR knew that it would soon face competition from other railways built to the West Coast. The Grand Trunk Pacific was completed in April 1914 to Prince Rupert, and the Canadian Northern Pacific Railway to Vancouver in January of the following year. (Both companies were soon nationalized to form Canadian National Railways.) Critically, both were built through Yellowhead Pass, and as such enjoyed considerably lower gradients than the CPR, which had only in 1909 got rid of its "Big Hill" in Kicking Horse Canyon with its 4.4 percent gradients using the new Spiral Tunnels (see page 286). Gentler gradients meant lower costs and hence the CPR would lose competitiveness. It still had steep gradients (2.2 percent, considered the maximum for main-line operation) in Rogers Pass, which had been addressed by the use of multiple crossings of the Illecillewaet River and the loops near Glacier. The railway thus planned the Connaught Tunnel, which was completed in 1916, as a way of reducing these gradients. In the 1980s, congestion was becoming a problem, and so the CPR planned an extensive project to separate eastbound and westbound traffic by building the Mount Macdonald and Mount Shaughnessy Tunnels, connected by a long viaduct, the John Fox Viaduct (*right*). Eastbound traffic normally uses the Connaught Tunnel but westbound trains use the Mount Macdonald.

776. EAST PORTAL CONNAUGHT TUNNEL, MT MACDONALD

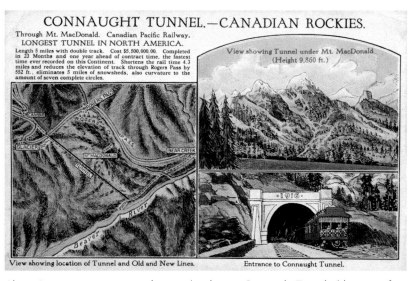

CONNAUGHT TUNNEL.—CANADIAN ROCKIES.

Through Mt. MacDonald. Canadian Pacific Railway.
LONGEST TUNNEL IN NORTH AMERICA.

Length 5 miles with double track. Cost $5,500,000.00. Completed in 23 Months and one year ahead of contract time, the fastest time ever recorded on this Continent. Shortens the rail time 4.3 miles and reduces the elevation of track through Rogers Pass by 552 ft., eliminates 5 miles of snowsheds, also curvature to the amount of seven complete circles.

View showing Tunnel under Mt. MacDonald. (Height 9,860 ft.)

View showing location of Tunnel and Old and New Lines.

Entrance to Connaught Tunnel.

Above. A contemporary postcard promoting the new Connaught Tunnel with a map of the old and new routes.

Left. A train exits the Connaught Tunnel sometime in the 1920s.

Left. The John Fox Viaduct. Part of the new track leading to the Macdonald Tunnel, this 1,229-m-long viaduct was installed because normal cut and fill would have undermined the track from the Connaught Tunnel above it. Some 45 steel spans, each 27 m long and weighing 82 tonnes, had to be brought from Calgary via the Crowsnest Pass because they would not fit through the Spiral Tunnels in Kicking Horse Pass (see page 287).

Right. Railfan Matthew Robson took this photo of a westbound freight train exiting the Mount Shaughnessy Tunnel onto the John Fox Viaduct.

Kicking Horse & the Rockies

East of Golden to the Alberta border, the Canadian Pacific and the Trans-Canada Highway follow the valley of the Kicking Horse River, named by the Palliser Expedition in 1858 after a horse kicked geologist James Hector in the chest.

The Trans-Canada has been improved a great deal in recent years, and as a result has some spectacular bridges, most notably Park Bridge, opened in 2006. But the major engineering feature of the Kicking Horse valley is undoubted one that the tourist sees very little of: the CPR's Spiral Tunnels, completed in 1909 but still very much an essential part of the railway's path to the coast. In the early 1900s the CPR finally resolved to rid itself of the "Big Hill," a section of track with 4.4 percent grades, twice that normally allowed for main-line use. The Big Hill had been intended as a temporary measure, as were many of the first wooden bridges, just to get the line into operation and begin earning sorely needed revenue. CPR engineer John E. Schwitzer came up with the idea of reducing the grade by lengthening the path and creating two circular tunnels. Called the Spiral Tunnels, they were modelled on similar loop tunnels on the approach lines to the Gotthard Tunnel in Switzerland, built in 1882.

Above, top, and *above.* The 10th Avenue bridge in Golden, built in 1951–52 over the Kicking Horse River.

Left and *below.* The Kicking Horse Pedestrian Bridge in Golden, built in 2001. It is the longest free-standing wood-frame bridge in Canada. Pedestrian bridges are becoming popular: the Golden Skybridge, two suspension pedestrian bridges, opened in 2021 in Golden.

Above. The Park Bridge on the Trans-Canada, about 10 km east of Golden, was completed in 2007 together with reconstruction of 26 km of highway, which before had been considered one of the worst stretches of road in the province for accidents. The bridge is 405 m long.

Above. The building of the Canadian Pacific Railway through the Rockies entailed not only many bridges, but many tunnels. None were more troublesome than the Corry Brothers Tunnel at Palliser, now a ghost town between Field and Golden. The photo shows it during excavation in 1884. This tunnel kept contracting in size and had to be abandoned in 1887. A second tunnel, which was later concrete lined, still managed to keep contracting. Finally, in the 1950s, a solution was found—remove the entire hill, leaving just the concrete shell as a stand-alone structure more akin to a snowshed.

Left. The Ottertail River Bridge as first built by the CPR in 1885. The Ottertail is a tributary of the Kicking Horse River. This wooden bridge was not replaced until 1922.

Below. This map appeared in *Saturday Sunset*, a popular Vancouver magazine, on 28 March 1908 to explain to its readers what the CPR was doing in the Kicking Horse valley. The *Present Line* is the Big Hill, complete with switches and spurs of runaway tracks similar to runaway lanes of steep hills on today's roads. The *New Line* is the reduced-grade line that would be produced once the Spiral Tunnels were complete. *Tunnel No 1* is the Upper Spiral Tunnel and *Tunnel No 2* the lower.

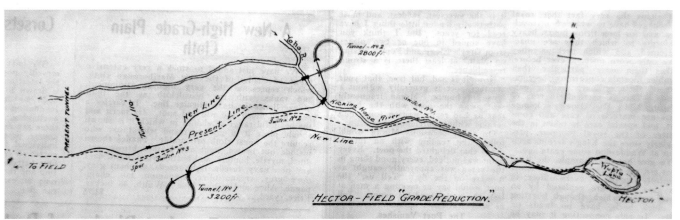

Above. This three-dimensional map was published by the CPR in the 1930s to explain the Spiral Tunnels, which it does better than a regular map or a regular photograph, although the lower tunnel, on the left, looks higher than the upper tunnel, on the right.

Below. In the summer of 1969 railway photographer Dave Wilkie took this excellent photo of a freight train emerging westbound from the Lower Spiral Tunnel. In the early days trains were not long enough to take a photo like this, so CPR photographers would pose two trains to look like they were one.

British Columbia also has a *natural* bridge. Here, on the Kicking Horse River 3 km from Field, the river is actively cutting down its channel. The natural bridge was formerly a waterfall. Water found its way through cracks in the surface rock to a softer rock layer beneath it and eroded it faster than surface rock, creating a new channel underneath. Over time, the passage will deepen and eventually the bridge will collapse, leaving a gorge. In the meantime, the natural bridge makes a very scenic view for photographers.

Left. The Yoho Valley Road Bridge over the Kicking Horse River must be one of the most scenic in the province. Mount Stephen is in the background. This road is closed during the winter months. *Above*, one of the local inhabitants seen taking advantage of the bridge to cross the river!

Above. Just 7 km from the BC boundary in Alberta is this footbridge across the Bow River—mundane looking, perhaps, but it has an interesting origin. For it was built in 1912 to carry the Lake Louise Tramway from the CPR station at Lake Louise to Chateau Lake Louise, then a Canadian Pacific hotel on the shores of the lake. The railway, aware of the tourism possibilities of the Rocky Mountains, built a number of imposing hotels for its clientele, even employing Swiss mountain guides. A tram is pictured in front of the hotel in 1929, *right, centre,* and an open-type tram at Lake Louise Station, *right.*

Left. In 2018 the world's longest wildlife bridge was built over the Trans-Canada Highway in BC, less than 3 km shy of the Alberta border. Unlike those on the Alberta side, this bridge covered the whole roadway with a single arch; the Alberta ones all have two arches. This view, from the road, is looking westward. In recent years much attention has been given to avoiding wildlife on BC roads, both here and in the Crowsnest Pass on Highway 3, where underpasses have been constructed.

Kootenay National Park.
All of the images on these two pages are from BC's premier national park, the Kootenay. All are pedestrian bridges.

Above, far left and *left.* The Simpson Bridge across the Kootenay River to the Simpson River Trailhead, which gives access from Highway 93 to the adjacent Mount Assiniboine Provincial Park. It is a beautiful simple curved-beam bridge. The railings yield a plethora of shadow patterns, photographed, *far left*, with an 8 mm fisheye lens, and, *left*, with a normal lens, for totally different effects.

Shadows also make for an interesting photo at Numa Falls, on the Vermilion River, a Kootenay River tributary, *below, left*. The "normal" photo of the bridge is included, *below*, for comparison.

This page. Marble Canyon in Kootenay National Park, 89 km north of Radium Hot Springs on Highway 93, is part of the headwater tributaries of the Kootenay River. Here it flows through a limestone and dolomite gorge, and the trail has no fewer than seven bridges, all across Tokumm Creek, which flows into the Vermilion River, which in turn flows into the Kootenay River. Some of the bridges are shown here in their spectacular environment. Forest fires have been here, however, as evidenced by the alarming amount of burned trees. This beautiful spot is, like all our parks, threatened by the effects of global warming.

Victoria & Vancouver Island

One of Victoria's first bridges, the James Bay Bridge, was a low wooden structure that carried Government Street over James Bay to new legislative buildings, called the "birdcages" after their distinctive style, that were built in 1859. It was replaced by another wooden bridge in 1900, but it was itself replaced only three years later by a stone causeway. James Bay at that time was a tidal mud flat, and the decision had been made to fill it in, and the CPR built its now famous Empress Hotel there in 1908.

Victoria's most prominent bridge, the Johnson Street Bascule, was first built as a wagon bridge in 1855, and was called the Victoria Bridge. It didn't last long because it blocked navigation, and in 1862 it was torn down and, unusually, replaced by a ferry. The second bridge was only a railway bridge, though pedestrians were allowed to cross. But it was a swing bridge to allow boats to pass. It was built in 1888 to carry the extension into Victoria of the Esquimalt & Nanaimo Railway (E&N) across the harbour.

This bridge lasted until 1923 when a bascule bridge was constructed for both road and rail. It was actually two bridges side by side. It was designed by Joseph Strauss, a leading bridge designer of the day, who was later responsible for the design of the Golden Gate Bridge in San Francisco. This steel bridge was prefabricated in Walkerville, Ontario, and shipped in pieces by rail to Victoria, where it was reassembled on site.

This bridge was officially opened on 11 January 1924. The original wooden bridge deck absorbed water, which made it heavier to lift than it was designed for, so in 1966 it was replaced by an open steel grid. It was painted blue in the 1970s with a paint found to weather without changing colour, which had been used for Victoria's street lights. Then, to many, it became known as the Blue Bridge.

The 1923 bridge lasted a respectable 95 years. When replacing it began, one span was removed in 2014, leaving the other to carry traffic until the new bridge was ready. The present bridge is also a bascule, but a much more elegant modern structure, with the counterweight more hidden instead of menacing the traffic from above as the old one had. It opened to traffic on 31 March 2018.

Victoria was the site of one of the worst bridge accidents in the province. On 26 May 1896 a streetcar overloaded with 143 people travelling to attend celebrations at Esquimalt for Queen Victoria's birthday crashed through the Point Ellice Bridge; 55 were killed. It was the worst streetcar accident ever to occur in North America. The first bridge here, built about 1859, had been removed by 1863 because it obstructed marine traffic. Its replacement, a higher span, carried recently laid track of the Consolidated Electric Railway Company, but the bridge had not been built for such weight. As a result of the accident, the company was forced into receivership and, reorganized, emerged in April

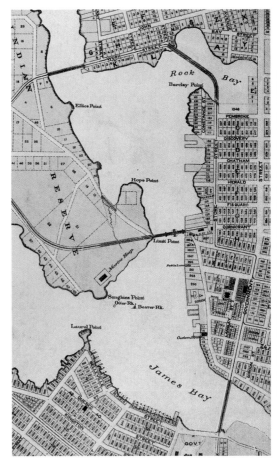

Left. The bridge of Victoria Harbour in 1893. The James Bay Bridge is at bottom, the E&N swing bridge at centre, the Point Ellice Bridge, three years away from its disastrous collapse, is at top left, and the Rock Bay Bridge, connecting Bridge and Store Streets, top right.

Above. The first E&N train arrives in Victoria on 29 March 1888; the swing bridge can be seen in the background.

Below. The 1900 James Bay Bridge, a photo taken from the legislative buildings.

1897 as the British Columbia Electric Railway, the predecessor of BC Hydro.

The bridge was rebuilt in 1903 and lasted until 30 November 1957, when a new one opened. It is now generally known as the Bay Street Bridge, though it has never been officially renamed as such.

There was also an early bridge curving across Rock Bay just east of Point Ellice, built in the mid-1880s and rebuilt in 1887 when the bay was much larger than it is now. It connected Bridge Street to Store Street.

Left and *right, centre.* The 1924–2018 Johnson Street Bridge photographed in 2010 when it was painted blue. *Right, top,* the bridge is under construction in 1921. The 1888 swing bridge is behind the construction work.

Right, centre bottom. The 2018 Johnson Street Bridge, an artistic addition to Victoria's Inner Harbour.

Below. The massive concrete piers of the 1924 bridge left in place with the 2018 bridge behind.

Below. The new Johnson Street Bridge makes a nice frame for this view across the Inner Harbour. The BC legislative buildings are at left.

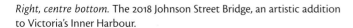

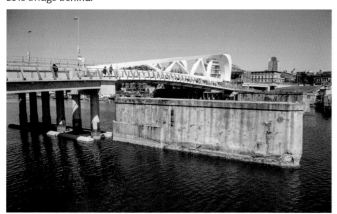

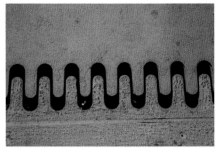

Left and *above*. The workings of the 2018 bascule bridge are a great subject for photographers. Here are three details, with the one at left rendered in black and white.

Below. The day after the Point Ellice Bridge tragedy, the streetcar has been beached beside the bridge. Well-known early Victoria photographer Richard Maynard took this photo.

Above, top. Boats full of would-be rescuers line the site of the submerged streetcar after the bridge collapse on 26 May 1896. Some 55 people died.

Above. Victoria's Gorge Bridge, shown on a postcard from 1911.

Above. The Bay Street Bridge, the 1957 third bridge at the Point Ellice location, looks a great deal more substantial than its predecessor.

Above. In 1967, a new steel Sooke River Bridge stands beside the one it was to succeed, built in 1946. When the 1946 bridge was built, its predecessor, a bridge built in 1921, was summarily blown up.

Left. This bridge across the Jordan River near Victoria carried both a narrow-gauge railway and a flume, the latter channelling water for the powerhouse from a diversion dam down to a reservoir. It was completed in 1911 by Vancouver Island Power Company, a subsidiary of BCER, as part of a hydroelectric scheme supplying power to Victoria. The railway's principal responsibility was to inspect and maintain the box-type wooden flume. The rails and the flume were on trestles for most of their 8.5-km length. The railway initially used horses for motive power, then a steam locomotive, then gas locomotives and cars. The flume was replaced in 1971 by a 7-km-long tunnel delivering water to a new generating station.

There are a quite a number of railway trestles and bridges on southern Vancouver Island, many of which have been restored as part of trails. They are the result of the Canadian Northern Pacific Railway's (CNoPR) decision to build a line from Victoria to Muchalat Inlet, an arm of Nootka Sound. This line only ever reached as far as Kissinger, 18 km from Youbou, on Cowichan Lake, which it did in 1928, built by the CNoPR's successor, Canadian National. The line never was economically successful despite the introduction at one point of a passenger railcar fondly called the Galloping Goose (after which the trail is named) and was closed down in 1979, although the line from Youbou to Cowichan Bay survived until 1988 because of its use in the logging industry. One notable trestle is the Kinsol Trestle, near Shawnigan Lake, built in 1921 and at the time the highest curved wooden structure of its kind in the British Empire.

Right, top. The deep Niagara Creek Canyon at Goldstream, 16 km north of Victoria, meant that the E&N had to build a high trestle, shown here. In 1910 when the first bridge, built in 1884, across the Fraser at Cisco was replaced (see page 204), the original bridge was disassembled and brought to Goldstream to replace the trestle.

Right, centre. The ex-Cisco Niagara Canyon Bridge in 1978 with the daily E&N train.

Below. The restored Selkirk Trestle in Victoria, once part of the CNoPR railway line, has been restored as part of the Galloping Goose Trail. The rise in the middle of the bridge, with a drawbridge, is a modification to allow sailboats to pass.

Right. The Kinsol Trestle, the CNR's bridge over the Koksilah River (and sometimes referred to as the Koksilah Trestle), was completed in 1921 on the "Galloping Goose" line that never reached farther than the Cowichan Valley. It is 44 m high and 188 m long, making it one of the largest railway trestles in the world. The sheer mass of timber is astonishing. It was restored in 2009–11 and reopened as part of the Galloping Goose Trail on 28 July 2011.

Above. The Kinsol Trestle with a train of logs, an evocative photo taken by prolific train photographer Dave Wilkie in 1958; a black-and-white version is displayed on an information sign at the site.

Right. A train loaded with logs crosses the Kinsol Trestle on 16 September 1958. This photo, also by Dave Wilkie, was selected to be part of a mural for the new Senate Building in Ottawa.

Far left, bottom. The other major trestle on the CNR line is the Todd Creek Trestle, north of Sooke. It is shown with a very short train crossing in October 1972 in a photo by Dave Wilkie.

Left, bottom. The Bear Creek Bridge, a logging bridge in the San Juan Valley on the west coast of Vancouver Island, was 74 m high, probably the highest wooden logging bridge ever, and only 10 m lower than the CPR's 1885 Stoney Creek Bridge in the Selkirks (see page 282). The Bear Creek Bridge was also 167 m in length and consisted of trestles and three 27.5-m-long Pratt truss spans. It was built in 1939 and was a particularly amazing structure, considering it was intended only for temporary use.

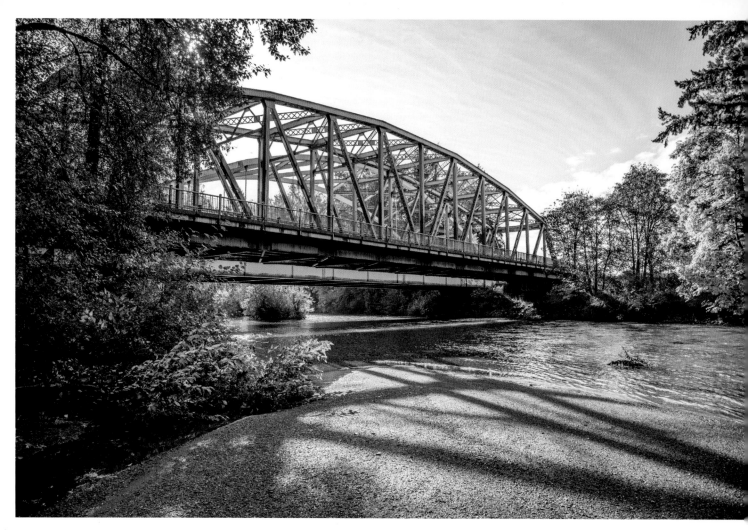

Above, top, and *above.* The Trans-Canada Highway bridges over the Chemainus River. A number of the bridges in this area were doubled up when the highway was upgraded. Here, the newer bridge, on the left, was completed in 1980. The older bridge, on the right, was built in 1950.

Below. This heritage single-lane wooden-truss bridge over the Koksilah River south of Duncan was built in 1939, replacing one built in 1876.

Above. The Duncan Wagon Bridge, a wooden bridge over the Cowichan River at Allenby Road, on the Old Island Highway, was built in 1926 and lasted until 1952 when it was blown up, to be replaced by the current steel-truss bridge. This is a BC Department of Public Works photo from its 1926–27 annual report.

Right. This interesting bridge with the trusses tied together overhead is the E&N railway bridge over the Koksilah River south of Duncan. It replaced the original E&N bridge here, which was washed out in 1892. The bridge's rust colours are complemented by the surrounding fall foliage. The Koksilah is, barely, a tributary of the Cowichan, joining the south arm of that river just before it enters Cowichan Bay.

The 1950 bridge at Duncan was known as the Silver Bridge, and its distinctive colour is well shown in the photo *above, left*. Local lobbying prevented the bridge from being painted some other colour because of the number of nearby businesses named after it, such as the Silver Bridge Inn.

Above, right, top. The bridge was doubled in 1978 when the east span was built. *Above, right*. Depending on how it is photographed, the bridge can naturally look more black than silver, though this image was converted to black and white to emphasize the structural patterns.

Left and *above*. The Cowichan River railway bridge in Duncan, surrounded by fall colours. This bridge replaced an earlier wooden-truss bridge in 1907 and is considered to be the result of a CPR experiment with recycling two obsolete light spans, dating from about 1880, into one single medium-capacity span. As can be seen in the photos, the trusses are in pairs. The bridge is built with a rare form of structure called a Whipple truss, with all the compression posts being what is known as Phoenix columns, a distinctive and very rare patented type of multiple girder once made by the Phoenix Iron Company of Pennsylvania. This 67-m-long bridge is thought to be one of only three bridges with these columns in Canada and the only one in the world of this design, with four separate trusses. Although Whipple truss designs are uncommon today, they were invented in the 1840s by Squire Whipple, an American engineer who designed and built many bridges, including over 70 on the Erie Canal.

Left. This old postcard, dating from about 1910, shows the two bridges over the Nanaimo River south of the city. In the foreground is the E&N railway bridge, and in the distance the road bridge. *Right, centre.* The railway bridge as it is today.

Above, right. The Nanaimo River Canyon. This photo was taken from the railway bridge, which can be seen in the foreground looking towards a modern bridge, neither road nor rail. It is a purpose-built bungee jumping bridge. It is 46 m high and was opened in March 2006 as North America's first legal bridge for this purpose.

Right. The more mundane nearby twinned Trans-Canada Highway bridges over the Nanaimo River. The earlier one, on the right, was built in 1957, while the one on the left opened in 1977, a replacement for one built in 1955.

Close to the Nanaimo River at this point is its tributary Haslam Creek, over which there is a recent pedestrian suspension bridge a bit further downstream. *Left* is the E&N railway bridge across the creek; the Trans-Canada Highway bridges (*right, centre*) can be seen just beyond it. *Right* is a detail of the steel truss under the railway bridge. The Trans-Canada bridge is, like many in this area, doubled. The green arch bridge dates from 1946 and the flat-concrete-beam bridge from 1977.

Left, centre, top. North of Nanaimo in Lantzville the E&N crosses Green Lake on this low trestle, and *left, centre, bottom,* French Creek in Parksville on a much higher

one. The track north of Nanaimo was laid down in 1909–14 but is now in as bad a state as the rest of the disused line.

Below. The Old Island Highway (19A) goes over French Creek on this tied-arch steel bridge just north of Parksville. It was built in 1947.

Right. At Oyster River, between Courtenay and Campbell River, is this wooden-truss bridge, on Regent Road.

Below. At Courtenay the Old Island Highway crosses the Puntledge River, which flows into Comox Harbour, on what looks like a regular modern flat-concrete bridge but which has a section, covering less than half of the bridge, with this bascule, built in 1981, which allows boats upriver to a slough. Some 850 m farther north is the 5th Street Bridge, a 1960-built steel truss. The bascule has an open steel-grid deck.

Above. This 1947 steel-truss bridge carries the Old Island Highway (19A) over the Englishman River in Parksville.

Right. The bridge over the Nimpkish River 6 km east of Port McNeill, built in 1964.

Above and *above, right*. The Pashleth Creek Bridge was built in 1981 near Rivers Inlet and, at 102 m high, was the world's highest logging bridge. It was designed by Buckland & Taylor and built for BC Forest Products by Dominion Bridge. The 102-m-long bridge still exists, but its use for logging ended in 2005. The east side was only accessible by helicopters, which lifted all the equipment required there. The three-span deck truss was assembled on the west side of the canyon and then launched in a single piece across to the other side. The newspaper image *above, left*, shows this in process. The supporting posts and cables underneath were folded down. In 2001 a similar bridge was built across the Machmell River nearby, lasting only four years before logging was shut down.

Above. Two Englewood Railway diesels lead a train across the Kokish River Bridge. The river flows into Beaver Cove on Northern Vancouver Island. This was the last logging railway in North America when it shut down in November 2017 following an accident, and it had a network of lines in the region, including many bridges like this one.

Above. The remains of an old logging railway bridge across Skidegate Lake on Moresby Island, Haida Gwaii, photographed in 2009. The line was built in 1936–37 and took logs to Cumshewa Inlet, where they were shipped to Powell River. It was operated by the federal government during World War II, as the spruce it shipped was critical to the war effort. It shut down in 1955.

There have been a number of proposals for bridges to replace ferries along the coast. One, in 1980, proposed two possible routes from the Saanich Peninsula to replace the Mill Bay ferry. In 1995, an ambitious scheme to connect Vancouver Island to the mainland was promoted by ex–provincial cabinet minister Pat McGeer. It involved a causeway from Steveston; a tunnel, to allow ships to pass; and a 24.2-km-long floating bridge to Valdes Island, which would then connect with Vancouver Island near Duke Point in Nanaimo via several other island-connecting bridges. The project was resurrected by the government in 2000—perhaps motivated by a threatened ferry workers' strike—and examined in detail, but in December 2002 the Ministry of Transportation and Highways issued a report prepared for them called *A Potential Fixed Link to Vancouver Island*. The report concluded that cost-effective technology to build a bridge connecting the mainland with Vancouver Island was not yet available. The potential cost with the technology of the day was calculated at $12 billion and would take 25 years to build. Options considered included a bored tunnel, a floating tunnel, a pontoon bridge, and a multiple cable–stayed bridge with floating piers. The potential for earthquakes was a major safety consideration. Needless to say, the existing ferries looked like a much easier and cheaper option, and so the fixed-link idea was shelved.

Below. The proposed bridge route on a model made by McGeer, with a graphic showing the floating bridge at the tunnel and a suggested design for the floating bridge, a sort of double-hull catamaran design.

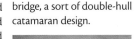

The Big Flood of November 2021

In late 2021 British Columbia's reliance on its highways, railways and their bridges was brutally exposed. Between 14 and 16 November, a two-and-a-half-day storm—an atmospheric river—dumped between 200 and 300 mm of rain on southern British Columbia, more than the normal total for the whole of November. With snowmelt added, it caused mountainsides to collapse and rivers to take out bridges, killing five people in the process. On the Coquihalla Highway a number of bridges were heavily damaged or washed away, as were major sections of the highway. On Highway 8, between Spences Bridge and Merritt—which had to be evacuated—the highway was obliterated in 18 locations and four bridges were lost. Many drivers were stranded for days.

The Hope-Princeton Highway was reopened quickly, but this route was restricted to essential traffic and had intermittent closures from 19 November until 21 December. Highway 99 north of Pemberton also opened to essential traffic but was then closed for extended periods again several times because of bad weather and slide clearing. Amazingly, the Coquihalla was opened to essential traffic by 20 December, the result of 24/7 construction by a myriad of workers, and was opened to all traffic on 19 January 2022. The Trans-Canada reopened to all traffic on 24 January 2022. However, the permanent replacement of many bridges remained to be done, and the expected final cost of the flooding is likely to be in the billions.

Left. A massive slide obliterated Highway 1 at Jackass Mountain. A temporary 80-m-long Acrow bridge was used to bridge the gap quickly, allowing for single-lane traffic. *Left, top,* the easily transportable sections of the bridge were assembled into a strong single-truss structure before being hauled across the gap. *Left, centre,* a sectional steel deck is laid between the trusses. *Left, bottom,* the length of the bridge is apparent in this aerial view as it nears completion.

Right, top and centre. The scene at Tank Hill, about 12 km east of Lytton, after the devastation. An underpass under the Canadian Pacific Railway has been compromised, and some of the railway line itself is hanging in mid-air. The mayhem was caused by a landslide that turned into a torrent. *Right, bottom,* the temporary solution here was not a bridge at all but a barrier-controlled grade crossing.

Right. This aerial view with information from a survey camera was taken by the BC Ministry of Transportation and Infrastructure on 21 November 2021. It shows extensive damage to the Coquihalla Highway and the Bottletop Bridge over the Coldwater River.

Right, centre top. This was the scene at the Bottletop Bridge on 27 November, only six days after the aerial survey, *above, top.* Massive amounts of earth have been moved, and the collapsed end spans of the bridge are awaiting removal. Crews worked 24/7 to restore the highway.

The railways reacted even faster than the government, although they suffered less than the roads. CPR had 30 damaged locations, not all bridges, and by 23 November managed to reopen its line from Kamloops to Vancouver. Because of line-sharing agreements, this opened up the pathway to the Port of Vancouver again to both CPR and CNR, although at a considerably reduced capacity. CNR reopened its line a week after the storm but pre-emptively closed it again because more rain, causing debris flows, landslides and washouts, was presenting danger to trains. The CNR line finally reopened on 5 December.

Left. The Jessica Bridge over the Coquihalla River on Highway 5 has its collapsed span removed preparatory to installing a temporary bridge.

Left, bottom. Curnow Bridge, on Highway 8 in the Nicola Valley near Spences Bridge.

Many smaller bridges were destroyed by the flooding. *Right* is the remains of a bridge across the Sumas River in Abbotsford, on the northern side of what used to be Sumas Lake before it was drained in the 1920s (see page 178). *Below*, a new single-span steel-beam bridge nears completion; this was the scene on 1 February 2022, just two and a half months later.

The Other Ferries...

Although this book has excluded coastal ferries for reasons of space, the reality is that BC Ferries is an enormously important link in our province's highways and will likely remain so in the future. British Columbia has the largest fleet of ferry vessels in the world. Created in June 1960, BC Ferries now has about 40 vessels that serve points all along the coast but charges what are in effect tolls for their use, unlike the inland ferries, which are free.

Above. MV *Kwuna* unloading at Alliford Bay in July 2018. The ferry service here connects the two main islands of Haida Gwaii. This vessel, unlike others in its class but in similar fashion to many inland ferries, has large loading ramps attached. Otherwise, as a K Class ferry, it is the same as the two vessels that used to cross the Fraser River at Albion (see page 97). *Kwuna* was built in 1975.

Left. On a completely different scale is *Northern Adventure*, seen here arriving at Skidegate, Haida Gwaii, also in July 2018. This ship was purchased from European owners in 2006 and, after refit, began service in 2009 on northern coastal routes. The vessel had been purchased originally to replace the *Queen of the North* on the Inside Passage route. The latter ship sank on 22 March 2006 at Gil Island, some 135 km south of its destination, Prince Rupert.

Bibliography

British Columbia Ministry of Transportation and Highways. *Frontier to Freeway: A Short Illustrated History of the Roads in British Columbia.*
  Victoria: Ministry of Transportation and Highways. Online PDF c. 2001.
Burkinshaw, Robert K. *False Creek: History, Images, and Research Sources.* Vancouver: City of Vancouver Archives Occasional Paper No. 2, 1983.
Conn, Heather, and Henry Ewert. *Vancouver's Glory Years: Public Transit 1890–1915.* North Vancouver: Whitecap, 2003.
Dawe, Alan. *Richmond and Its Bridges: Fifteen Crossings of the Fraser River.* Richmond: City of Richmond Archives, 1996.
Denison, Edward, and Ian Stewart. *How to Read Bridges: A Crash Course in Engineering and Architecture.* New York: Rizzoli, 2012.
Ewert, Henry. *The Story of the B.C. Electric Railway Company.* North Vancouver: Whitecap, 1986.
Harvey, R.G. *The Coast Connection.* Lantzville: Oolichan Books, 1994.
———. *Carving the Western Path: By River, Rail, and Road through B.C.'s Southern Mountains.* Surrey: Heritage House, 1998.
———. *Carving the Western Path: By River, Rail, and Road through Central and Northern B.C.* Surrey: Heritage House, 1999.
———. *Head On!: Collisions of Egos, Ethics, and Politics in B.C.'s Transportation History.* Surrey: Heritage House, 2004.
———. *Carving the Western Path: Routes to Remember.* Surrey: Heritage House, 2006.
Hayes, Derek. *Historical Atlas of Vancouver and the Lower Fraser Valley.* Vancouver: Douglas & McIntyre, 2005.
———. *British Columbia: A New Historical Atlas.* Vancouver: Douglas & McIntyre, 2012.
———. *Iron Road West: An Illustrated History of British Columbia's Railways.* Madeira Park: Harbour Publishing, 2018.
Hind, Patrick O. *The Pacific Great Eastern Railway Company: A Short History of the North Shore Subdivision 1914–1928.*
  North Vancouver: North Vancouver Museum and Archives Commission, 1999.
Jamieson, Eric. *Tragedy at Second Narrows.* Madeira Park: Harbour Publishing, 2008.
Lavallée, Omer. *Van Horne's Road: The Building of the Canadian Pacific Railway.* Second Edition. Calgary: Fifth House, 2007.
McCombs, Arnold M., and Wilfrid W. Chittenden. *The Fraser Valley Challenge: An Illustrated Account of Logging and Sawmilling in the Fraser Valley.*
  Harrison Hot Springs: Treeling Publishing, 1990.
Pole, Graeme. *The Spiral Tunnels and the Big Hill: A Canadian Railway Adventure.* Canmore, Alberta: Altitude Publishing, 1995.
Rees-Thomas, David M. *Timber Down the Capilano: A History of the Capilano Timber Company on Vancouver's North Shore.*
  Victoria: British Columbia Railway Historical Association, 1984.
Rothenburger, Mel. *Friend o' Mine: The Story of Flyin' Phil Gaglardi.* Victoria: Orca Publishers, 1991.
Sandhouse, The. Journal of the CRHA Pacific Coast Division. Vancouver: Canadian Railroad Historical Association, Pacific Coast Division. Various issues.
Sanford, Barrie. *McCulloch's Wonder: The Story of the Kettle Valley Railway.* North Vancouver: Whitecap, 1977.
———. *Steel Rails & Iron Men: A Pictorial History of the Kettle Valley Railway.* North Vancouver: Whitecap, 2003.
———. *Royal Metal: The People, Times and Trains of New Westminster Bridge.* Vancouver: National Railway Historical Society, 2004.
Stevens, G.R. *Canadian National Railways: Towards the Inevitable: 1896–1922.* Toronto: Clarke, Irwin & Co., 1962.
Turner, Robert D. *West of the Great Divide: An Illustrated History of the Canadian Pacific Railway in British Columbia 1880–1986.*
  Victoria: Sono Nis Press, 1987.
———. *Logging by Rail: The British Columbia Story.* Winlaw: Sono Nis Press, 1990.
Watt, K. Jane. *Surrey: A City of Stories.* Surrey: City of Surrey, 2017.

Right. BC Ferries' *Queen of Alberni* approaches the dock at Tsawwassen in the fading evening light of 5 July 2018. The ship is one of an older class of vessels now slated for replacement. The C-Class ferry was built in North Vancouver in 1976 with a single deck, and it was in this form that she went up on the rocks at the western end of Active Pass on 9 August 1979, killing a racehorse in a horsebox on the open deck. The author happened to be flying to Victoria on a float plane that morning, and the pilot flew low over the ship so that his passengers could get a good look. Oh, how I wish I'd had my camera with me that day!

A second deck was added in 1984, and the hull lengthened. The ship has spent most of its life on the Tsawwassen–Swartz Bay or Tsawwassen–Nanaimo Duke Point runs connecting southern Vancouver Island with the mainland. The bottom deck, once the single deck, is particularly accommodating for overheight vehicles.

Sources

All photos and other images not otherwise credited are by Derek Hayes or from the collection of Derek Hayes.
Photos from BC Department of Public Works annual reports are credited in their captions.

Abbreviations

BCA	British Columbia Archives	MRMCA	Maple Ridge Museum & Community Archives
CA	Coquitlam Archives	NVMA	North Vancouver Museum & Archives
CCA	City of Chilliwack Archives	NWA	New Westminster Archives
CRA	City of Richmond Archives	PCH	PoCo Heritage
CSA	City of Surrey Archives	UBC	University of British Columbia Special Collections
CVA	City of Vancouver Archives	UNBC	University of Northern British Columbia
DA	Delta Archives/Delta Heritage Society/City of Delta	VPL	Vancouver Public Library
JMABC	Jewish Museum & Archives of BC		
LAC	Library & Archives Canada		l=left; r=right; c=centre; t=top; b=bottom.
LTSA	Land Titles & Survey Archives		

8 tl	BCA C-08818	32 cl	CVA 1376-456	52 b	CVA 228-383
8 br	BC Ministry of Transportation*	33 b	CVA SGN 936	56 t	CVA 447-2386
9 b	BC Ministry of Transportation*	34 t	CVA Pan N95	56 c	DA CR-101-1970-1-138
10 t	CVA BO P62	34cr	CVA 228-446	56 bc	CVA 99-3970
10 c	NVMA 5451	34 b	CRA 1999-4-1-250	57 tl	DA CR-101-1970-1-365
10–11	CVA PAN N172	35 bl	CVA LP 203.2	57 tr	DA CR-101-1970-1-363
11 tr	CVA 371-1077	35 br	Triathlon Mapping Corp (Pacific	57 br	CRA 1984-6-4
11 rcb	NVMA 15932		Survey Corp) CVA 59-06	58 t	DA CR-101-1970-1-139
13 t	NVMA	36 t	CVA 228-540	59 t	DA 101-1970-1-144
14 tl	CVA 1477-101	37 t	CVA 228-548	59 b	DA 1979-26-319
14 cl	CVA 99-1335	37 cl	CVA 228-352	60 t	CRA 1984-6-20
14 bl	CVA 371-2831	37 bl	CVA 228-211	60 b	CRA 1984-3-1
14 tr	CVA Br P9.5	37 br	VPL 13218	61 tl	CRA 1984-6-35
14 cr	CVA 99-2152 Stuart Thomson	40 t	CVA 260-1541	61 tr	CRA 1984-6-23
14 br	CVA Br N4.1	40 c	CRA 1999-4-3-2254	64 t	NWA IHP9563-0478 Betty McVie
15 t	NVMA 9736 J. Wardlow	40 b	CVA Dist P135.5	69 t	NWA IHP10217-007 Croton Studio
15 bl	CVA 232-07	43 cr	DougVancouver	69 c	NWA IHP10217-009 Croton Studio
15 br	CVA Map 700	44 crt	CVA Van Sc P128.3-128	71 b	NWA IHP10217-018
16 tl	CVA 260-302	44 crb	CVA Br P25	74 b	CSA 203.04
16 tr	CVA 447-110	44 b	CVA SGN 1545	75 c	NWA IHP3769
16 cr	NWA IHP10001-0354	45 tl	CVA SGN 996.4	75 b	CVA 102-17
17 b	CVA Br P68.3 Leonard Frank JMABC	45 tc	CVA Br P16.2	76 t	NWA IHP2986
18 bl	CVA Br. P66	45 tr	CVA 99-1888	77 t	CRA 1999-4-3-928
18 br	VPL 3042	45 lct	CVA 800-2435	77 b	CRA 1999-4-3-339
19 tl	CVA Br P73.11 No. 22	45 lcb	CVA 800-3619	78 t	NWA IHP0868 Basil King/*Columbian*
19 tr	CVA Br P68.10	45 rct	CVA 800-2573	78 c	NWA IHP9078
19 cl	CVA Br. P68.14 Leonard Frank JMABC	45 rcb	CVA 800-3837	80 t	NWA IHP7427 L.B. Elliot
19 b	CVA Br P73.23 Leonard Frank JMABC	45 b	CVA 800-3446	80 b	CVA Br P29-1937
19 cr	CVA Br P73.25 Leonard Frank JMABC	47 tl	LTSA 14T3 Roads & Trails	84 t	CSA 2017.0049
20 tl	CVA 134-115	47 bl	CVA 1376-451	88	CRA 2010-87-49
20 bl	NVMA 10006 W.J. McDonough	47 tr	CVA Str P247	89 t	CSA 2013-0061
20 t–21	CVA 180-5254.4	47 br	CVA Van Sc P147	89 bl	CSA 1992.036.986
24 bl	CVA Add. MSS-492	48 tr	CVA Br P54.1 9420	89 br	CSA 203.20
24 tr	CVA 265-12	48 c	CRA 1999-4-3-1010	90 bl	BC Ministry of Transportation*
24 cr	CVA 260-773	48 b	CVA Pan N158	99 tl	CSA 192.69
24 br	CVA 260-805	49 cl	CVA Pan Nxx	99 tr	CSA F83-0-0-0-0-0-0-452
25 tl	CVA Br P81.21	49 b	CVA 500-2	100 t	CVA Out P366
25 tr	CVA Br P81.27	49 tr	CVA Map 191	100 b	CVA Out P101
26 tl	CVA 6-103	50 t	CVA Pan Nxx	101 t	CVA 1123-2
26 bl	CVA 288-025	50 bl	CVA 2011-010-1721	101 c	CVA Pan P49
27 b	*Vancouver Sun* Craig Hodge	50 br	CVA 371-2242 Claude Dettloff	101 b	CVA 371-928-6
30	CVA PD 1044	51 t	CVA Pan N100A	102 t	CRA 1977-1-108
31 tl	CVA PD 682	51 c	VPL 6617	102 b	CRA 1999-4-2-853
31 tr	CVA PD 682	52 tl	CVA 447-374 Walter Frost	103 tl	CRA 1999-4-2-586

103 tr CVA Br P63.3
103 b CRA 1999-4-3-2082
104 t CRA 1999-4-3-28
104 b CRA 1988-17-83
105 b CVA Br P63.1
106 tl CRA 2008-36-2-27
106 tr CVA Br P74.12 Leonard Frank JMABC
106 c CRA 2008-36-2-25
111 cl CRA 2008-36-1-92
112 t CRA 1988-10-339
113 t CVA 371-903
113 c CVA 371-902
113 b CRA 1996-0008-00001
114 t CRA 1977-15-28
116 b CVA LEG 1256.3-1256.2
117 b NWA IHP6387
117 c NWA IHP7950 Croton Studio
119 bl CRA 2010-87-36
119 br NWA NWPL 0454 Croton Studio
124 cr CRA 1984-0017-00084
126 t CVA 3-37
126 b BCA PR 0878
127 t CA 2005.50.10
127 b BCA PR 0878
128 t BCA PR 0878
128 b BCA PR 0878
129 t BCA PR 0878
129 b BCA PR 0878
132 t PCH 2003.009
132 b–133 CVA 99-125
133 t CVA 99-315
137 t PCH 2008.001.48A
142 cr Henry Ewert
142 b CSA 203.01
144 br CSA 121.027
149 t NVMA 3604
152 tl CVA Out P808.2
152 tr CVA 312-11
152 c CVA Br P78
152 b BC Ministry of Transportation*
154 t NVMA 11298
158 cl NVMA 5216
159 t Squamish Public Library 036
162 cl UNBC 2020.08.002
162 cr UNBC 2020.08.019
164 cr UBC G354.P3
164 bl UNBC 2020.08.09
166 b Whistler Question
167 t Powell River Museum & Archives
168 b MRMCA P01829
170 t MRMCA 1829-2
170 bcr CVA Pan N03
170 b MRMCA P01479
171 t CVA SGN 1479
171 tcr CVA AM54-S4-Out P45
172 tl NWA IHP10001 Don Whistler Columbian
172 cr NWA IHP10001-103 Columbian
177 c BCA H-06885
179 b CCA Chilliwack Progress
183 t VPL 1939
183 b CCA 1983.083.008.098
184 t Emil Anderson Group
184 c City of Chilliwack

187 b CRA 1999-4-1-127
190 b CVA 586-649
194 br CVA 260-1259
195 tl CVA 260-1255
197 t BCA I-17014
198 CVA A-6-169.9
199 tl CVA 586-5297
202 t CVA 3-16
203 tl Weixi Zeng
203 tr BCA D-01467
204 tr BCA B-04968
205 t Owen Laukkanen
205 bl CVA 289-004.346
210 UNBC 2020.08.32
210 b BCA 04189
211 tr BCA B-02676-0287
212 c Fabrikov
213 cr CVA Br P56.4
215 t Chris Harris
216 b Quesnel Archives 1977.14.1
218 bl BCA D-00068
218 tr Dave Wilkie
222 Prince George Railway Museum
224 t CVA Br P44
224 bl BCA A-06048
224 bc BCA F-09849
224 br BCA B-01381
226 t Google
226 t inset Google
226 br Kitimat Archives 2001.18.14
227 tl UNBC 2002.1.9.2.105
227 cl BCA E-02778
227 tr BCA B-01382
227 cr BCA D-07540
229 t BC Ministry of Transportation*
229 b BC Ministry of Transportation*
230 t Canadian Geotechnical Society
230 c Canadian Geotechnical Society
230 b Jerrye and Roy Klotz
231 clt BCA B05438
231 tr BCA H-06869
231 br South Peace Historical Society 13158
232 br BCA NA-08399
233 t McElhanney
233 c McElhanney
233 bl McElhanney
233 br BC Ministry of Transportation*
234 b Marty Bernard
238 rct Kamloops Museum & Archives
238 rc Kamloops Museum & Archives
238 bl Ken Favrholdt
241 c Kamloops Museum & Archives
241 b Kamloops Museum & Archives
244 tl CVA Out P753.3
244 cr Mike Danneman
244 br Doug Smith, kamloopstrails.net
248 br SS Sicamous Museum
251 cl KWH Constructors
251 cbr Halmyra
251 br Darren Kirby
253 t Penticton Museum
253 c Penticton Museum
254 tl Penticton Museum

254 tr Penticton Museum
255 tl CVA 289-002.425
255 tr CVA 289-002.433
255 cl CVA 289-002.449
255 cr CVA 289-002.427
256 tl Eric Sakowski, highestbridges.com
256 tr Eric Sakowski, highestbridges.com
257 b Princeton Museum
258 t James Fowler
268 tl CVA Can P174
270 b Dave Wilkie
272 c SS Moyie Museum
273 tl Touchstones Nelson
274 t Land Titles office, Kamloops
274 b Garry and Roz Miller
275 t Garry and Roz Miller
275 b Garry and Roz Miller
278 l Revelstoke Museum and Archives
278 cr University of Calgary CU 1129899
278 cbr LAC PA 66570
278 br BCA E-00333
282 bl David R. Spencer
283 t LAC 3194173
283 bl BCA E00301
284 tl London News 24 July 1886
285 br Matthew Robson
287 b Saturday Sunset 28 March 1908, BC Legislature Library
288 t Chung Collection, UBC Special Collections
288 b Dave Wilkie
294 t LTSA 9T8 Old Maps
294 c Victoria City Archives
297 t CVA Out P247
297 bl Colin Stepney
298 bl Dave Wilkie
298 cr Dave Wilkie
299 tl Dave Wilkie
299 b Dave Wilkie
304 bl rslocationshub.com
305 tr COWI
305 cl Drew Jacksich
306 (all) BC Ministry of Transportation*
307 t BC Ministry of Transportation*
307 lc BC Ministry of Transportation*
307 lb BC Ministry of Transportation*
307 rtc BC Ministry of Transportation*
307 rbc Abbotsford Police Department
315 BC Ministry of Transportation*

*Ministry of Transportation and Infrastructure, Province of British Columbia.
Copyright Province of British Columbia.
Reproduced with permission of the Province of British Columbia.

Bridge Finder

Page number refers to principal entry. For multiple entries see index.

Right. This view from the Big Eddy (Wilson Street) Bridge in Revelstoke shows two other bridges that cross the Columbia River here: the railway bridge and the suspension road bridge. See page 280.

Index

Above. Simon Fraser Bridge, Prince George. This is the original bridge, built in 1963; at left is its twin, built in 2009 (see page 223). The bridge is named after the North West Company explorer Simon Fraser, who embarked from this spot on his epic journey to the mouth of the river (also named after him) in 1808.

Above. Curves and lines. In Princeton, the Bridge of Dreams at the location of the original railway bridge, and, at left, the Princeton–Merritt Highway 5A bridge. See page 258.

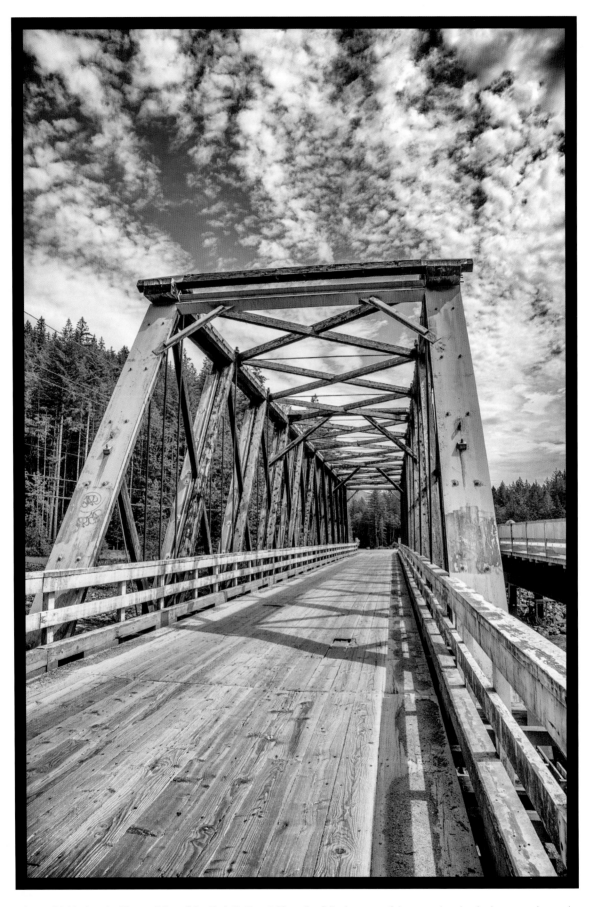

Above. This black-and-white rendition of the Chehalis River Bridge takes full advantage of the streaming clouds above to enhance the image. This photo, taken on 15 June 2022, shows the bridge that will soon replace it under construction at right. See pages 9 and 176.